MW00712454

Poetics of Opposition in Contemporary Spain

To Audrey —
One of my first and forever
most influential teachers of
irony and literature, even if
I started at Agatha Christie.

All my love,
Jon

Madrid, January 2017

HISPANIC URBAN STUDIES

BENJAMIN FRASER is Professor and Chair of Foreign Languages and Literatures in the Thomas Harriot College of Arts and Sciences at East Carolina University, North Carolina, US. He is the editor of the *Journal of Urban Cultural Studies* and the author, editor, and translator of book and article publications in Hispanic Studies, Cultural Studies, and Urban Studies.

SUSAN LARSON is an Associate Professor of Spanish at the University of Kentucky, US. She is Senior Editor of the *Arizona Journal of Hispanic Cultural Studies* and works at the intersections of Spatial Theory and Literary, Film and Urban Studies.

Toward an Urban Cultural Studies: Henri Lefebvre and the Humanities
Benjamin Fraser

Poetics of Opposition in Contemporary Spain: Politics and the Work of Urban Culture
Jonathan Snyder

Poetics of Opposition in Contemporary Spain

Politics and the Work of Urban Culture

Jonathan Snyder

POETICS OF OPPOSITION IN CONTEMPORARY SPAIN
Copyright © Jonathan Snyder, 2015.

All rights reserved.

First published in 2015 by
PALGRAVE MACMILLAN®
in the United States—a division of St. Martin's Press LLC,
175 Fifth Avenue, New York, NY 10010.

Where this book is distributed in the UK, Europe and the rest of the world,
this is by Palgrave Macmillan, a division of Macmillan Publishers Limited,
registered in England, company number 785998, of Houndmills,
Basingstoke, Hampshire RG21 6XS.

Palgrave Macmillan is the global academic imprint of the above companies
and has companies and representatives throughout the world.

Palgrave® and Macmillan® are registered trademarks in the United States,
the United Kingdom, Europe and other countries.

ISBN: 978–1–137–53679–2

Library of Congress Cataloging-in-Publication Data is available from the
Library of Congress.

A catalogue record of the book is available from the British Library.

Design by Newgen Knowledge Works (P) Ltd., Chennai, India.

First edition: October 2015

10 9 8 7 6 5 4 3 2 1

For Miguel

Contents

Figures

Preface

After tugging at the wrists of his gloves, the artist opened an envelope of graphite filings, scooping them in spoonfuls onto an oversized sheet of white paper. He then suspended the material above a record player; on its turntable rotating at slow speed was a magnet and positioned next to it, an electric amplifier. Although he could hardly be seen over the crowd standing in the dark warehouse, the image of this apparatus, captured on closed-circuit video, was projected on the wall where it would remain for the next three hours. When the bassist plucked a chord the filings scattered around the paper, some standing on end as they drew wobbly, jagged patterns in circles. The band would play intermittently, amid screenings and other distractions to be discovered around the warehouse—projected slides of landscape photography in muted colors, videos of everyday objects presented as trompe l'oeil, a painted display of pop icons glowing under ultraviolet light, and so on. Occasionally, the digital silhouette of a monumental pack of elk would race around the perimeter of the wall where it met the ceiling and at other times, a flock of ravens. This warehouse was one of the many vast spaces in Madrid's former slaughterhouse El Matadero, renovated in 2007 to become the capital's largest cultural center, something of a small city housing several exhibition spaces, theaters, an auditorium, a cinema, a library, and a media center, among others.

The public invitation to this one-time event announced "No hay banda" citing the master of ceremonies from the unusual stage show in David Lynch's film *Mulholland Drive.* Curated by Abel H. Pozuelo for some ten participating artists and musicians, *No hay banda* promised "un experimento en el tiempo" [an experiment in time] in an announcement that told readers what *not* to expect, or then again, a rather playful denial of all that it would entail: "No es un concierto ni una exposición colectiva, no es un happening ni una performance ni tampoco una improvisación multidisciplinar" [This is not a concert or a collective exhibit; it is not a happening or a performance, nor inter-disciplinary improvisation]. The event delivered what it promised as both a (non-)happening and a temporal experiment, harkening back to the "radical juxtapositions" of unlikely assemblages, according to Susan Sontag, characteristic of happenings in the 1950s and 1960s. Much like them, it was unclear when the nonhappening started or ended while visitors would come and go as they pleased, with simultaneous events taking place around the room in overlapping succession. And the crowd, guided to move through the warehouse by interest or surprise, seemed as much to form part of the performance, too. As such, when the band took pause a spotlight focused on participating artist Fran Mohíno who dialed a number from his cell phone to activate the sculpture *We_Love_You*. Positioned on a crane above the crowd, a towering black cylinder spoke, in a thundering male voice, a random sequence of three words accompanied by flashes of strobe light: "We, Love, You." Like Mohíno's other work on childhood subjectivity and memory, this piece had spectators momentarily blinded and deafened, one might say smothered in most senses, by an overpowering iteration on love. The arrhythmic blasts at intervals long enough to ready oneself for the next flash also provoked some irritation and much amusement among visitors. The crowd retracted from the tower in a movement that seemed comparable (at least to me, looking away to see the projection on the adjacent wall) to that of the graphite filings shuffled around on paper.

Sometime later, I spoke with Fran Mohíno when I had the chance to ask him some questions about his own work and this group show. "This kind of event would have been unthinkable a couple of years ago," he noted—if readers will allow me to paraphrase Mohíno's words—that is, the invitation to experience this nonhappening simply wouldn't have made sense. This observation on sense-making struck me, given that two parties could agree in conversation on what seemed to be sensible change in the present without knowing how to articulate precisely the factors at play in making this so. Under what changing circumstances did the occurrence signify in ways that seemed to "work" for its audience, if not *on* its audience? In what ways, if at all, did this sensible change dialog with the turn to the experiential, alternative practices of a collective bent becoming more commonplace in Madrid amid times of austerity? What did this assemblage of cultural works that resisted narrative and instead invited visitors to collective experience in this space, accomplish in form and function? Beyond the context of the performance alone, these general questions prompted by sensing that "somehow" things are different than only shortly ago, could be said to outline the essays in the following chapters on cultural analysis and the political.

The global financial crisis and recent social mobilizations, such as the 15M mass protests in Spain, have inaugurated renewed interest in critically rethinking Spain's present cultural, social, and political circumstance, from the democratic *Transición* to its adhesion to the European Union. In the wake of the crisis in Spain, critical readings of and responses to the present scenario take at least two main stages of activity: cultural production in urban centers, often of an alternative status, and protests and assemblies in public spaces throughout Spanish cities. The essays gathered in the following chapters address how recent cultural production in Spain (fanzine poetry, video performance, photography, theater, from 2008 to 2013) grapples with the conditions and possibilities for social transformation in myriad ways that dialog with the ongoing crisis, neoliberal governance, and political culture in Spain's recent democratic history.

In his proposal for microcultural studies, Chris Perriam argues that ephemera can prove a "weighty witness" to the times. "What the ephemeral witnesses and documents above all," Perriam writes, "is the combination of the unknown cultural configuration which preceded it, surrounded it, and gave it momentary meaning" in the present of its production (2010, 292). Consider, for example, fanzines and some independent self-publications from the scene of cultural activity often regarded to be the urban underground. In the first decade of the twenty-first century, self-publishing in Spain has received renewed interest among amateur and professional creators alike. Augmented uses of desktop publishing software have facilitated accessible, do-it-yourself production supports for creative work in print and online distribution. Among the most fringe independent self-publications, fanzines today exhibit more polished layouts, illustrations, typesetting, and even binding than their predecessors from the 1970s and 80s (Compitello, 2013, 203–31), a circumstance attributable, in part, to digital production. Still, many retain the manual and analog practices, true to fanzine origins, in cut-and-paste design, mixed-media collage, cartoons, and illustrated fiction of an underground aesthetic (Duncombe, 2008; Librería Bakakai, 2006). Of a much wider panorama than fanzines alone, the great variety of independent print matter today—hand-sewn literary journals, artist books, and pamphlets categorized as ephemera—range in support from bound cardstock to sleek, glossy color prints, which on the whole demonstrate that self-publishing has traveled in multiple low-budget projects from the underground to the commercial upstart.

Independent self-publishing today provides an illustration of Perriam's claim for its alternative status in relation to institutional supports and funding sources, and to the markets that make some established circles of cultural and literary production a more sustainable, if not at times lucrative, business by comparison. For many creators, self-publishing provides alternative, inexpensive channels to distribute work against the publishing crisis in recent years, which has writers and artists face increasingly limited possibilities to see their work in traditional print media (Martínez Soria, 2013, 12–14; Rodrigo et al., 2012). These practices hold an alternative regard and readership appeal that stand in opposition to the established, exclusive publishing circuits and their authors in the arts and literature (Acevedo et al., 2012). In this sense, although fanzines oppose and critique commercial culture for its potential to absorb almost any material of marketable value, as Stephen Duncombe has noted, it seems that in times of crisis, to the contrary, fanzines may have subsumed the commercial aesthetics of some independent self-publishing (2008, 159). On the other hand, many self-publishers and independent presses, though by no means all of them, are committed to the distribution of cultural material as public domain against copyright restrictions, known as the *copyleft* movement (Martín Cabrera, 2012, 583–605; Moreno-Caballud, 2012, 535–55). In these practices, there exists an oppositional tension between some official spaces of cultural production (sponsored creation, exhibition, distribution, publishing, and so on) and their alternative counterparts whose works seldom reach channels of public visibility, other than through local circuits of readers and collectors (Guirao Cabrera, 2013, 5). To return to the nonhappening of Pozuelo's group show, many artists, acutely aware of the material limitations and languishing institutional support in times of austerity, pool their resources collectively in order to continue practicing and exhibiting their work. Their production can provide a weighty witness to the times, as Perriam notes, a point I take up in this book, less from the position of how economic factors alone can shape cultural production with material limitations and contribute to emergent practices among artists, noted all too briefly here, than from that of questioning the *work* that cultural production accomplishes as it imagines worlds shaped by conditions and possibilities for change from the sociopolitical circumstances in which it materializes, at present.

What follows is an attempt to think through the relationships between cultural production and political culture in the urban milieu during this time of crisis. The gravity of the economic crisis and the still-emerging social mobilizations have incited a process of change that may yet amount to a paradigm shift, which raises the question of precisely how and why this is so. These essays aim to contribute modestly to this sense-making of the present circumstance in which over time, writes Lauren Berlant, "a process will eventually appear monumentally as form—as episode, event, or epoch [—] while living in the stretched out 'now' that is at once intimate and estranged" (2008, 5). At my time of writing, the essays take up this line of inquiry from a present sensed as one enduring historic change at great speed, for both everyday life in urban centers in Spain and possibly for scholarship on interdisciplinary approaches to contemporary Spanish culture, politics, and society. In this sense, they have also been written from a sense of urgency in order to address Spain's crisis, neoliberalism, and the relationships between culture and politics at present, particularly where I view my own teaching and scholarship striving for the tools to address the current conjuncture. First drafted between September 2012 and February 2014, they date from the adoption of Spain's deepest cutbacks to social programs in its democratic history, to elected officials' first proclaimed indications of an economic recovery, the social effects of which have yet to be seen. To place a date on these essays is, referring to the work of interpretation in the following pages, to situate them within the circumstance of their production at a time moving with great speed.

Acknowledgments

I would like to thank the Department of Spanish and Portuguese at New York University for providing me with necessary access to research materials as a visiting scholar from 2013 to 2015. Also, my acknowledgment to Taylor and Francis for the authorization to reprint the latter portion of chapter 3, originally published under the title "About Time: Sensing the Crisis in Nophoto's *El último verano*" in the *Journal of Spanish Cultural Studies* (2014). For the epigraphs, the University of Chicago Press and Semiotext(e) kindly granted their permissions to include the quotations by Ross Chambers and Franco "Bifo" Berardi, respectively.

Several authors and artists generously agreed to have their work reprinted in this volume; I am especially grateful to them. My appreciation to the poet Gregorio Apesteguía, photographer Vicente A. Jiménez, and the Nophoto Photography Collective, especially Jonás Bel, Paco Gómez, and Eduardo Nave, for their generosity. Thank you to Nina Shield who provided masterful translations of Apesteguía's poetry in English and as an excellent editor, also gave me insightful comments on an earlier draft of chapter 3. All other English translations of original Spanish texts, unless referenced otherwise, are my own. My warm thanks to coeditors Benjamin Fraser and Susan Larson, as well as to Shaun Vigil, Erica Buchman, and Leighton Lustig at Palgrave Macmillan, whose invaluable feedback and encouragement throughout the publishing process made it a delightful one.

This book would not have been possible without the support of many friends, family members, and colleagues who deserve special mention for our continued conversations, not least their patience and encouragement during my time immersed in this project. They deserve more acknowledgment than can be expressed here. Very much present throughout the writing of this book are the many things I have learned from them, and so I wish to dedicate it to them in part, to those who in one way or another have taught me. This book is also, of course, for Miguel.

INTRODUCTION

Urban Multitudes: 15M and the Spontaneous "Spanish Revolution"

I.

Cities have become more than simply the *locations* for peoples to protest common social injustices, notes Manuel Delgado (2010, 137–53). As demonstrators gather in the streets to practice forms of resistance, urban life is also *reshaped* in these oppositional struggles against the city's prescribed economic functions as "a mere source of revenue" and profit alone (2010, 152). The practices of demonstrators reconfigure the city as multitudes congregate and move spontaneously through space, as they collectively express emotions and their intensities in great numbers, as they settle in encampments and strongholds, as they scatter in displacements and make vertical climbs to post banners on building surfaces. To transform the city in protest, even if briefly, before routine commerce and transit take hold again, is also to accelerate and intensify common production among people who share their status as subject to the everyday priorities of capital in the urban milieu. Common production materializes when demonstrators take the public square, when they perform coordinated gestures at the same time and place, and when they assemble to take action toward specific aims in opposition to the sources of collective domination they decry, reshaping the city all the while in its look, feel, and meshwork of relations (2010, 141).

The global financial crisis of 2007–8 has come to bear upon Spain with regional and local particularities that continue to unfold in interrelated crises—an urban crisis, a housing crisis, a labor crisis, a state crisis of sovereignty, a political crisis of governance to neoliberal policy aims, an everyday crisis of survival for many, and so on. In times of crisis, the mass demonstrations consolidated after May 15, 2011, known as the 15M movement, drew unexpected multitudes of protesters before the local and regional elections. Outrage and the slogan "¡No somos mercancía en manos de políticos y banqueros!" [We're not goods in the hands of politicians and bankers!], were understood to be the common denominators among protesters, called the *indignadxs*—the angry ones.[1] Demonstrators occupied public plazas and raised self-managed encampments throughout Spanish cities, communicating among them through social networks, cell phones, and the web. Mobilizing against the government's austerity measures, rising unemployment, political corruption, restrictive copyright laws, among numerous other reasons, the protesters endured confrontations with the police through passive resistance and the National Election Board's verdict that declared the demonstrations illegal. By mid-June, protesters in Madrid's kilometer zero at La Puerta del Sol lifted the encampment voluntarily, for the 15M movement had transformed into a network of local assemblies and working groups coordinating sustained actions, which since then have received widespread sympathizers across demographics (Sampedro and Lobera, 2014). Across Spain to date, self-organized networks of civilians have stopped forced evictions for homeowners and the deportation of immigrants, rallied against privatization and cutbacks to public education and healthcare, and organized debates, textbook exchanges, and neighborhood film screenings, to name a few lines of action. Though unexpected, May 2011 marked an event that reinvigorated direct democratic participation in public affairs in which according to Spanish public television (TVE), an estimated 6 to 8.5 million residents in Spain had participated to some degree in a matter of three months ("Más de seis millones," 2011).

Although Spanish cities served as their *stages* for protest, the 15M demonstrations likewise *transformed* the urban environment through oppositional practices that released the potential for common production in assembly, experimental problem solving, and concerted action toward change. As the primary civilian response to Spain's compounded crises, the 15M mobilizations have forcefully "irrumpido desde la primavera de 2011 como un actor nuevo en la ciudad" [irrupted as a new actor in the city ever since the spring of 2011] (Observatorio Metropolitano, 2013, 171). I take as my point of departure the premise that multitudes in 15M and its derivations have proved capable of reshaping urban space through oppositional practices in assembly and protest—configured in their fixed encampments and swarmlike movements in the city, their performed gestures and chants, their standoffs before the police and parliament, their networked actions and sensible intensities, all matters explored in this book.

In the urban setting, 15M and its derivatives have reappropriated and resignified space (Sampedro and Sánchez, 2011), that is, they have produced space toward the protesters' aims at once *within* and *in opposition to* the existing capital flows and regulatory policies of the city. Although the protesters' reshaping of the city may be precarious, forever on the shore of its own disappearance, to paraphrase Jacques Rancière (2010, 39), what persist when demonstrators no longer occupy the square, and when the urban milieu may succumb again to routine commerce, private enterprise, and property speculation, are the transformative practices of protesters who *read* their common subjugation critically and, in the process, make the sources of domination *legible* as a collective circumstance, with material consequences. There exists no one material that is read and made readable in these practices but an array of singularities bound together by the common circumstances of production across them, in the sinews between them. Protesters read and denounce the processes of gentrification and privatization in the urban landscape, rhetoric on austerity circulating in the media by government officials and policy makers, precarious conditions of everyday work-life, economic-political consensuses forged against the interests of the represented, social inequalities recast in media analysis as the personal failings of the poor, and so forth. Reading, it seems, plays an important role in constituting and reconstituting multitudes that mobilize toward change.

What are the mechanics of these readings? How are they produced, and what work they *do* across different publics? An inquiry into the relationships among oppositional readings in 15M, or the question of what holds these critical practices together and what makes them tick, is one main line of investigation in this book. In approach, this work examines the mechanics of how these readings are practiced in form and function as the urban landscape is reshaped in protest, and, conversely, what demonstrators can and have accomplished collectively as their practices articulate desires for change—taken up together, the *poetics* of oppositional practices at my time of writing.

II.

Each chapter of *Poetics of Opposition in Contemporary Spain: Politics and the Work of Urban Culture* explores the relationships between culture and the political in an attempt to understand how the former works through current change and imagined alternatives, with their short-comings and liberating possibilities, from a present in which government officials and policy makers have denied repeatedly the existence of any alternative, at all. Across the chapters, the project explores the practices of urban protest in Madrid, the roles of affect/emotion in demonstrations, and the critical activity of "reading the crisis" by protesters, as part and parcel of the urban transformations in the public square. The analytical drift of this line of research interrogates how creation, or the poetics of the cultural production examined in each case study, configures both the liberating and policing functions of the current circumstance within the prevailing powers that shape, in part, the real. Culture, it seems, accomplishes a kind of immeasurable, uncountable work for viewers and readers in critical opposition to a pervasive "political rationality that tries to render the social domain economic" amid the neoliberal governance of contemporary times (Lemke, 2001, 203).

Readers interested in an overview of the global and Spanish crises since 2007–8 will find these matters addressed in chapter 1, Lessons Felt, Then Learned, which approaches the role of affects/emotions, among them outrage, as potentially mobilizing forces for the 15M demonstrations. Although "anger" and other emotions could easily be regarded as the personal feelings of protesters, I caution against this presumption by exploring the collective circumstance of their production in times of austerity. Sketching out a system of thought on the crisis, the chapter examines official state discourse on austerity during the tenure of socialist (PSOE) and conservative (PP) rule, which draws from "humility," shame in "living beyond one's means," and "the honorability of sacrifice" whereby policy aims are asserted as an intimately personal matter. Considering the frequency and volume of these iterations in circulation in the media, and their potential emotional pull, this chapter lays the basis for further discussion on neoliberal governance and the oppositional practices of protesters, respectively. In doing so, I address existing scholarship on how affects, emotions, and feelings are produced, and their potential role in moving actors to take action in political mobilization.

The second part of the chapter examines Gregorio Apesteguía's free-verse poems published in literary fanzines, which situate readers in an imagined future after a financial collapse. The poetic voice registers the detached experiences of an automated life in the postcrisis city—among them, precarity, insolvency, and commercial desire. Apesteguía's verse exploits what Franco "Bifo" Berardi calls the immeasurable "process of emancipating language and affects" in poetry and the sensory

experience privileged in poetic voice, against the accountable financialization of the economy in which almost everything, even emotion in
marketing strategies, is capitalized upon for calculable profits (2012,
16). The present of an immeasurable social catastrophe, it seems, cannot be charted by the forecasting logic of capital accumulation, which
works to destabilize any affirmation on positive economic recovery. In
verse, Apesteguía's poetry turns to "others" by viewing their condition
as one's own under the rule of capital, which provides the mechanics for
the poetic "I's" eventual transformation that has this voice recognize
its own voluntary participation in sustaining "The Great Fraud" and
financial collapse. In this *becoming-other* for the poetic voice, to take
stock of the present is also to provide an emancipatory knowledge for
change, one that must be committed to remembrance of the present
crisis in posterity.

Ángel Luis Lara described the encampment raised by 15M demonstrators as a miniature "city within a city" in Madrid's La Puerta del Sol
(2012, 652). Requiring ample space, chapter 2 also takes the form of a
mini-book within this book in order to address the 15M Sol encampment's practices of protest and assembly, the role of affect/emotion in
them, and their shaping of the urban milieu in 2011. In it, I pay particular attention to the plural responses from protesters who read critically
and refused the official state discourse on the crisis amid the deteriorating conditions of life in the economic downturn. In the protest actions
and banners of the *indignadxs*, there is no one subject position that can
be claimed to produce these oppositional statements, of course, which
rather form a field of discursive production from multiple positions, as
a *practice* of reading among many. In one possible approach to the 15M
protests, then, I examine the demonstrators' language and performative
actions in assembly as a form of *oppositional literacy* (or, a knowledge
and practice of reading) that bears the possibility for transformation
examined in Ross Chambers's *Room for Maneuver* (1991). Chambers
interrogates the oppositional practice of *reading* as a cognitive one of
self-education capable of producing changes in desire and, thus, desirable change. In 15M, taught and learned from one another in assembly,
and by doing things together without the need for formal education,
the knowledges and practices of oppositional readings (or, "literacy")
might confront academic endeavors with a challenge to reassess the task
of criticism in order to account for the transformative capacity of what
is already being practiced in the streets.

Reflecting on the lessons of the 1968 uprisings in Paris, Chambers
tempers the claims made by Deleuze and Guattari that resistance can

escape *outside* the existing structures of power (the "line of flight"). One might also look to the experience of modern history in the West from the French Revolution to twentieth-century totalitarianisms, or elsewhere in the world, to observe that as resistance struggles secured positions of power they tended to reproduce the very regimes of violence, repression, and terror that their followers sought to topple. Chambers proposes a nuanced understanding of how critical interpretation, in narrative reception and address, partakes in an oppositional practice capable of producing desired change *within* predominant power structures that, in turn, can shape them. The effect that oppositional reading has, in practice, is one that shows power to be relational and necessarily mediated wherever it lays a claim to its authority. Extrapolating from Chambers's argument, in the first instance, to read oppositionally is to question from the reader's subject position how desires are shaped or repressed by the prevailing structures of power, that is, to conceive of their authority as necessarily mediated in order to become "an object of interpretation" (*Room for Maneuver*, 179). And secondly, once the latter are constructed with readability, it is to articulate oppositional maneuvers in speech and action within these predominant power relations, thereby mitigating them wherever they work to repress or police the possible.

To argue this point, I look to different scenes of readerly activities in the 15M protests, and their mechanics, that respond to authority with oppositionality in speech, space, and affective intensity: first, in the demonstrators' critiques of how existing powers (political, economic, financial) shape the conditions of life at present and, then, in the liberating possibilities of collectively imagining and creating alternatives that maneuver these conditions wherever they are identified for producing a policing or repressive function. Opposition to authority, notes Chambers, is discursive in part, in which "'narrative' opposition [...] has as its distinguishing feature the power of 'authority' to affect people, mentally and emotionally, and by that means to change states of affairs in general" (1991, 12). The forms of opposition, nonviolence, and care developing in assembly procedure and the protests, in this light, consist in what Deleuze and Guattari understood as a *minoritarian politics* capable of transforming the majority in opposition to it. In afterword, the section closes with an audiovisual analysis of the televised 2011 General Election campaign by the conservative Partido Popular (PP) that would secure an absolute majority in parliament. Notably, the campaign evokes emotions for change and "hope" without stating an explicit platform, other than through its "warm" values on perseverance and industriousness amid difficult times. My hope is that these reflections on 15M and its oppositional practices can contribute to analyzing some of the mechanics and defining features of the mobilizations as one possible take on the events of 2011, without intending to speak for or "represent" the movement.

In closure, chapter 2 addresses the inheritance of Spain's *Transición* from dictatorship to democracy through a critique of the Culture of Transition and its consensuses—among them, the bipartisan turn between socialist and conservative rule—challenged by the practices of 15M. I explore the urban performance *Los encargados* by Santiago Sierra and Jorge Galindo, of a Situationist bent, in which the video recording of a simulated presidential motorcade down Madrid's Gran Vía calls into question the relationship between spectators (pedestrians) and state security in urban space. The spectacle of democracy critiqued in this intervention, as Spain's heads of state since the *Transición* parade solemnly down Madrid's emblematic boulevard, resides in the spatial distance between citizens (spectators) and the state (the motorcade), and the latter's ceremonious demonstration of power and security—indeed immunity—over the interests of its constituents. The mechanics of what the parade accomplishes in sight, sound, and space are examined for the contradictions that arise when reading the parade through the lens of political ideology.

From the pressing need to address neoliberal policies, among them austerity, chapter 3 endeavors to analyze the governing logics of neoliberalism and some myth-making assertions around the policies that call for the autonomous self-care of the population through private investments. In Spain, as elsewhere, rhetoric on neoliberal policies often justifies privatization initiatives and reduced public expenditures—generally, the dismantling of the welfare state—as an intensely personalized matter that upholds "empowering" narratives on enterprise, equal opportunity, and economic self-sufficiency for life. This chapter revisits Michel Foucault's lectures on the biopolitics of neoliberalism, in the history of the twentieth-century equation between free-market policies and democratic freedoms, and since the time of his lectures, in recent attempts to pin together, metonymically, certain social judgments about welfare, un/employment, and the model behaviors of an ideal economic subject (*homo oeconomicus*). That model behaviors and values for the population are crafted around neoliberal policy aims, it can be said, operates as a *dispositif* to correct others and oneself in alignment with the discourse of power. Informed by an extensive review of the publications from neoliberal think tanks in Spain, among them the Fundación para el Análisis y Estudios Sociales (FAES) that guides the policy agendas for the ruling PP, this reading does not intend to be exhaustive but to generate some critical tools in order to approach the social production of neoliberal thought operating beyond, and conversely in relation to, state policy aims—or, their biopolitics.

Aside from the oppositional practices of protest, what happens in everyday life amid austerity when it seems that, generally, not much is happening at all? To close the chapter, I look to Nophoto's collective photography project *El último verano* on downward mobility, precarity, and emigration. Drawing from Lauren Berlant's writings on the *impasse*, I read how these photos expose *la crisis* through the subject's affective attachments to perceptible losses and then in strategies for survival developed amid an ongoing crisis. To take stock of the present at an impasse, I argue, is to immerse oneself in a strong sense of temporality in which induced change and loss destabilize the present, evoking senses of return, nostalgia, future projection, escapist fantasy, and anxieties about projected risk. In Nophoto's photographs, the composite character of this project indexes plural ways of viewing times of crisis that assemble a collective, shared circumstance of everyday life amid austerity. The indexical character of the photographs, which has them move from capture to the *production* of such effects in viewers, muddies any strict dichotomy between the viewing subject and viewed photograph in ways that tend to suggest, as David Levi Strauss (2003, 23) has noted, that images "exist and operate on an axis of selection meaningful in relation to other photographs in proximity," and perhaps in relation to other viewers, too.

Reading and (il)legibility is the main thrust of the final essay, in chapter 4, House Rules, in which I read stage theater and the impunity of political and capital interests in the Spanish state at my time of writing. To begin, I propose rethinking political theorist Carl Schmitt's classic formulation of the "state of exception" in an attempt to account for the current practices of *selective exemption* and self-impunity in the Spanish State for measures that are paradoxically called "exceptional" even as they escape Schmitt's historical definition of sovereign exceptionalism. Some of these undemocratic measures include parliamentary mandate by decree, the cancellation of the State of the Nation debate, parliament's refusal to hold public hearings for corruption charges, the conservative party's purging of journalists from Spanish public television and radio (RTVE), and recent laws that criminalize protest, to name a few. Returning to Nicos Poulantzas's writings on state authoritarianism amid the economic crisis of the 1970s, I propose straying from Poulantzas's original proposals to reconsider the current conjuncture as a form of (il)legible exception that, instead, could perhaps be understood more accurately as a plural, micropolitical field of struggle against the practices of selective exemption and impunity within and beyond the state.

Questioning how desires for transformation alone are not enough to enact substantive change, the book concludes with a discussion of Abel Zamora's stage-play *Temporada baja* and his microtheater production *Pequeños dramas sobre arena azul*. In both works, I explore how Zamora invites his audience to view the characters' frustrated, unrealized desires for change and the missed encounters among them, as conditioned by the prevailing structures of power (social class, gender, sexuality) that speak through the characters' interactions. Policing each other and themselves, the characters expose for the audience their own participation in conditioning possibilities for substantive change, even paradoxically, against their own desires. The characters' inability to read their relationships to each other and to the modern hotel they inhabit, or the *non-place* that frames their encounters, per Marc Augé, leaves them largely atomized from each other, pigeonholed and incapable of viewing their collective circumstance in this tightly controlled space of surveillance. The prevailing structures of power, then, are not presented as abstract conditions for these exchanges but are located in the characters' actions and speech, and in their own participation in reifying the disciplinary forces of their environment.

Poetics in literary and cultural analysis, writes Justin Crumbaugh, is eclipsed, if not subsumed by a contemporary interest in *praxis*, often privileged as the social and political nexus to a given work's circumstance of production by standards of authorship (2012, 41–53). The attribution of authorly responsibility for creation, notes Crumbaugh in his reading of Marx—that is, the individualization of the creative act in industrial and advanced capitalism—tends to collapse creative production (*poiesis*) into authorly decision and intention (*praxis*) in the modern cult for an attributable subject responsible for creation itself.[2] For Marx, notes Crumbaugh, to ignore the collective character of production (*poiesis*) is also to disregard its transmutative possibilities in which *poiesis* can not only transform the makers in the process, but also the material and social environment of production itself; that is, it is to overlook the entangled character of practice and creation, never in diametric opposition, as a transformative process of "consciousness" (for Marx) upon which work depends. Tracing a brief but excellent comprehensive overview of *poiesis* in Aristotle, Marx, and Agamben, Crumbaugh proposes revisiting poetics in critical analysis, then, as a way of considering creation "un fenómeno radicalmente desindividualizado" [a radically de-individualized phenomenon], capable of suspending "la subjetividad moderna y [abrir] paso a otros esquemas conceptuales y nuevas condiciones de posibilidad" [modern subjectivity and opening ways to other conceptual schematics and new conditions of possibility] (2012, 42). Or, to restate Crumbaugh's proposal for my scope here, an endeavor into poetics would require, on certain terms, forms of analysis that take into account the transformative capacity of creation and practice wherever the capitalist mode of production serves to represses *poiesis* (and its possibilities to engender *becomings*) from *praxis*.

An inquiry into poetics, as I refer to the term here, supposes approaching cultural production, in part, as an ensemble of operations and mechanics that have produced a given work and, in turn, *can work on* viewers and readers as a kind of device. In this way, I analyze these operative parts, at times, for how political rhetoric slides together concepts (metonymically) from one to the next in order to pin them together in the social imaginary, for how oppositional readings by protesters are performed into existence or displaced (in metaphor), and for the ways in which demonstrators assemble a string of ideas together (polysyndeton) to express desirable change across conjunctions. It also requires, at times, taking a look at how visual and narrative stories on the crisis fit together and speak to each other (indexically). What the work of culture can do, on the other hand, bears no specific formula, of course, and it requires a turn to its context of production and reception, which can never be a total or complete endeavor. But nor does the context of reception presume the critical activity of reading as a form of passive intake. Rather, the work of culture viewed or read, heard or perhaps even consumed, is not conceived of as an object per se, but as the result of an assembled configuration of processes in which reception of its so-called product likewise configures multiplicities of readings from its mediated context of reception. This result of what viewers may see and hear, read and interpret, is not an end-object itself, but another assembled moment in movement, of processes of delivery and reception that bear possibilities for interpretation within the subject-object world in which it is reassembled (or, in interpretation). Implied in the language of the term, the *work of culture*, then, moves from the object of study as an isolated "work" or product, to the relational processes of production in the *work* that it can accomplish for readers and viewers in different contexts—its mechanisms *at work*—as a device that questions possibilities for change.

The politics of dissent today, as well as the collective projects forged in opposition to decried injustices, may have carved out an alternative regime of signification in contemporary Spain. This observation is not an abstraction but rather bears material forms, such as those processes of change "enfleshed" in city areas transformed by protests and mobilizations defending the public "right to the city" (Feinberg, 2014, 8–10, 14). Much like the city, shaped and reshaped materially in relation to and conversely by inhabitants, the production of culture can be said to bear some traces of this resignifying process. Cultural production, particularly that of an alternative urban bent, partakes in these critical practices by imagining the very conditions of possibility and limitations for desired change. And much like the resignified city, this production (fanzine poetry, video performance, collective photography, stage- and microtheater) explores changes that must necessarily embark from what is already being practiced at present, from at once *within* and *in opposition to* the predominant power relations shaping everyday life. Cultural production, then, is not simply an expression or representation, but shows itself as bearing some working parts and mechanisms of this resignifying process *as* it resignifies. First, though, what were the 15M protests, and how have these demonstrations been read by others?

III.

"Nobody Expects the Spanish Revolution" reads one sign from a widely circulated photograph of the first 15M demonstrations. In it, a protester masked as Guy Fawkes from the film *V for Vendetta* offers a political twist to Monty Python's comedy sketch ("Nobody Expects the Spanish Inquisition!"), for a movement characterized by its seriousness of action and occasional irony of forms. In protests, demonstrators have used the term "spontaneous" to describe their actions when interviewed by the media, as have commentators and journalists. Its usage, however, implicitly skirts the difficulties that arise in any attempt to describe a field of possibilities, actions, and contingencies from which mass mobilizations emerge seemingly overnight, gain supporters, lose them, and disappear from public view until the next demonstration appears visibly in the streets. Spontaneity and its many synonyms have become the shorthand to describe the time with which the May 2011 protests irrupted with great intensity and specific demands, in an unexpected tempo of "sudden" emergence.

In some sense-making narratives on the spontaneous character of 15M, the search to pinpoint the movement's origins contributes indirectly to portraying the multitude as an anomaly—unusual, out-of-the-blue, and destined to disappear in due time—thereby taming it through prediction. In others, readings rely on the operative concepts in liberal democracy and class struggle to explain a movement that problematizes these analytical frameworks. And for many protesters, spontaneity is a powerful choice of words to express the incalculability of the multitude's actions against the speech of government officials who attempt to criminalize the demonstrations in public opinion. In all cases, however, the use of the word "spontaneous" grazes over the field of contingencies from which the protests emerged.

Here, I set out to address how some news media, official state discourse, and critiques on the 15M phenomenon have portrayed or analyzed the movement through operations that tend to assimilate its sudden emergence and intensity within specific logics that somehow fail to explain it. The shortcomings of these readings may speak more to the methodological displacements required to analyze mobilizations or the conventions of class struggle and liberal democracy, than to the authors' own responsibility for them. In this regard, by reading them against their moment of production, one may begin to articulate a narrative over time of how 15M was interpreted from different perspectives in its first few months of existence in order to arrive at a discussion of what critical tools are available to understand its emergence. After all, 15M is a critical moment that questions operative notions of the public, the media and digital culture, and direct democratic participation in ways that exceed institutional knowledge of the kind deployed in state decision making, all of which entails revisiting the ways in which 15M *has been read*.

One of the earliest substantial attempts to make sense of the spontaneity of the 15M movement is that of journalist Alicia G. Montano, director of *Informe Semanal* (TVE) news program at that time (2011). Delivered less than four months after the first demonstrations in Madrid, G. Montano's exposition is a necessary interpretation of the movement's origins and consequences for partisan politics. The events of 15M proved powerful enough to require politicians to address mass demonstrations that had spoken first with the cry "¡No nos representan!" [They don't represent us!], in great numbers, and then with specific demands for government officials. G. Montano's analysis cites footage from *Informe Semanal* dating to April 2011 in order to explain the economic conditions that laid the foundations for the protests in May, as well as the organization and literature that influenced protesters. Moving through the backdrop of the financial crisis, she traces the first appearance of the 15M movement in part to the unemployed university-educated founders of Democracia Real Ya! (Real Democracy

Now! – DRY), one of many platforms participating in 15M, and the great influence of Stéphane Hessel's bestseller *¡Indignaos!* [Time for Outrage!] published in Spanish translation in 2010. In his timely reflection, Hessel speaks to his readers as the surviving author of the Universal Declaration of Human Rights, calling for peaceful insurrection against human rights violations today, specifically, on the discriminatory laws of European states against immigrants and the military offenses against civilians in the Middle East. Reading 15M through Hessel's influence, then, G. Montano's analysis and dual attribution—on the one hand, to a university-educated leadership core, and on the other, to a human rights guru calling for peaceful insurrection—is spoken from specific coordinates in time. This analysis dates to the end of summer 2011, after the Sol encampment was lifted, when the movement had not yet demonstrated its endurance with sustained actions over the year; when public speculation wondered if 15M would turn into a political party; and when its participants were likewise faced with a potential reinsertion into everyday routine in the fall season. In this sense, my reading of G. Montano's analysis takes into account both the operation that must identify the materialization of a movement with definitive leaders and a specific literature, and the time of her reading the movement against its potential disappearance.

However involuntarily, to assign the movement leaders and locatable origins recasts 15M as a replicated extension of class struggles and positions within civil society. For, although it is clear that the reported name given to the *indignadxs* shares the title of Hessel's manifesto, it is not certain that demonstrators in late May 2011 found in Hessel their very reason to join the protests, or if a significant number had read his work before migrating to the encampments. At the root of this operation is a direct cause-effect relation, which shuttles from circumstance to production, from Hessel's bestseller to direct action, in a suture that explains the multitude's sudden mobilization. As does the necessity of locating a specific origin for the movement in a leadership core, which known with greater clarity in hindsight was dispersed among multiple platforms with different causes, addressed in chapter 2. At my time of writing as then, the governing norms of debate and organizational structures of 15M rely on mechanisms that actively disable the concentration of power within a specific leadership, as its popular assemblies and working groups are open to all participants whose administrative responsibilities rotate among volunteers. It would seem as though a first analysis, spoken from a specific time inflected by the movement's potential reinsertion into daily routine, or its presumed transformation into a party, would find in 15M a microscale reproduction of civil society's hierarchies engaged in class struggle: a certain cohesion among the socially stratified masses, an educated elite at the helm, and an influential text. To stretch this comparison in terms translatable to the state, the movement is seen through a lens that likens its components to a class alliance, a party, and an ideology, all of which constitute the analytical tools of institutional hegemony and political strategy in state theory, for a movement that at that time resisted both institutionalism and the standing system of partisan politics. G. Montano's important analysis, in my view, is inflected by the circumstance from which it was produced and the operative procedures required to assimilate its inexplicable spontaneity and direction. This reading that tends to normalize the movement within class struggle "as usual" is spoken from the time of its possible disappearance or institutionalization as its participants again assimilated into everyday routine after summer 2011.

Departing from G. Montano's analysis then, one can begin to approximate a concept of the *multitude* that has since proved resilient to class definition and institutional structuring within the existing partisan channels. In their work *Multitude: War and Democracy in the Age of Empire*, Michael Hardt and Antonio Negri argue that the accelerated distribution of labor in advanced capitalism and its de-territorializing effects have contributed to new forms of transversal solidarity across workers in different sectors and classes. Such solidarity among socioeconomic segments and labor sectors certainly describes the composite picture of the multitude of protesters and participants in 15M, who in demographic terms, come from diverse socioeconomic backgrounds and labor markets. Ultimately, Hardt and Negri (2005, 107) explain, this potential for cross-segment solidarity stems from the regime of productivity in late capitalism in which all workers participate, whether by providing services or manual labor. Whereas notions of class difference and class alliance may have been fundamental concepts to explain past labor struggles, today the lack of political priority for forms of labor in advanced capitalism bears the potential to render this distinction a secondary consideration to all workers' productivity. That is, despite class difference, workers share in common their proletarian condition as laborers and producers. Therefore, "the multitude is an open and expansive concept. The multitude gives the concept of the proletariat its fullest definition as all those who labor and produce under the rule of capital." This is not to say that the social production of class difference is erased in the multitude, but that one point of transversal solidarity binding its multiplicity together resides in the collective recognition of a shared exploitation (one source of outrage) and common production in assembly. As such, the encampment in Sol had achieved a creative accomplishment for common production: it suspended the rhythms of everyday life in the open plaza, reconfiguring its functionality as a space for protest, dialog, reflection, and collective labors for the demonstrators' plural aims (Corsín Jiménez and Estalella, 2013; Sánchez Cedillo, 2012).

Perhaps it is this creative potential of the demonstrations, together with the movement's aims, which has led some academic criticism to construe a form of humanist ethos from 15M. In this vein, another critical contribution on the movement within months of its appearance comes from the architect Cristina García-Rosales and professor of philosophy Manuel Penella Heller (2011, 66) in their coauthored work *Palabras para indignados. Hacia una nueva revolución humanista* [Words for the *Indignados*. Toward a New Humanist Revolution], which projects 15M as a revitalizing project for liberal humanism. As such, the spontaneity of the movement is erased through a procedure that grafts it within a homogeneous, historical time. As the title implies, the text is addressed to both those interested in learning about the movement and those already participating in it, as a dual appeal to readers who might join or sympathize with its aims, on the one hand, and their education on the movement's humanist precedents, on the other. Constructing a "history of humanism" that originates in Greek stoicism and continues in Christianity, the Enlightenment, and antifascist resistance in the twentieth century, the authors build a philosophical and moral tradition for the movement through an astonishing act of imagining the community for the community, the very task upon which nation building has historically depended. Their project is borne from "la necesidad histórica de salvar la parte noble del liberalismo" [the historical need to save the noble part of liberalism] for the common good. If precedents for 15M exist, however, they are located in the *practices* of demonstrators and in the assemblies, which have brought together participants from both the antidictatorship struggles and a new generation of cyber activists, and draw from the established resistance movements of the 1970s Madrid Neighborhood Associations to the activist networks mobilizing in defense of the commons at present (La Parra-Pérez, 2014; Sampedro and Lobera, 2014; Vilaseca, 2014).

Nevertheless, to describe 15M as a phenomenon arising from a historical tradition of humanism—and to inscribe the movement within a revitalized liberal project rooted in "where we came from"— performs however unintentionally a sleight of hand that reintroduces

the movement within the logical schematics of modernity's most exclusionary machinery: liberal notions of the "common good" and humanist
universalisms that slip dangerously into moral judgment. The myth-
making that ensues in *Palabras para indignados* finds its justification
in the sutured, homogeneous narrative of a timeless humanist history
across millennia. The text in this sense proposes a return to projects past
without a critical take on their violent, exclusionary results in history.
Stated otherwise, any proposal to return to the falsely universal axioms
of humanism should confront its greatest critique in Max Horkheimer
and Theodor Adorno's *Dialectic of Enlightenment*. García-Rosales and
Penella Heller's work, however, is also written from a specific moment,
published within six months of May 2011, and as such proves important
for its attempt to foster the movement's expansion through interpretation, in which sympathizers will find reasons to participate through
identification, in this case, with a sense of timeless humanism. Yet, even
as 15M's practices in assembly procedure and direct democracy break
away from the conventions of liberalism, the authors' critical lens recap-
tures it as a new imagined community of the People, as a historically
determined product grounded in two millennia of resistance struggles
in the West.

As Hardt and Negri argue in their work *Empire*, the multitude differs
from the concept of the People imagined historically in nation states:

> The multitude is a multiplicity, a plane of singularities, an open set of
> relations, which is not homogenous or identical with itself and bears an
> indistinct, inclusive relation to those outside of it. The people, in con-
> trast, tends toward identity and homogeneity internally while posing its
> difference from and excluding what remains outside of it. Whereas the
> multitude is an inconclusive constituent relation, the people is a consti-
> tuted synthesis that is prepared for sovereignty. The people provides a
> single will and action that is independent of and often in conflict with
> the various wills and actions of the multitude. Every nation must make
> the multitude into a people. (2000, 103)

The concept of the People in liberal democracy is inherently imagined from an exclusionary principle, required historically to define a
nation, that constructs categories of difference to Others—with both
interiority to its marginalized and exteriority to "foreign" peoples and
nations. Conceived as a singular entity united by will, the People is
constituted for and by the nation state as a collective subject of governance. As every nation state must mold the multitude into a People it
can govern, the conditions of its subjecthood for rule are reproduced in a

social relation imagined as the governed who must be governable to the state. In 15M's refusal of this presumption, however, feelings of outrage and anger are named for a shared condition among protesters, produced from the sense that sovereignty has been usurped, specifically, by state decision making that has the burden of the financial crisis come to bear upon Spanish residents through cutbacks to social programs, healthcare, education, and so on, denounced in the slogan, "¡No pagaremos vuestras crisis!" [We won't pay for your crises!]. Though perhaps an inheritance from national projects past, today the state must govern the multitude as a collective subject, as the People. In contrast, however, the multitude is irreducible to a singular identity, subjectivity, or homogenizing principle, thereby bearing the possibility of constituting itself within a multiplicity of social relations by refusing collectively the sovereign "We" of this People. In doing so, the multitude deploys this "we" in a collective refusal of its condition as a subject (in this case, reduced to an object), "We are not goods in the hands of politicians and bankers!"

Among responses from the state, government officials were left with little recourse other than to comment on the mass protests, particularly during the final stretch of an election campaign. Among statements from the conservative Partido Popular (PP), Soraya Sáenz de Santamaría seconded the protesters' "indignation," recasting their outrage as a tool to criticize the ruling Socialist Party's responsibility (PSOE) for high unemployment rates,[3] while the PP's leader Mariano Rajoy, when pressed to comment on 15M, dismissed the protests as facile criticism of politicians.[4] Among candidates on the left, Tomás Gómez (PSOE) and Cayo Lara from Izquierda Unida (IU) both empathized publicly with the protesters' aims, contributing indirectly to a far-fetched conspiracy theory in the rightwing media that the ruling PSOE had engineered protests that were neither chance nor spontaneous (Seco et al., 2011; Cué, "Los indignados," 2011). On the other hand, President Zapatero of the ruling Socialist party (PSOE) expressed the need to listen and be sensitive to the demands of protesters, while stressing the need for a representative democracy with a party system (Cué and Díez, 2011). In different ways, despite much partisan finger-pointing, elected officials of all stripes found a form of appropriation in the mass mobilizations, either to seek potential votes in the coming elections or to bid lessons on conserving the status quo of the standing partisan system. In this way, President Zapatero's words indeed drove at the heart of a perceptible antagonism between the direct democracy of assembly procedure practiced in the 15M encampments and the representative democracy of the Spanish state that protesters claimed was in need of considerable reforms.

Tellingly, in the following months, the PSOE's presidential candidate Alfredo Pérez Rubalcaba would elaborate the most direct response to the movement in his proposal for the "351st seat" in parliament, which would have allowed for one civilian representative to participate in parliamentary debates, an initiative that never came to fruition (Garea 2011). In theories on hegemony, Rubalcaba's proposal, at least in design, would have equated to an attempt to co-opt the movement into the existing representative channels, for participants in a movement who had largely refused their condition as the governed in the standing electoral system. In all cases, then, the public address of politicians demonstrated that institutional knowledge rested upon addressing the multitude from a hegemonic position toward the People, presumed naturally to be partisan voters of one political color or another in the standing party system. And in these cases, their language showed traces of the undeniable force with which the multitude had pronounced itself with great international projection. For, the presence and visibility of the demonstrations proved capable of interpellating politicians in a manner that incited a direct response to channel voter interests into partisan lines. These responses spoken from the Spanish State were not addressed to the multitude's positions of negation that had refused the deteriorating conditions of life and their status as "the represented" by the prevailing partisan system, but instead were articulated from a hegemonic position when speaking to the electorate, a potential constituency, as the People (Hardt and Negri, 2012).

Symptomatic of the need to make sense of the multitude's composite character, the mainstream news media offered countless portraits—photo reports, televised interviews, and news columns of an artistic and informative bent—of the individuals participating in the events of spring and summer 2011 (Alcaide, 2011; Gil, 2011; "Indignados," 2011; Santaeulalia et al., 2011). "Citizens demand rebuilding democracy," summarizes the title to one article in which protesters young and elder, employed and seeking work, lawyers and executives, teachers and students of different socioeconomic backgrounds, list their desires to change the present circumstance and construct a different future than the one envisioned by government officials (Alcaide, 2011). In a sense, the attention paid to the professions in the article may be said to underwrite an appeal for a middle-class readership to identify with 15M's aims. Similarly, the *El País* photo report released during the first encampment in Sol and, one year later, in the country-wide march to Madrid, may be read as evidence of a certain investigative necessity to describe not only the diversity of profiles and causes comprising the "outraged" multitude, but their accumulative desires for change, written on notes, categorized by theme, and released for publication in the mainstream press (Comisión de Información, 2012; García de Blas, 2012). The chance for readers and viewers to identify with specific profiles and faces, diverse backgrounds, and reasons for joining the protests, speculatively, may have benefited the 15M movement to mobilize others, as much as it also speaks to a certain necessity to conceive of the multitude as a composite of desiring individuals, rather than an amorphous, ungovernable mass.

The desires for social change that characterized the demonstrations are conveyed in some news coverage on the initial protests. In one remarkable example, the opening sequence of *Informe Semanal*'s first report on the *Indignados* (broadcast May 21, 2011 and cited in G. Montano's analysis) displays a series of close-up shots of the faces of protesters, who open their eyes in a gesture of political awakening while the camera zooms into focus to show the outward appearance of diversity among its participants (figure I.1).

The narrator's voiceover is reinforced by sound clips from interviews with the *indignadxs* (to paraphrase the words of one protester, "it's a spontaneous movement without any political party," and another, "all of us learned about it on the Internet"), as the crescendo of Calexico's protest song "Victor Jara's Hands" is marked by accelerated camera shots of different faces. The camera then cuts to a fast-paced sequence and slow panorama of the massive concentrations in Sol. As a document to its time, the news clip is extraordinary, in my view, for having conveyed in this crescendo of song and image, the affective intensity with which the demonstrations took place. In this sense, the magnitude of

Figure I.1 15M portrayed as a political awakening. Sequence of still images from *Informe Semanal* (TVE), "Indignados," broadcast on 21 May 2011.

the protests, the creative productivity among unknown others who also desired change, and the suspension of disbelief in the first mobilizations are conveyed to viewers in the audiovisual sequence through a portrait of its most immeasurable feature: the intensity of its affect, of its ability to move and trigger movement in others. The audiovisual sequence does so, in part, through camera and editing work that builds in intensity by showing the rapid succession of scored images, which establishes a rhythm simulating a narrative arch, its climax and denouement in the thousands of protesters gathered in Sol. This sequence aptly conveys the time of the multitude's seemingly spontaneous appearance for its affective potential to stir awe or disbelief in viewers, which the report casts in a positive light as enthusiasm for uncertain change.

Now, in stark contrast to the affective intensity of the mass demonstrations and the encampments, there also exists a patent fear of the masses, evident in the political discourse about civilian protests since 2011. For government officials, particularly among the political right, the unpredictable appearance of mass demonstrations has stirred significant anxiety for its incalculable potential for action. This anxiety is made clear in the apocalyptic discourse of politicians who attempt to criminalize protesters as "radicals" and antisystem, violent types who desire "urban guerrilla warfare" and even "terrorism" (Gobierno de España, Congreso de los Diputados, 2012, 12–13). The potential ungovernability of multitudes that refuse the subjecthood of state rule can be said to reside at the core of legal provisions in response to these anxieties. This cataclysmic picture upheld by government officials not only infringes on the democratic right to demonstrate peacefully, but has materialized in the reforms to the Penal Code (Gobierno de España, Ministerio de Justicia, 2012). When proposed in 2012, the Judges for Democracy (JpD) spokesperson Joaquim Bosch denounced that these reforms criminalize certain forms of protest thereby turning "a social state to a penal state" (Fabra, 2012). Since passed into law, the Ley de Seguridad Ciudadana [Law of Citizen Security], commonly known as the "Gag Law," interprets passive resistance and other forms of protest as infractions punishable by prison and heavy fines, as it also outlaws demonstrations from raising encampments again, specifically, in La Puerta del Sol. Violent police interventions in demonstrations, as well as persecution and intimidation tactics used against organizers and the press attempting to cover them, have become increasingly commonplace at my time of writing.

The state response to the multitude further demonstrates that institutional political strategy continues to operate within the dualities of hegemonic power by treating the multitude as a singular subject that must be forged into a People. The multitude, in other words, is a project for the state. It must be constructed in speech and law as the state's adversary, according to this logic, in which the People is a friend of the state insofar as it concedes to its subjecthood for state rule. This friend/enemy distinction is perhaps nowhere more evident than in the words of Valencia's Chief of Police Antonio Moreno, who refused to disclose to the press the number of security forces dispatched to disperse, by violent force, the secondary school teachers, parents, and students protesting cutbacks to education, since one should not "proporcionar esta información para el enemigo" [provide this information for the enemy] (Ferrandis, 2012). In response, however, demonstrators mobilized in opposition, proclaiming, "¡Yo también soy el enemigo!" [I too am the enemy!]. As government officials attempt to legitimize state authority through the bellicose friend/enemy distinction in speech, force, and law (Schmitt, 1996, 19–45), it paradoxically undermines the very legitimacy of democracy in the state. In this sense, when peaceful protesters use "spontaneous" to describe their actions, it proves an empowering gesture on the incalculability of the multitude. For, although this may not be the protesters' aim, the unpredictable time of the multitude's spontaneity destabilizes the state's potential to police effectively that as Chief Moreno exposes in his statement, is required for the state's own administrative time-cycle to produce a calculated response with political and policing strategy.

Moving toward a conclusion, then, it seems that different narrative logics aiming to make sense of the 15M movement and its spontaneous character have tended to analyze the phenomenon through the lens of liberal democracy, class struggle, and hegemonic power, assuming that the movement operates within a certain conceptual domain that it tended to resist in its first few months of existence. Surely, the political strategy deployed by the state to forge the multitude into an enemy and thereby reconstitute its legitimacy of rule for the People, demonstrates that its operative power-knowledge rests on engaging the multitude from a hegemonic institutional position. However, the transversal solidarity that characterizes the composite multitude (understood as a cross-sector and -class proletariat) and the production of its temporal and affective incalculability, tend to overflow the conventions of analytical frameworks required to explain it. The multitude's emergence and crystallization into an operative network for mobilization constitutes an event that exceeds institutional knowledge on governability, in which state powers respond, noted by sociologist Manuel Castells, with coercion and the construction of (negative) meaning in people's minds, if not fear (*Networks*, 2012, 5–7).

What escapes these analytical procedures is a critique of how a given mobilization first crystallizes and manifests itself visibly, undeniably present, with force. Here the force to which I refer is specifically bound to an action (protest) and subsequent demand, summarized largely as that of the multitude's collective, plural grievances against the Spanish state for its pursuit of neoliberal policies and the elite who benefit from them, explored in subsequent chapters. Articulated with increasing complexity in the wake of 15M, the movement's proposals and actions call for significant reforms to both the structure of the state and its policy positions, which constructively question directly or indirectly, democratic sovereignty itself. Furthermore, although the actions and demands of 15M have been articulated with particularity to the Spanish state, they also respond directly to the increasingly exclusionary consequences of austerity, privatization, and widening class disparity as a systemic crisis, which—as all power is a paradox—strengthen the movement's potential solidarity within a network of other groups that make likeminded claims articulated from the local and regional.

Passing, then, from the first mass mobilizations to common production, 15M and its many derivations have since materialized into plural demands, actions, and operative working groups in Spain. Its political survival—or, rather, its constant transformation to *becoming* something other than it was—resides in the crystallization of operative horizontal governance (structure), sustained by the inclusive debates of popular assemblies, commissions, and working groups that generate specific demands and proposals (enunciations and actions) on a local level. It is this particularity of the local that may be the movement's greatest motor for continued action and community involvement in which a sense of common ownership of the public (public space, services, education, healthcare, and so on) constitutes its transversal solidarity with similar actions organized in defense of shared, inclusive public ownership and rights on a regional and international scale. Its nonhierarchical, networked structure endows the movement with its possibility to reenact mobilization with new initiatives, proposals, and demands. This has been achieved with remarkably great speed as the movement transforms continuously, and as such, so do its trajectories of proposed actions and the locations of its enunciations. They emerge from a diverse range of collectives and individuals within and beyond the so-called movement, from platforms, neighborhood associations, parents and teachers, state employees, and so on. It is, after all, organized within a networked social field in constant flux, in motion, in contradiction, which the sociologist Manuel Castells has aptly suggested, in language he attributes to a 15M protester, as bearing the form of a rhizome ("12M#15M," 2012; *Networks*, 2012, 110–55).[5]

Following the 1968 uprisings, Gilles Deleuze and Félix Guattari theorize some of the organic properties of the *rhizome* as a conceptual model to understand social interconnectivity and the seemingly unlimited maneuvers provided by its distribution. The rhizome is conceived as a multidimensional space in which any point may be connected to any other with networked, heterogeneous multiplicity; thus, unlike the roots of a tree, the rhizome grows horizontally in lines and curves, and tends to be resilient to the structuring of rigid hierarchies within it. Resisting specific coordinates, its properties are never static or total, but bear the possibility of transformation through motion and contact, a moving-through with no specific beginning or end. The rhizome is always both the middle from which it grows and *in medias res*, exceeding the trajectories from which it grew. When a line within the rhizome comes into contact with a separate plane, its properties transform to become something else but not wholly other, in a trajectory that bears the possibility of constant metamorphosis, that is, a *becoming-other*. Organically speaking, the rhizome cannot be reduced to a single element within it, nor can its multiplicity be traced to a single origin. "It is not a multiple derived from the one, or to which one is added (n+1). It is comprised not of units but of dimensions, or rather directions in motion. [...] It constitutes linear multiplicities with *n* dimensions having neither subject nor object, which can be laid out on a plane of consistency, and from which the one is always subtracted (n-1)" (Deleuze and Guattari, 1987, 21). Abstracted in mathematical terms, n-1 is the formula of multiplicity and difference in the rhizome, in contrast to a purely accumulative principle (n+1).[6]

Viewed through Deleuze and Guattari's conceptual model, the rhizomatic form of 15M's organization is indeed cited within some of the communication platforms related to the movement, notably the self-managed N-1 network. Named after Deleuze and Guattari's principle of subtraction that gives way to multiplicity in the rhizome, N-1 is an open-source platform for registered users (called "inhabitants") to share documents, audiovisuals, and archived resources, to establish self-managed working groups, and to disseminate information among other inhabitants. Its subtraction consists in its parallel structure to, and removal from, other social networks (such as Facebook, Twitter, Tuenti), allowing for specific organizational initiatives to develop in communication within it and in dissemination to other public sites, social networks, and webs. Activities on N-1 develop in tandem with, and separately from, 15M and other participants in international movements, as well as the former's public domains: the documentation center maintained in collaboration with MediaLab Prado, the launching of the 15M-pedia, the development of WikiLibro, the operative network of popular assemblies across Spain and their activities on the TomaLaPlaza web, and a long list of etceteras. Within this networked fabric, the "spontaneity" with which initiatives may be articulated and enacted in any given local node of activity, with any precise quantification of its total magnitude within and among these or other domains, is incalculable to administrative logics that require temporal precision and specific measure.

The following chapters are dedicated in part to a brief, incomplete account of 15M that attempts to map the "force" of outrage arising from the circumstance of the crisis, to the movement's crystallization as a structure of horizontal governance. On a precautionary note, however, all contemporary activism in Spain should not be attributed to the organizational structures of the 15M movement as though the notion of the multitude has only one voice and site of activity, rather than a plurality of enunciations. Nor should the heterogeneous, composite character of the 15M movement be reduced to one unified platform or entity, or a static structure. It would be an impossible and mostly undesirable task to grasp a totality of the so-called movement, a term I try to use sparingly hereafter, for its multiple particularities in the local and its diverse actions coordinated within its virtual and physical assemblage of networks. These points are ultimately what make the 15M phenomenon difficult to pinpoint, as it slips into a transformative field of social relations on the move. Here, I focus exclusively, at the risk of reductionism, on the urban site of Madrid as one networked node of activity, itself an intensely plural site of networked activity, which should not be collapsed into the entirety of 15M per se. Nevertheless, the local and regional interconnectivity of platforms, commissions, and working groups has become the sort of channel for an operative plurality of demands that productively revitalize direct democratic participation at my time of writing.

I hoped to have shown briefly here that the question of reading the multitude's "sudden" emergence escapes the terms used to describe, and sometimes can contribute to confining by prescriptive language, a phenomenon that resisted assimilation into some normalizing discourses projected upon it. Instead, as in the following chapters, I look to the protesters' actions and language from which, potentially, cultural analysis can learn. How to read the transformations implicit in an act of becoming, on the other hand, while related to this matter, would require questioning critically the act of reading and, informing this activity, the analytical tools already known to readers. In this sense, paying attention to the act of reading and to the conclusions it provides, can point to the ways in which analysis is undergirded by power-knowledge. I should like to suggest throughout this book, then, that the political instance of the 15M phenomenon might also entail a crisis of interpretation, said in a positive light, in its invitation to read the ways in which these oppositional practices, readings, and re-significations by protesters have produced and can produce change, whatever the scale. My approach is largely concerned with examining how they work in the operative mechanics, forms, and functions of oppositional practices and readings—that is, their *poetics*—as one kind of material from which to analyze their relation to the current conjuncture of Spain's crises.

CHAPTER 1

Lessons Felt, Then Learned

Those who will not bend to the Great Necessity (Competition and Growth) will be out of the game. Those who want to stay in the game will have to accept any punishment, any renunciation, any suffering that the Great Necessity will demand. Who said that we absolutely must be part of the game?

—Franco "Bifo" Berardi, *The Uprising*

Organiza la rabia, pero no te olvides de defender la felicidad.
(Organize your anger, but don't forget to defend your happiness.)
—Juventud Sin Futuro, protest flyer

La(s) crisis

I.

From 2008 to 2011, the burden of the financial and economic crisis, well underway, came to bear on residents in Spain with inseparable economic and social significance. In 2007, Spain's unbridled construction boom ended abruptly, bringing the so-called housing bubble to a close, which contributed to halting credit-lending from banks while indebted homeowners saw their properties devalued—two issues that characterized the particular gravity of the crisis for Spain.[1] Successive state interventions to rescue semipublic savings banks seemed not only to echo first news of a compounded crisis rippling out from the United States and the European financial economy, but of a greater crisis for business ethics and practices at large that favored a wealthy elite. In cities and suburbs across Spain, the construction boom had produced countless abandoned or unfinished construction sites, tourist destinations, ghost airports, and housing developments—the subject of artist Hans Haacke's installation "Castles in the Air" and Markel Redondo's photography[2]—in exchanges benefiting contractors and local government officials from public coffers. Semipublic savings banks that had overestimated their possibilities for loan and investment required state intervention and rescue, whereas directors and their leadership teams often received healthy severance packages with benefits. News of unethical, if not allegedly criminal, practices from big business and government officials of all political colors, in corruption scandals such as Gürtel, Malaya, or Pretoria, among countless others, had served in part as the primer for growing distrust in confluent interests between the business and financial sectors and government officials. Many of these figures' apparent immunity from expedient trial further deepened popular distrust in the judicial and political mechanisms that seemed to protect them. When exposed publicly, widespread *clientelismo*, or the "cronyism" of favors exchanged within elite spheres of influence, harkened back to the dictatorship years, or in other comparisons, to dubious business practices likened to systematic, organized fraud.[3]

During these years unemployment rates surpassed historic records and would continue to rise thereafter.[4] Fearing that businesses would fold, the ruling Socialist party (PSOE) passed into law urgent labor reforms of a neoliberal stripe, which among other concessions allowed employers greater leeway to fire employees at less expense to companies (Gobierno de España, Boletín Oficial de Estado, 2010). Underpinning these measures was the justification of an end—that of diminishing the state's juridical role in guaranteeing job security, furthering the deregulation of the labor market as one speculative, neoliberal remedy to the crisis. Following the logic of this decision at that time, it was more advantageous for the economy to suffer a short-term rise in unemployment than to face the long-term consequences from companies forced out of business. And so the Socialist government advocated a law that would cut Spain's expected losses by providing employers with greater freedoms to downsize. In September 2010, the labor unions Unión General de Trabajadores (UGT) and Comisiones Obreras (CCOO) called for a national strike, denouncing labor reforms that would indeed contribute to precarity for workers across all sectors. That this scenario should repeat itself after May 2011 in a second general strike—against the "urgent labor reform" decree-law by the conservative Partido Popular (PP), which allowed companies to fire employees based on projected future losses—seemed to confirm the common assumption that government officials ignored mass demonstrations and labor actions altogether (Gobierno de España, Boletín Oficial de Estado, 2012). In parallel to Sergio Vilar's argument in *La década sorprendente*, if the

Socialist administrations from the *Transición* era (1982–96) had disenchanted constituents by abandoning the party's founding ideological principles in favor of neoliberal policies, then the PSOE's navigation of the financial crisis proved an evocative reminder of recent history, both in the administration's cutbacks to the social programs it championed and in the popular disenchantment this provoked.[5]

During Zapatero's administration, parliament passed into law a battery of neoliberal interventions in response to the crisis, which were pursued thereafter with sharpened severity by the conservative PP: cutbacks to social programs, tax reforms favoring the wealthy, bailouts of public funds for the banking sector, and further deregulatory measures for the labor market were among other corrective instruments to sustain the markets. The dismantling of social programs and the welfare state was inaugurated amid public speculation about a new wave of privatizations in the regional autonomous communities, primarily in healthcare and education. Demonstrators holding signs with "PPSOE," which fused the letters of the conservative Popular (PP) and Socialist (PSOE) parties into one, pointed out the lack of distinction between these parties' economic policies and the growing popular disenchantment with bipartisan politics in a plural representative democracy. One indicator of this equation between parties materialized four months after the first mass demonstrations in 2011; the PP and PSOE together would agree to amend the Constitution, without calling for a popular referendum and despite opposition from minority parties, to include a future cap on the deficit that limited public spending to European regulation. This measure was applauded by the German Chancellor Angela Merkel, as Spain had "chosen the path of reason" for "the common good" of the European markets ("Merkel alaba," 2011). It became increasingly evident in policy making from Spain's major right and leftwing parties that both were subservient to the influence of banking and financial capital, whose objective was to conserve the neoliberal projects of the Euro Zone at great social and economic costs for residents.

Those who remained active in the workforce faced the precarity of a job market that enabled potential abuses by employers against the threat of being fired, one motive for the demonstrations in Madrid called by unions UGT and CCOO in 2009. Some common consequences for workers who consented to measures in order to keep their jobs were the suspension of contracts for unpaid vacations, the demand to work extra hours without compensation, the negotiation of extended leaves for a company to avoid reporting a collective dismissal (*Expediente de Regulación de Empleo*, or ERE), and the restructuring of positions to distribute greater job responsibilities among fewer personnel. For workers in the public sector who generally benefitted from greater job security (in education, healthcare, social services, justice, administrative offices, and so on), the government announced later that state employees could expect to receive one monthly paycheck less in 2012, which consolidated mobilizations across these sectors. Residents in Spain were told ad nauseam that they had lived lifestyles well beyond their means ("los españoles han vivido por encima de sus posibilidades"), echoed in the assertion by the politician Jaime Mayor Oreja (PP),[6] and according to the neoliberal axiom, that either increased productivity or lower wages were the only viable solutions to the crisis (Erlanger, 2010; "Spain: After the Fiesta," 2008). Facing growing expendability, employees were expected to be "overworked but thankful" while mindful of sacrifices required for downsizing and cutbacks, which describes the discourse of power-subservience permeating the workplace, if not fear. On parodying the expectation of servile gratitude from the employed, with relevant Christian undertones, the comedian Eva Hache joked in one televised stand-up routine that summer vacations had changed since the crisis, given that workers who returned to find the office still in business kissed the ground as Pope John Paul II would have done (Hache, 2011).

In domestic affairs, the economic forecast that warned of a long-term crisis eroded popular support for the PSOE and Zapatero's administration, which had initially downplayed these reports in light of a "robust" European and Spanish economy on the whole (Romero et al., 2008). The Bank of Spain, which supported this assertion, became another focus of popular skepticism, echoed by analysts in debates on television and radio, and in humor. Early on, late-night television host Andreu Buenafuente summarized this popular distrust in his monologue on the Bank of Spain, political corruption, and loaning agencies whose representatives had abused credit-lending ("subprime mortgages") with a soothing smile worthy of Michael Landon's character in *Little House on the Prairie* (Buenafuente, 2007). On a more serious note, in his recognition of the immense hardship experienced by many, President Zapatero reminded Spanish citizens that combined "great effort and sacrifice" were the only viable solution to the crisis ("es un gran desafío que exige un gran esfuerzo y sacrificio"), an assertion that would be taken up in the rhetoric of the conservative PP and also cited verbatim every year in King Juan Carlos I's televised Christmas Eve address since 2009 (Narváez and Lucio, 2010; Casa Real, 2009–12). The assertion that government officials were left with "no alternative" but to adopt austerity measures and neoliberal labor reforms circulated with growing political currency among government officials and media commentators, and even inspired a direct replication from economists Vicenç Navarro, Juan Torres, and Alberto Garzón who dissented with alternative proposals to sustain the welfare state in their reply *Hay Alternativas* (Navarro et al., 2011). Later, the affirmation "Sí hay alternativas" would come from state-employed tax analysts in the Finance Ministry, who released a largely ignored report by the same name to propose pursuing higher taxes for the wealthy, international tax havens, and fiscal fraud as sources of revenue, to counteract the current "unjust" and "socially regressive" measures to reduce the deficit (GESTHA, 2012, 1–3). Lifted directly from 1980s Thatcherism in the neoliberal adage "There Is No Alternative," the dominant discourse of "no alternative" was recast as a powerful pedagogical tool to legitimize the Spanish government's choices in policy making and to a certain degree acquired its status as truth through habitual repetition. The burden that there is "no alternative" would be contested later in 15M Sol's open call for new proposals on change as the very possibility from which to imagine alternative models of direct democratic participation, constitutionalism, and inclusive social well-being.

For university students, the Bologna Process had sparked an awareness for local, national, and European politics in the public university, including the rising costs for higher education, the standardization of degree programs across Europe, the elimination of others (particularly in the Humanities) to tailor academic programs to market demands, and the exclusion of substantial faculty and student involvement from the plan's design and implementation. The homogenizing effects of these reforms in higher education followed the logic in advanced capitalism seeking "freer flows" for exchange, one in which the business model is taken to be transferrable to any other system or organization and is largely implemented as such. The Bologna Process's objective to standardize academic programs across European universities echoed the globalizing trend in the business sectors, one of systems integration aiming primarily for greater mobility across borders—whether people, in this case students, capital investments, goods, or workers of European origin. In response, renewed activism in the university provided the grounds for networked communications among protesters to mobilize in specific actions, in which the use of online social networks (Twitter, Facebook, Tuenti, and so on) played a key role to draw supporters, project the visibility of a given cause, and ultimately organize against national and European measures adopted without local democratic participation.

From 2008 to 2012 alone, over 170,000 forced evictions were processed through the courts (Muñiz, 2012), which by Spanish law required most evicted homeowners to retain the burden of debt after foreclosure on a home that they no longer owned, the reason for many suicides. Due to a constricting job market, many Spanish citizens in the active workforce became "emigrants again" in ways that newspaper editorials associated with a strong evocation of the years of emigration from dictatorship; similarly, many immigrants in Spain likewise returned to their countries of origin for greater work opportunities (Huete Machado and Collera, 2011). Many of Spain's nearly 50 percent of young adults without jobs had fewer possibilities to become independent from their parents, while many others moved back to the nest. Although *convivencia* in the family and neighborhood community was a common theme in television series well before the crisis (*Aída, Aquí no hay quien viva*, etc.), other programs have come to make this circumstance—as well as bartering and exchanges of favors without currency, the defense of one's home from eviction, relocations, and so on—the very premise of episodes and series (*Con el culo en el aire, La que se avecina, Stamos Okupa2*, etc.).

As unemployment lines grew, rightwing politicians and media sources spoke of the abuses of those collecting unemployment from the government, thereby promoting the perception that those who could not find work were not demonstrating sufficient effort to do so. Keeping in mind that wages in Spain are notoriously low—with more than 7.8 million *mileuristas* earning less than one thousand euros per month (Instituto Nacional de Estadística, 2010)—the imperative to assume greater expenses equated to a vital threshold into poverty for many middle- and working-class households and retirees.[7] The derogatory term "estómagos agradecidos" [thankful stomachs] circulated in the rightwing media, which aimed to portray labor union affiliates, their leaders, and leftwing voters in general, bundled into one, as dependent on "a free handout" from the state in exchange for their vote.[8] In a direct attack on labor struggles, social welfare programs, pensioners, and persons receiving some form of government aid, statements such as these aimed to justify the elimination of social welfare programs through a false logic that implied a tacit exchange (or, social services for one's vote) among citizens presumed to be uncritical thinkers, on the one hand, while they also accuse voters of cronyism, which in hindsight has become more apparent among the political classes making this very claim. This colorful language is not unique to welfare, as other statements commonly stigmatized participants in strikes and labor actions on moral grounds, recasting them as "vagos" (lazy) who do not desire to work, while ignoring the motivations behind the strikes altogether (Carmona et al., 2012, 139, 150).

In the same vein, the alleged abuses of the welfare system by the unemployed acquired powerful political leverage to inaugurate the dismantling of social services by criminalizing the jobless. The oft-repeated phrase "chupan del bote," which describes welfare recipients as "moochers" or "slackers" living from state funds (*bote*), tended to shift public attention from the labor markets to the unemployed. The president of the Madrid Autonomous Community Esperanza Aguirre (PP) insisted that "Lo que tiene que hacer este país [es hacer una reforma] que permita contratar a quien quiera trabajar y ser contratado" [What this country has to do is to make a reform allowing (employers) to hire those who want to work and be hired]—an assertion that, at once, justifies the neoliberal labor reform to which she refers, while portraying the unemployed as undesiring to work (qtd. in Carmona et al., 2012, 145). The suggestion that the jobless must be policed would materialize later in a statement from Madrid's appointed mayor Ana Botella (PP) who proposed that the unemployed take up obligatory volunteer work, from cleaning streets to staffing public libraries, a plan designed to minimize the alleged abuses on unemployment pensions (Agencia EFE, 2012; S. C. Agencias, 2013). By personalizing one's own employment status and compliance with austerity, these statements attempted to shift attention from the labor market to individual responsibility, behaviors, and attitudes for one's own circumstance, that is, as personal successes and failures attributable to the properties of the "self." Feelings of outrage in response, it could be said, may have also taken shape around this individuation, at least initially, as the address of these statements constructed "personalized" assessments toward one's own socioeconomic or employment status, and that of others. This point on making the crisis a personal matter might help readers understand why, then, attributes like "humility and modesty" in times of austerity were touted by the conservative politician Soraya Sáenz de Santamaría (PP) as the crisis's saving grace, for in her view Spanish society had "recuperated important values once lost" (Blanco, 2012).

In turn, the PSOE and PP leaders' successive attempts to demonstrate their commitment to the solvency of European neoliberal projects constituted a dual crisis of sovereignty, on the one hand for Spanish citizens who are to assume the social expense of the crisis for generations to come, and on the other for government officials faced with the increasing intervention of European administration into domestic affairs, whether economic, social, or political. Some peripheral indications of the deterritorializing effects of late capitalism were evident in the Spanish State's weakened autonomy in policy-making decisions before the European Union. In 2011, the European Commission evaluated Spain's economic and fiscal policy in at least two public reports, which urged greater liberalization of the labor market and tighter centralized monitoring and controls of the autonomous regions' decision making on public spending (Comisión Europea, *Diario Oficial*, 2011; *Documento de Trabajo*, 2011). However, in the public eye, the Spanish government's displaced role in its administration became more evident only after the first demonstrations in 2011, in successive news stories in which domestic affairs were addressed not with Spanish government officials, but directly with European administration: in Chancellor Merkel's exceptional meeting with union leaders Cándido Méndez (UGT) and Ignacio Fernández Toxo (CCOO) who denounced the Spanish government's deregulatory measures for the labor market and the deteriorating welfare state (Unión General de Trabajadores, 2012); in the European Central Bank's conditions for the government to reduce spending on social programs in preparation for a potential bailout (Navarro, "The Euro," 2012); and in the European Commission's position on Catalonian independence, to name a few (Agencia EFE, 2013). Whereas the deterritorializing effects of capital contributed to a crisis of sovereignty for the state, they also laid the conditions for new forms of transversal solidarity across segments of the population to mobilize, both locally and on an international scale. Democracy, to use retrospectively the words of the first demonstrations, had been "held hostage by the elite" political class governing for the interests of the few ("¡Manos arriba! ¡Esto es un atraco!"). The demand for "Real Democracy Now" embodied the estrangement from democratic participation—in the university, in state politics, in the public—from a field of juridical and economic interests that protected financial and banking capital, neoliberal European projects, and the standing partisan system.

Anger is the very tone of author Juan José Millás's controversial article "Un cañón en el culo" [A Gun Barrel in the Ass] published one year after the first 15M demonstrations, which rails against the financial sector and the government's drastic austerity measures compromising residents in Spain.[9] In metaphor, Millás equates this detriment to the *terrorismo* to which citizens are subjected on several accounts, as though one is "taken hostage at gunpoint" by a captor who plays sadistic games of torture: the dismantling of social protections; government officials' subservience to the financial and banking sectors in Spain and abroad; the growing repression by state security forces against peaceful demonstrators; and a justice system that seemingly protects politicians and bankers despite the criminal allegations against them. Rife with allusions to the historical violence of totalitarianism and terrorism alike (among them, the armed Basque separatist group ETA, the 11-M Atocha train bombings by an Al-Qaeda cell, and European fascisms in the twentieth century), Millás's text stands as an outraged response that conveys—as it spits—more than a social malaise, but the subjection to an oppressive totalitarian rule of the markets through the article's succession of analogies to violence in memory and history. Millás notes, "la economía financiera es a la economía real lo que el señor feudal al siervo, lo que el amo al esclavo, lo que la metrópoli a la colonia, lo que el capitalista manchesteriano al obrero sobreexplotado" [the financial economy is to the real economy what the feudal lord is to the serf, the master to the slave, the metropolis to the colony, the Manchesterian capitalist to the overexploited laborer]. Following Millás' linkage across historical eras, whether readers call it feudalism, slavery, colonialism, or neoliberalism, the author proposes that the present is witness to a new form of financial authoritarianism produced as a "reign of terror" in subjective and collective experience. The notion of "being taken hostage" in Millás' article conveys both the threat of violence and the impossibility of having a choice in the matter, as though one is held at gunpoint—a telling comparison for the violence implicit in the usurping of autonomous decision.

The subtext of the Millás's biting exposition, in his claim that billions of euros are being funneled into German banks, refers to the 100 billion-euro bailout package approved by the European Central Bank (ECB) in order for Spain to pay off interest owed on its estimated 200 billion-euro debt at that time, primarily to financial institutions abroad. The Spanish State ended up accepting 41.3 billion of this sum as it pursued drastic cutbacks in state spending. The economist Vicenç Navarro warns, however, that the ECB "bailout"—a term that government officials refused to call by at that time—does not alleviate the credit crisis in Spain by making loans more available to small business owners, homeowners, and individuals.[10] Rather, Navarro argues, the capital allocated to circulate from the ECB to Spain to abroad ends up strengthening, primarily, public bonds in Germany and financial institutions in Europe. It indirectly contributes to the growing polarization of uneven economic cycles between "northern Europe" and its periphery, the so-called PIIGS (Portugal, Ireland, Italy, Greece, and Spain), to use the notorious acronym coined by the *Financial Times* ("Definition," n.d.). The epithet is undoubtedly one palpable example of neoliberal thought's potential to conjure up chauvinist forms of nationalism. It also captures, however, the sense of subjugation that has stirred much enraged skepticism about the European Union, and the Troika, by European parties on both the political left and right that have been labeled "Euro-skeptics."

On the other side of the same coin to austerity in Spain, one observes narrative and audiovisual accounts of hardship, bearing a potentially emotive pull, which unsettle the individualist rhetoric on economic self-sacrifice and retribution for living beyond one's means. Intimate life stories told by or about those most affected by economic hardship have circulated widely in alternative, mainstream, and social media, in *Callejeros* TV-documentary programs, newspaper editorials, and Facebook, among others. Germán Labrador Méndez has argued compellingly that these stories of the crisis on strife, suicide, and slow death bear a narrative genre that confounds clear distinctions between authorship and reception and between the isolation of individual experience and the collective, as a potentially mobilizing technology in the social imaginary. The author calls them *subprime* life histories, which by granting public visibility to personal accounts of strife, allow individuality to be socialized from the material, economic, and political circumstances of the crisis (2012, 563). In growing circulation, personal narratives shift the focus of public attention towards shared experience, in sharp contrast to the abstractions of economic indicators ubiquitous in the media:

> Ya no solo estaríamos hablando de inmolaciones, sino de personas que mueren tras serles denegada la asistencia en urgencias por falta de medios, cánceres que se agravan porque se demoran los plazos de intervenciones quirúrgicas por culpa de recortes presupuestarios, ancianas desahuciadas de las casas donde vivieron toda su vida, trabajadores embargados con deudas que no van a poder pagar nunca, jóvenes con formación específica que trabajan de teleoperadores o que acumulan decenas de contratos temporales sin llegar a obtener salarios viables para vivir, un conjunto de narraciones que podrían enmarcarse como "relatos del final del Estado de bienestar."

> [No longer would we be speaking of self-immolating suicides, but of people who die after being denied emergency medical attention for lack of funds, cancers that worsen because of prolonged waiting periods for surgery due to budget cutbacks, elderly women evicted from homes where they lived their whole lives, workers sequestered by debts they will never be able to pay, young people with specific training who work as telephone operators or accumulate temporary contracts without obtaining a viable salary to live on—a set of narratives that could be framed as "stories on the end of the welfare State"]. (2012, 563–4)

In elaboration from Labrador Méndez's argument, these intimate stories introduce an immeasurable "life scale" to the accountability of austerity and the dismantling of social welfare in general. Whether about modernization, development, economic strife, migrations, or ecological disasters—in Spain or elsewhere—subprime life histories give meaning to macropolitics and macroeconomics that at once shape and take shape through the story being told (2012, 564). As they are told and retold in circulation, they draw attention to the (biopolitical) experience of the subject and collective as bound together and dissolved in each other, which blurs the distinction between the two in multiplicities of authorship and reception. After all, whose story is being told? Not that of one person, but of many, in which storytelling and reception of subprime life histories are no longer (auto-)biographical in nature but instead may stand in for others' stories or perhaps even one's own. Indeed, to borrow from the author's terms, the visibility of these narratives in circulation may prove a powerful technology of political imagination for their mobilizing capacity to forge "empathetic bridges" (*un puente empático*) with others through association and critique of a collective, and inherently political, history of the crisis (2012, 563). Their social circulation would charge the task of criticism, then, with considering what these narratives and their affective potential can prove capable of doing across audiences.

Repeated in the media, in official state discourse, in social exchanges with great frequency, were some common discursive threads of a pedagogy on the crisis in individuated narratives on sacrifice, humility, excess, and self-responsibility, to name a few. It was asserted, time and again, that there exists "no alternative" to resolve the crisis other than the "sacrifice" of labor rights and social services (healthcare, education, social security, disability); that the crisis is recompense for Spanish residents having "lived beyond their means," except for the greatest fortunes; that the employed working "to lift Spain up" should be grateful despite managerial abuses; that the unemployed and demonstrators are "irresponsible," "indolent," or even "criminal" in their actions or socioeconomic status; that demonstrations are "not the solution." Pointing generally toward a system of thought on the crisis, these suppositions in circulation can bear an emotional pull, which are not wholly "subjective feelings" but are shared in their collective circumstance of production, Labrador Méndez notes, as one of common subjugation.

Those who are called *indignadxs* do not read this official discourse on the crisis literally, by any means. So, although the social and economic burden of the crisis contributed to generating what could be called a tipping point for outrage, it is the critical practice of reading the government's policy making and public statements, and those of likeminded commentators and analysts in the media, which can further regenerate the intensity of critical response and the mobilizing potential for action. In other words, outrage may be reactivated when watching the news to hear a politician make similar claims, or to learn first on Twitter that the monarchy is also allegedly involved in a multimillion-euro corruption scandal. Emotions like Millás's sensible outrage can be associated with *critical* responses that identify and reject the everyday corrective instruments of discursive power—an *oppositional practice*—particularly wherever they bear burdensome effects as a form of social conditioning to garner acceptance for "the way things are." As these imposed "truths" are cast, in part, to legitimize state policies for the governed, they also become fodder for demonstrators who read critically—and oppose—the discourse of power from the mobilizing potential of anger and outrage, which may be "felt" first, but then are decried in protest: "We are not goods in the hands of bankers"; "They don't represent us"; "We are the alternative!" These discursive formations are never static but are mimicked in this or that news source or online social network, are interpreted with difference in the context of specific social interactions, are spoken publicly in press conferences, and thereby transform over time as the circumstances of the crisis create real economic hardships, on the one hand, and shape the perceptible magnitude of an unfolding *crisis*, on the other.

Regarding this sensible magnitude, television viewers in recent years can count on at least 20 minutes of the afternoon and evening news, on any network, dedicated to rapid-fire coverage of these issues and their developments in succession. Making sense of them, on the other hand, also presumes having followed a backlog of news coverage to situate readers and viewers within the present gravity of the crisis. It is this speed and volume of information that proves challenging to take stock of the present with critical reflection. One might call it a sense of "shock" leading to numbness in repetition, or a great volume of noise that at once informs and conceals what it informs through its "pandemonium," in the words of David Levi Strauss (2003, 156).

Amid the cacophony of news—interest rates, financial indicators, forced evictions, severance bonuses for executives, lost savings and pensions, boardroom meetings in Brussels, and so on—the pandemonium of information at great speed moves faster than can be assimilated, as Strauss argues, and just might require the present to develop ways of critically detaining this speed of communications in order to differentiate other voices above the noise it conveys (2003, 157–8). If discursive formations on the crisis can be said, in a sense, to work on their audience through the speedy succession of information in frequent repetition, then the relevant question of how publics are addressed may no longer be uniquely one of individual reception, but rather one that asks to discern above the volume, across and among publics, as Strauss asks, "Can you hear me?" (2003, 156). News on the crisis, and its saturation in the mainstream and social media, may be sensed overwhelmingly as one of the deterrents to making meaning of the present circumstance, but it also provides a point of reflection, perhaps an invitation, to reconsider the role of audiences for what they do and can prove capable of doing.

II.

Outrage, or *indignación* in Spanish, has become somewhat of a reductionist buzzword in the mainstream media that substitutes for naming the countless, multiple reasons that motivated 15M protesters to take to the streets.[11] Reasonably, it is shorthand to describe the political emotions of protesters on the whole who have likewise been coined for their political anger as *indignadxs*. Emotion, it follows, is both an expression of personal feeling ("outrage" and "anger") and a name that describes what compels protesters into action, or a certain drive. It is this reductionism which I should like to explore briefly for its possibility to approach the terms of political affect, emotion, and feeling for analysis, which takes as its point of departure the assessment, akin to the *indignadxs*, that much "of the engine of politics consists of the surge that comes from structures of feeling attached to objects of political anger or hope that demand change" (Amin and Thrift, 2013, 211). To paraphrase the authors' nod to the cultural theorist Raymond Williams, one political motor for change is constituted in the intensities—or affects—from the "structures of feeling" shaped around the perceived sources of political anger and hope.

One of the organizations established before and a participant in 15M comes to mind. Its name *Estado de Malestar* tropes the language "welfare state" (*estado de bienestar*) to convey a social malaise (*malestar*) in linkage between the austerity measures pursued to dismantle the welfare state and, in consequence, a general social unease—that is, between the political and the affective. Is social malaise an emotion? Probably not, unless it is attributed to perception from a subject that "feels" or "senses" malaise, that is, that comes into contact with this circumstance to perceive a sensible unease in particular. It follows that "feeling," as I use it here, refers to the activity of sensing, of perception, of interface with one's surroundings. How, then, are things "felt" to be uneasy? And in what sense is an affect different from emotion, if at all?

To clarify the matter, I refer in the first instance to Brian Massumi's definition of Deleuze and Guattari's term "affect" in *A Thousand Plateaus* in which affect describes the "ability to affect and be affected" into action or movement. "It is a prepersonal intensity corresponding to the passage from one experiential state of the body to another and implying an augmentation or diminution in that body's capacity to act" (Deleuze and Guattari, 1987, xvi). Affect is considered an intensity, magnitude, or force capable of moving bodies into action or stasis (*becoming*), and is often sensed by the body before cognitive activity can register or name it. By this definition, affect is "in the skin," hair-raising and pupil-dilating, or on the whole, indexed in the body's sensory stimuli before cognition, and hence language, can process it. Affects can thus give rise to "mixed emotions" as Lauren Berlant notes, in which the "structure of an affect has no inevitable relation to the penumbra of emotions that may cluster in the wake of its activity" (2008, 4). Goosebumps may come with terror, awe, pleasure, fascination, and vice versa, in which affect overspills the sensations felt and the emotions named. In this light, for Massumi, affect is radically open, and when named as emotion(s), the act of naming grounds it in a qualitative, fixed property:

> An emotion is a subjective content, the sociolinguistic fixing of the quality of an experience which is from that point onward defined as personal. Emotion is qualified intensity, the conventional, consensual point of insertion of intensity into semantically and semiotically formed progressions, into narrativizable action-reaction circuits, into function and meaning. (2002, 28)

Many critical approaches to affect notably bear a temporal dimension that refers to neuroscience, as does Massumi: to the precognitive, prelinguistic activities of the body-mind before judgment can be formed, and before language can construct meanings around affect. Much existing literature draws from, or presumes, this time lapse of stimulus-response in order to distinguish between the precognitive intensity of affect and the posterior naming of emotions given to it in language. Nevertheless, affective attachments to other bodies, things, places, and ideals can be shaped: "*Affect* is the evolved cognitive and physiological response to the detection of personal significance" (Neuman et al., 2007, 9).[12] Beyond laboratory experiments in stimulus-response, as Michael Hardt notes in his foreword to Clough and Halley's *The Affective Turn*, "Affects [...] offer a complex view of causality because affects belong simultaneously to both sides of the causal relationship [...to] both our power to affect the world around us and our power to be affected by it, along with the relationship between these two powers" (2007, ix). There exists, in other words, a potentially political dimension to affect in the reciprocal capacity of bodies to move and be moved into action in their surroundings, and in the shifting relations (affective attachments, emotions, and signified meanings) that bodies learn to have or make with the world. The possible transformative capacity between creation and practice, or, taken up together, the doing that praxis and *poiesis* suppose, is one that should not be overlooked for its intensities formed around the political instance.

However, affects cannot simply "exist" somehow in the world. They must be produced in perception, through "feeling," and must be formed in attachments, whether they take shape or deflate in intensity, wither away, or persist by habit. Affective attachments can be produced in and from powerful forces that shape the world through which subjects move. One is inclined to remember the perceptible malaise-unease-discontent to which *Estado de Malestar* refers in the context of Spain's economic crisis as an example, which would not be perceptible as such were there not materially sociopolitical conditions shaping sensibly uneasy times. In this light, some scholarship explores affects in reference to the immeasurable magnitude of moods persisting for more than the split-second of perception required for bodies to respond to them in the laboratory. For, affects can be shaped by existing and enduring relations of power, whether in the impending threat of an escalated notch in a national security warning on terrorism (Massumi), or in the numbness of coasting through precarious conditions of work-life (Berlant). In the work of Cristina Moreiras-Menor, affect is understood as an index, or a psychological and social symptom that points toward something other than what it shows, a Lacanian displacement, as it "works on" the subject. In Moreiras-Menor's scholarship, affects are produced in the subject and social body, whereby cultural forms (film, literature, photography) grapple with articulating the social, political, and economic forces disavowed for the ways in which they continue to work on subjects in the present (2002, 2011). In summary, power relations are mediated through the sensible information they can provide to subjects, in part, in the form of emotions and affects.

In this light, affects (or emotions, for that matter) should not be pried from their contexts of production, treated somehow as independent variables from their circumstance. As the urban geographer Nigel Thrift notes, reviewing Daniel M. Gross' scholarship on this point:

> In opposition to the idea that the passions are something that are housed in a body and shared by all human beings equally, affect consists of the contours of a dynamic social *field* "manifest in what's imagined and forgotten, what's praised and blamed, what's sanctioned and silenced." They are constituted *between* politically and historically situated agents. In turn, this suggests that it makes a difference "not only what sort of passions are distributed to whom, but also how they are hoarded and monopolized and how their systemic denial helps produce political subjects of a certain kind." (2007, 225)

Affect cannot be considered a free-floating "sentimentality" but an intensity produced relationally among political and historical agents in specific ways. To assume the contrary would presume abstractly, in a similar vein, that power exists in the world as a static object, independently of its relational production between agents and environments in particular scenarios. Rather, when affects and emotions are produced, they can be appropriated and harnessed, cannibalized and vindicated, and are intimately related to shifting power relations within their social field of production: they may be legitimated, denied, or channeled toward political and economic ends—as in the intensity of a threat (affect) and the fear (emotion) it provokes capable of debilitating autonomous decision—or rather, they can constitute the sinews of solidarity in opposition to the relations of power that attempt to harness their production toward specific ends.

It is from Massumi's distinction between emotions and affects that I refer to "outrage" as reductionist term, which effectively *captures* (emotion) and stands in for the intensities compelling protesters to mobilize (affect). "Formed, qualified, situated perceptions and cognitions fulfilling functions of actual connection or blockage," writes Massumi, "are the capture and closure of affect. Emotion is the most intense (most contracted) expression of that capture" (2002, 35). If affects are named in their emotive responses, and yet overspill them in the act of naming, then it would seem that the relationship between affect and emotion in Massumi's formulation could be described as one of metonymic capture, that is, a figure of speech that names a related attribute or quality that stands in for a greater implied whole. The OED defines metonymy as "the action of substituting for a word or phrase denoting an object, action, institution, etc., a word or phrase denoting a property or something associated with it." For the linguist

Zoltán Kövecses, the statement "she got cold feet" illustrates an example of how "fear" is expressed in language, metonymically, through one of its attributes: a drop in body temperature that stands in for the corporal experience associated with it (2000, 5). Etymologically rooted in the Latin *metōnymia* from the Greek μετωνυμία (*meta-* "in common," "together with," and *-onymy* "to give a name to"), metonymy literally means a "change of name" that in speech and literature, can provide illustrative sensory form or figuration to the inferred concept being described. After all, to name emotion is a complex matter that comes in mixed shades and tones, which shift over time and circumstance: one might feel self-deprecatingly amused at one's own embarrassment in a social setting, or feel reluctantly pleased and alleviated by the outcome of a decision, which is remembered later as contemptible—neither of which corresponds to simply "shameful" or "glad," respectively. The relationships between these elements, however (reluctance, contentment, and relief, and later contempt) arise from specific contexts, though they are expressed in more reductive, metonymic terms.

Here, one confronts a distinguishable characteristic of the possible political implications of emotion, particularly as emotion here is deployed as a powerful persuasive tool—not of intensity for action in this case, but of adherence to and alignment with the discourse of power (to legitimize the art of government for the governed), inasmuch as emotion can persuade or debilitate one into stasis or compliance without critical thought, say, on the authoritative effects of official state discourse on the crisis. To explore this point further, having detected that emotions play an important role in response to economic hardship, the think tank Fundación Alternativas published a study of some 250 participants in the 15M movement in 2011 in which the survey describes the participants' "fear of unemployment" and the emotions that "may energize mobilization" when thinking about the unemployed. Notably, "outraged" tops the list, followed by "angry," "sad," "guilty," and "hopeful," in what could be said within the limits of the study provides an indiscriminate grouping of emotional responses to economic hardship, comprising both critical reactions to the crisis and their more debilitating effects (Likki, 2012, 10). Otherwise, this approach that attempts to account for the emotions clustering around social mobilization (and potentially, affects) removes practices and critical responses from their contexts whereby "outrage" shares its place with moral judgment and its debilitating effects, "guilty" and "sad." Stated otherwise, the study does not distinguish between the emotive effects of public persuasion and social conditioning, indexed in the authoritative rhetorical instruments in circulation. Without greater context, the emotional responses to powerful discursive strategies on employment are treated as a variety of personal feelings, indistinguishable in the study from their affective potential for action and critical response.

Naming the "mixed emotions" clustering around an affective attachment, then, might be understood as attributes that together stand in for and likewise fall short of grasping an affect. However, this slippage could be said, to a certain extent, of all language, in that the act of naming exceeds and is insufficient to describe what is being named. This critical take on affect—as precognitive, prelinguistic—in relation to emotion runs the risk of overlooking how meanings are constructed through language or how language dually constructs and performs the meanings formed around affects/emotions. It is in this manner in which the cultural theorist Sara Ahmed argues in *The Cultural Politics of Emotion* that "'figures of speech' are crucial to the emotionality of texts" for the ways in which emotions can "stick together" by association or cluster around signs through the meanings invested in their relationships to other signs (2004, 12). For example, in the politics of the so-called war against terrorism after September 11, observes Ahmed, political discourse can perform the causes of "fear" by pinning together metonymically an implied relationship between Islam and terrorism in the social imaginary (2004, 76). The metonymic character of naming an emotion in relation to affect would inherently take as its point of departure, as Ahmed does, the assertion that emotions are not fixed states but rather bear figurative relationships to what they name in singularity "together and in common with" each other, which is, in part, a cultural matter.

Viewed in this way, emotions of "outrage" and "anger" relate metonymically to the "community" of unnamed emotional experiences captured and compressed into the term *indignación*, reductionist as it were, and more importantly, to the relationships produced in difference among them (their "communal" character). Keeping this in mind, then, folded within *indignación* is the set of named and unnamed emotions and their affective intensity to move bodies into action. In other words, *indignación* is both affect and emotion insofar as one considers that emotions, too, are capable of "doing things," as Jo Labanyi has argued (2010). Thinking affect, then, implies exploring the structures of feeling "as [a] means of thinking and as thought in action. Affect is a different kind of intelligence about the world, but it is intelligence nonetheless," one that is produced in part from the interstices of relational powers as a potentially productive—and political—force (Thrift, 2007, 175).

Or, summarized in one slogan from Juventud Sin Futuro, "Organiza la rabia, pero no te olvides de defender la felicidad" [Organize your anger, but don't forget to defend your happiness], a statement in which both "anger" and the affective attachments that give positive meaning to the world, compressed into the term "happiness," are named (metonymically) as the driving motors to organize for change.

The sociologist Manuel Castells underscores the role of affects and emotions as a motivating political force capable of mobilizing protesters to assemble in public space and in networked communications with each other. He writes,

> explosions of anger felt at the individual level have the potential of developing into an insurgent community by the instant networking of many different individuals who are united in their frustration, though not necessarily united around a common position or solution to the perceived unjust source of domination. (2009, 363)

Affects and emotions may forge compassion, empathy, and solidarity with others, or the interstitial social relations of a network mobilizing for change, as much as they are also subject to operations of hierarchical structuring, appropriation, performance, not always in a negative light, say, in the emotions of what an activist group considers "inappropriate" or lacking empathy toward some collective end. So, whereas "social movements move because they engage emotions and values" such as empathy (Eyerman, 2005, 50), emotions can also cling to values and, say, "happiness" of a conformist bent in ways that attempt to conserve one's own beliefs, views, or the status quo, to one's detriment (Berlant, 2011). To explore how emotions and affects can be motors for mobilization in political contexts, however, requires setting aside a few presumptions about them. It requires abandoning any classical conception that the emotions are volatile, irrational feelings in diametric opposition to "human rationality" (the form of struggle expressed in the statement, "anger overcame/overpowered him"), given that critical thought can inform the cognitive production of affects/emotions and, conversely, as Teresa Brennan has argued, affects/emotions can be shaped around critical thinking (2004).[13] On these terms, one might be compelled to consider, for example, the conditions under which learning becomes sorrow, or reading a joy. And it requires interrogating passionate and fixed "political convictions" rooted in moral judgment, of the kind instrumentalized toward the ends and aims of powers.[14] To explore critically what affects/emotions can do in political contexts is to consider them "*practices*, rather than as states that exist inside the self," or as inherent "properties of the self," that is, as purely subjective "feelings" (Labanyi, 2010, 223). Emotions are produced in specific relational (political) contexts and can also be transmitted to others with difference. They can affect others in circulation with relative intensity as affects that move bodies into action or stasis.[15]

If emotions bear the potential to spark assembly and a networked insurgent community, a possible condition to action for Castells, I view the affects and emotions clustering around issues in the first 15M protests in 2011 ("outrage and hope" for Castells, "indignation" for the media, and certainly many others), as inextricable from a critical practice of interpretation among protesters. The Introduction began to explore this point, in part, by demonstrating how the "spontaneous" character of the protests elicited responses from government officials, particularly formed around the perceived fear of the incalculable multitude, on the one hand, and speech and law that aim to criminalize protest, on the other—both of which can be said to attempt to construct negative meaning, or detachment, from the social mobilizations in the public view. In turn, the plurality of demands, actions, and issues around which 15M took shape in its early months, likewise responded critically to the relations of (state and economic) powers for the ways in which they shape, materially and affectively, the real: the risk of losing one's home, the improbability of securing steady employment, the uncertainty of whether one will have access to healthcare and education due to their rising costs, and the cluster of emotions and affective intensities following in the wake of these and other vital concerns. One might call it a metonymy for collective social malaise, or *malestar*.

Reflections on an Automated Life in Apesteguía's Poetry

Before one can finish typing "why is poetry so..." into Google, the search engine turns up an ordered list of automated suggestions:

> why is poetry so important
> why is poetry so powerful
> why is poetry so hard to understand
> why is poetry so boring

Language, notes Franco "Bifo" Berardi, is increasingly automated by computer programming that interacts simultaneously with users. Programs also correct human error through conjecture about user intentions: "'Emotipn': Did you mean *emotion?*" For Berardi, today the "social body is wired by techno-linguistic automatisms" that contribute to guiding collective patterns of behavior (2012, 14). It is an observation that depends upon the understanding that "doing" can modify both, reciprocally, the agents performing the action and the system in which the action is performed. To elaborate on his claim, the automated combinations of the online search engine can be generated from a set of organizing principles deduced from patterns of high-incidence behavior among other users. In other words, one might observe that programming today adapts increasingly to users (whether designed for convenience, speed, "user-friendliness," or so on), but not without limiting the semantic field, in the case of the search engine, to preexisting combinations across them—in prioritized order, users wonder why poetry is important, powerful, hard to understand, boring.

Berardi's observation, in my view, can be brought into other terms. If the technological conjectures about user behavior tend to limit the field of possible combinations, then in what ways are users prompted to view, if not "trained" habitually to search for what is already known? In other words, in what ways are worlds being shaped that lend themselves ergonomically to diminishing chance, error, or the encounter with an unexpected "other" (result), in favor of the existing possibilities already given within the system and hence delivered to the "self" (user)? On the other hand, Berardi argues, "Poetry is the language of nonexchangeability, the return of infinite hermeneutics, and the return of the sensuous body of language," that is, an "excess of language" that refuses its debt to the automated semantic field (2012, 139–40). Poetry, to restate his argument, works against the mimetic digital and machinic operations that limit the possible combinations of what can be said and how, which together define the economy of the automated word. The politics of Berardi's proposal reside in the pursuit of new conditions of possibility within a given system, with its restrictive organizing principles and existing patterns of user behavior, that tend to reproduce identity, homogeneity, and automatism in only slight variation.

By invoking indebtedness, Berardi also refers to the technologies that have made possible the financialization of the economy, which is reliant on automated computer programming to register and react to system activities by selling stocks, taking inventories, placing purchase orders, calculating price indices, and so forth, independently of human operators. It is a circumstance that, in his view, resonates with the digitalization of semantic combinations increasingly left up to machines. One might think of computer-aided translation memories, scripting language in programming, and automated voice recognition. In a provocative comparison between the techno-linguistic and financial economies, Berardi notes that in today's digital world—in the same way in which money has become immaterially digital and plastic, no longer corresponding to paper—the "semio-inflation" of language requires "more signs, words, and information to buy less meaning. It is a problem of acceleration[, . . .] a kind of hyperfuturism" forged by the economic forecasts and growth upon which capitalist accumulation depends (2012, 96). The task for poetry, then, is to assert "a process of deautomating the word, and a process of activating sensuousness (singularity of enunciation, the voice) in the sphere of social communication" as a potentially oppositional technology itself that seeks new combinations, new conditions of possibility (2012, 21). To clarify, my interest here does not reside in exploring the automatisms in digital technology to which Berardi alludes, but rather in the possibilities of poetry to critique the organizing principles of an automated life, and mitigation of it, that capitalist logic cannot account for. Then again, this premise would depend upon an understanding, as in the reciprocal interface between the user and system, that the act of creative production can potentially modify to some degree both the agents that create and the world in which creation is produced.

Here, I examine Gregorio Apesteguía's free-verse poetry as a weighty witness to Spain's recent crises as it constructs worlds shaped by the conditions of precarious life, automated routine, and the demeaning experience of barely scraping by. They are often framed by the time of collective waiting, at times of wandering, of unemployment and insomnia.

> Millones de cigarillos fueron encendidos durante el trayecto
> y nadie quería moverse de su sitio,
> tampoco había sitio alguno al que volver,
> y cada cual estaba allí a su manera,
> sin esperar nada
> sin conocer el precio exacto de las divisas.
>
> (*Explicaciones*, 2013, 76)

> [Millions of cigarettes were lit along the way
> and no one wanted to move from his place
> nor was there anyplace to return to,
> and everyone was there in his own way,
> expecting nothing
> knowing nothing of the exact rate of exchange.]

The poetic voice in Apesteguía's verse exploits what Berardi calls the unaccountability of "the process of emancipating language and affects" in poetry, and the sensory experience privileged in poetic language, against the accounting logic of the capitalist economy in which most anything, even emotion in marketing strategies, can be capitalized upon as some form of value, commodity, or investment (2012, 16). The social communication of affects in poetry is unaccountable by financial and economic calculation, of course. But, so too can this excess of poetic language disturb the forecasting logic of capital accumulation by capturing what the latter cannot chart or account for: the affective experience of enduring the crisis conceived in verse and the social imaginary as a rupture from any long-term economic progress or financial recovery in the perceptible future. In Apesteguía's literary fanzine *(Explicaciones) Acerca de lo que está pasando* [(Explanations) Regarding What Is Going On], the poetic voice grapples with this fantasy of progress—"El Gran Timo," or a collective fraud—at times with critical pessimism and at others with humor, in ways that explore the qualities of an automated life, and possible transformation from it, after a catastrophe of immeasurable social dimensions.[16]

Los magnates escaparon de Europa en sus yates,
desde entonces,
en las sedes centrales de sus compañías, vacías y desangeladas,
suben los pobres con sus abrigos

Por lo visto alguien está asando unas sardinas en la planta 19
y un exbróker ha dejado un cochino,
que acaba de comprar a unos contrabandistas,
en la sala de juntas,
se lo vigila un becario con fe de hierro que aún no ha abandonado
su puesto

Los del este tocan la balalaica por los pasillos
mientras las señoras ponen tiestos con geranios
donde antes yacían las computadoras

Pero que nadie se lleve engaños
en este nuevo contexto,
no hay nada idílico
nunca resulta sencillo captar el espíritu de la Convivencia
                                        (Explicaciones, 2013, 37)

[The magnates fled Europe on their yachts,
ever since,
at their companies' headquarters, empty and dreary,
the poor ascend in their coats

It seems that someone is grilling sardines on the 19th floor
and an ex-broker left a pig
in the boardroom,
which he just bought from some smugglers,
watched by an intern with ironclad faith who still has not abandoned
his post

The easterners play the balalaika in the halls
while *señoras* place pots of geraniums
where there once sat computers.

But let's be honest
in this new context,
nothing is idyllic
it is never easy to capture the spirit of Coexistence]

Apesteguía's verse situates readers in Europe after a financial collapse, a transitory space of precarity, insolvency, and resettled ruins.
The Magnates have fled in their yachts, the title of this poem, leaving
behind abandoned financial high-rises, empty and drab, that are now
occupied by the poor. Urban life seems more rustic to the senses, if
not premodern, in the smell of grilled sardines and the sight of geraniums potted by señoras where the office computers were once distributed among cubicles. From the sound of the balalaika in the hallways,
played by minstrels from the East (again, a premodern vision), one
has the impression that many residents populate this vertical space,
immigrants and the Spanish alike, not all of them seen. Among them,
an ex-broker remains steadfast in his office. His intern clings to his
position with an iron faith, keeping watch over the boss's contraband,
a pig kept in its pen, which, true to Apesteguía's humor, in times of
business past was once the office boardroom where executive decisions
were made. Living together on these new terms is not so idyllic, cau-
tions the poetic voice, nor is it simple to convey. Despite this difficulty
to capture the new terms of cohabitation among residents, one gets the
sense that old habits die hard, as the ex-broker hoards his black-market
purchase under the watchful gaze of an intern who still hasn't lost his
faith (*aún*). Perhaps a faith in the economic recovery, or in reaching his
superior's position one day, or otherwise; the reasons are unclear. What

remains within this post-digital vision, however, are the attachments to a way of life persisting in the aftermath of disaster. As in another verse, "entre tanto, / los ciudadanos del occidente, caminando entre grúas, / continuaban buscando chalés caros por las afueras" [meanwhile, / Western citizens, walking among the cranes, / kept on searching for expensive chalets in the outskirts] (2013, 53). Despite it all, the affluent continued in their ways.

As in other poems from the series "Coplas a la muerte de Europa" [Couplets on the Death of Europe], Apesteguía's verse positions readers in worlds shaped by the present economic downturn. Precarity, abasement, and detachment linger in a dystopian future, one that has no room, however, for apocalyptic panic. Rather, what predominates in these worlds, amid moments of irony, is the dullness of vernacular routine in which commercialism anchors subjects in reality, of waiting for nothing at all amid the impossibility of finding work, and of drifting seemingly as though "la vida permanentemente transcurriese / en un asiento de metro" [life perpetually passes by / from a seat on the subway] (2013, 53). To witness the framed images flit by, while seated behind the glass of a subway car, gives a sense of detachment and rhythm to automated accelerations, slows, and stops while one is carried along for the ride. Remembrance of a past romance, too, is uneventfully transitory, even numb: "Tú, le sacaste una foto a un torito desde la ventanilla del autobús de línea / fueron estas las cosas que tuvieron lugar en nuestras vidas ¿verdad?" [You, you took a photo of a little bull from the bus window / these were the things that happened in our lives, right?] (2013, 56). An automated life, and particularly its boredom, is considered critically in other instances as a pervasive social behavior, one of detachment from the world. An example exists in the photograph of the baby bull seen from the window of the bus. Is it the tenderness of this fleeting image that draws the lover to photograph the calf before it slips out of sight? If so, it goes unstated, and what remains is the action of capture in the photograph ("the things that happened in our life") as well as the call for affirmation ("right?"). Is the photograph taken mechanically, then, simply by habit, as a reflex to document these moments by affirmation, and perhaps the fleeting attachments to them, before they disappear?

It is from the projected present-future of aftermath in which Apesteguía takes up a critique of the past, of a project called Europe recriminated for its excesses at the cost of workers: "Mírate ahora, Europa / Tú y tus crisis / Otra vez se te cayó la botella de anís al suelo [. . .] / No has parado ni un momento hasta conseguir [...] / que los peor pagados / hagan posible / el triunfo de las multinacionales" [Look at yourself now, Europe / You and your crises / Once again you dropped the bottle of anisette on the floor... / You haven't paused for even a moment to realize... / that the lowest-paid / enable / the triumph of the multinationals] (2013, 47). The title of this series borrows from Jorge Manrique's fifteenth-century elegy of his father's death *Coplas a la muerte del maestro don Rodrigo*, notably, by substituting Europe for the father figure to establish a suggestive equivalence across historical times. The publication does so by calling attention consistently to imperial dreams in European history, the will to authority and power, whether in the volume's first illustration *Donation of Constantine*, which depicts the thirteenth-century king relinquishing his empire by forgery to Pope Constantine I, or in the final image, Lessing's nineteenth-century painting of an aged and lone surviving *Last Crusader* who returns from war. As do Apesteguía's illustrations on colonial conquests and the African slave trade behind the portrait of the explorer Henry Morton Stanley, who, rifle in hand, poses authoritatively before the camera with an offstage stare (looking yonder, one gets the sense, at landscapes unsettled by European man) while, behind him, an African boy interpellates the viewer by gazing directly at the camera lens. Apparent in the illustrations, the comparison of imperial projects across historical eras likewise takes shape in verse.

"Elegía a un albañil" [Elegy for a Mason] eulogizes the fallen construction worker, prefaced by the double image of Goya's tapestry cartoons *The Injured Mason* and *The Drunken Mason* in which, in both, an injured bricklayer is carried away in arms by fellow workers. The verse, which opens by invoking the *albañil* in repetition, traces his fall from scaffolding in historical comparisons between the builders and slaves in ancient Egypt, medieval Christian kingdoms, and Spain's construction boom of the pre-crisis years ("Esclavo en la catedral, / en la pirádime, / en el rascacielos / y hasta en el triste bloque de viviendas" [Slave in the cathedral / in the pyramid / in the skyscraper / and even in the bleak apartment complex]) (2013, 21). As the verse links together the figure of the worker and the slave over historical epochs, it highlights the exploitative character of advanced capitalism for workers, but it does so by calling attention to the monumental edifices constructed over time as demonstrations of power. The pyramid, the cathedral, the skyscraper— and their opposite, the sad lot of housing developments—provide a comparative history that inscribes the rule of capital today within the material remainders of past desires to power. Cemented within their structures, notes the poetic voice, are the skeletons of sacrificed laborers:

"Y te has quedado petrificado / En el cemento de la historia / Gracias a esa infinita solemnidad estática / Creada con tus manos" [And you have been petrified / In the cement of history / Thanks to that infinite static solemnity / Built with your hands]. The monumental remains of power, then, bear within them the fossils over historical time of these "otros héroes atemporales," that is, "other untimely heroes" whose fall from the scaffold and entombment in cement parallel those of the "fallen soldier" from past wars, but without commemoration.

Europe, when not addressed as an inebriated authority, is referred to throughout the poems as the author of "El Gran Timo" whose "humiliating concept of life reduces it to a graph of measured profits" (2013, 49). Beyond the charted growth at the cost of expendable workers, Europe, addressed in the second person, has also "mercilessly" "apropiarte de sus poemas, / de sus canciones, / y de sus escuálidas almas" [appropriated their poems / their songs / and their squalid souls], in a comparison that not only underscores the usurping of possibilities to secure work and economic sustenance but also of these laborers' poetry and song in the same stroke (2013, 49). In it, the verse links together measurable profits and the immeasurable (poetry), at once, by asserting that workers, their verse stolen, will no longer adhere to the Great Fraud: "Ya no queremos que nos times más, / [...] ni nos gusta ni nos interesa" [We will no longer be deceived by you / . . . we do not like it nor do we want it]. The provocative comparison across historical epochs, in illustration and verse, lays the very basis from which to reflect on the present circumstance of the financial crisis as a will to power under the rule of capital, one of pharaonic proportions and sacrifices. As the poetic voice draws this timely comparison, however, it employs verse as a refrain to refuse returning to the Great Fraud.

If Europe holds to a project of imperial proportions today, then it can be heard late at night, notes the poetic voice, in the crumbling foundations of cement beneath the apartment:

pude sentir claramente, que Europa estaba hundiéndose

En aquella noche oscura del alma,
en la que se escuchaba a lo lejos,
el sonido del último cercanías de la noche pasar,
pude oír nítidamente,
cómo crujían los húmedos cimientos de Europa bajo mis pies.

Mientras, el silencio encumbraba,
con su estricta rítmica,

el "clac" de cada gota de agua
que se colaba por la raja del techo
al caer sobre el suelo
    (2013, 32)

[I could feel it clearly, that Europe was sinking

On that dark night of the soul,
when I heard in the distance,
the sound of the last train of the night go past,
I could hear it clearly,
how the wet foundations of Europe creaked underfoot.

Meanwhile, the silence extolled,
with its strict rhythm,
the "clack" of each drop of water
that dripped through the crack in the roof
falling to the floor]

As the last commuter train rumbles by in the distance, the poetic "I"
hears the sharp cracking of cement within the apartment, paradoxically,
a concrete that is still damp. The crumbling of Europe's foundations
finds its expression in an allusion to Spain's recent construction boom
and bust, of concrete that has not yet dried. The poem constructs, then,
a present time on the heels of a crisis that has not yet been cemented. In
sound, the repetition of sharp stops ("estricta rítmica," "clac," "gota")
performs the "strict rhythm" that interrupts the late-night silence with
the clack of each drop of water falling from the crack in the roof. The
dilapidation of the apartment's impoverished structure, it seems, is
beyond repair. As silence was first broken by distant sounds (the train,
the crumble), now it extols the rhythmic measure of water dripping in
succession like a metronome, which gives the impression, following the
first signs of a shifting foundation, that something rather ominous is
"clearly sensed" for the immediate future ("pude sentir claramente").
Given that the poetic "I" is at home, to work with Apesteguía's figuration, one might say that if the first warning sign has been heard,
then this temporal sequence gives the impression that "I" is waiting for
the other shoe to drop. Readers might note, then, that as the subject
senses the collapse from home, the act of reading the conjectural signs
of an immediate present to-come, as catastrophe, is one that shares its
temporal logic with that of forecasting, that is, the economic conjecture of growth and profitability in the short- to long-term upon which

capital accumulation depends. The act of forecasting in verse, on the contrary, exploits the immeasurable sense of a pending crumble that erodes, like the building's foundation, any future vision of chartable economic recovery.

Readers will note that the verse "aquella noche oscura del alma" cites the mystic San Juan de la Cruz, but does so as it overturns the ecstatic spiritual union when the poetic "I" ventures outside his abode, as in San Juan's original. Rather, upon shifting the reader's attention to the street, this "I" encounters a defenseless army and a sea of detritus, the jettisoned objects remaining after the collapse:

> Europa aburrida de sí misma se hundió,
> Dejando un ejército de desamparados por las calles.
>
> Ahora,
> unos días después,
> algunas cosas flotan en mitad de la nada:
> tarjetas de débito, televisores de pantalla plana
> y unos pocos bolsos brillantes de tienda de chinos.
>
> Los becarios de Erasmus
> nunca más podrán ir a estudiar a las universidades de Europa
> de ahora en adelante,
> en vez de practicar un idioma,
> aprenderán a hacer guisos de patatas en un puchero abollado
>   (2013, 32)
>
> [Europe sank, bored with itself
> Leaving an army of homeless on the streets.
>
> Now,
> some days later,
> stuff floats in the middle of nothing:
> credit cards, flat-screen televisions
> and some shiny bags from the convenience store.
>
> Erasmus scholars
> will never again study in Europe's universities
> from now on,
> instead of practicing a language,
> they will learn to make potato stews in a dented pot]

The material residue of bank cards, plasma televisions, and flashy bags from any convenience store, provides the image of a sea of glittering junk, expensive and cheap alike, for items that may have lost their allure after the crash. In this imagined world, indebtedness by credit is now unviable, perhaps even undesirable. So too does the image suggest a predigital world, one in which the items for electronic transactions to purchase (credit card) and high-definition entertainment (television) are rendered useless. In its return to the future that lags with it the present-perfect collapse, European students will never study abroad again, destined instead to make potato stews in dented pots, the image of premodern times conveyed in the poem's opening line ("Tumbado en mi catre, con la estufilla encendida" [Lying on my cot, the camp stove lit] 2013, 32). Apesteguía's poetry imagines a post-crisis future without recovery, one whose experience of precarity and insolvency, in the present, takes up a return to a predigital, even pre-modern past. Within this coexistent future-present-past, the verse at once inhabits the temporal logic of the economic forecast on projected growth, while it unravels the assertion of progress in capital accumu-lation that would require clinging, like the intern in his office, to the ways of the present.

Hope comes in doses, but not as one might presume; hope is rather an expectation manufactured from the promises of a commercial guarantee. Readers are situated before the television in an insom-niac's early-morning-hour hope that his purchase from the home-shopping network, a hefty tome of theoretical self-help literature, will explain it all. "Me ha llegado el tomo de teoría por correo / La buena, la definitiva / La que explica muy bien el porqué de los hechos / (además de un montón de regalos estupendos)" [I received the theoretical volume in the mail / The good one, the definitive one / The one that really explains the way things are / (and it comes with a ton of fabulous gifts)] (2013, 17). There is no warranty despite the television announcer's sales pitch to buy, performed synthetically according to the genre of telemarketing, and yet convincingly enough for the poetic "I" to have placed an order. This definitive volume, states the advertisement, promises to reveal all "true" secrets on art, love, and one's personal life, as the announcement devolves into a parody of itself. The promotion explains that the volume contains theories "que usted necesita urgentemente" [that you need urgently] and comes with telemarketing gimmicks, including a free gift of cutlery and—as the commercial turns to the absurd—a camping tent so that the book can be read on some remote mountain, and so on (2013, 17). The televised marketing ploy is portrayed as the very "future of knowledge" commercialized and packaged for sale ("el porvenir del conocimiento"), which even compares its product humorously to "the leading brands" ("ni tendrá que estar al día de lo último que ha salido de Jacques Rancière o de Didi-Huberman" [nor will you have to keep up on the latest from Jacques Rancière or Didi-Huberman], with theses that surpass "con creces lo de la vida líquida y todo eso de Zygmunt Bauman" [far beyond liquid life and all that from Zygmunt Bauman]; 2013, 17). Taking aim at the conspicuousness of advertising messages, the mechanics of marketing ploys, and the desires that they promise to fulfill in the consumer, the verse critiques how advertising aims to manufacture feelings of individual satisfaction around the good or service being sold, one that promises self-help after all. These words accomplish their critique, however, by calling attention to the fact that the object being sold is ultimately a simple pretext for the unraveling sales pitch itself, that is, a mechanical discursive formation aimed at selling promises, and the feelings associated with them, for consumers.

Apesteguía's verse also pays great attention to constructing space through the senses, whether the distant sounds and smells in the vertical high-rise, the overheard rumble afar and crumbling below the apartment, the envisioned fall of the sacrificed *albañil*, or the unemployed who contemplate the outlying cityscape from their folding chairs. Space is often, like the city, necessarily organized by transitory commerce and consumerism. In the poem titled *"Elater Animi. El carrito de la compra, o del significado de las fronteras"* [The Shopping Cart, or On the Meaning of Borders], the Kantian notion of one's disposition to be moved to desire (*elater animi*) is today substitutable for the shopping cart. The verse provides a poignant image of the disposition to be moved (and to move, by pushing the cart) from consumer desire. Do not let go of the shopping cart handle, warns the poetic voice, for it is the last bastion of one's will ("El último asidero de tu voluntad"; 2013, 11). The shopping cart gives an image of the automated motion of wandering through the supermarket aisles were the verse not to defamiliarize this object for alternative uses in other spaces.

In the first instance, the addressee seems to wander, having come from far away and belonging nowhere in particular:

No tienes donde estar,
vienes de lejos y no existe un lugar para ti en esta ciudad.
El día es infinito cuando lo único que puedes hacer es
circular y circular por las calles

buscando algo que te ayude a ocupar tu tiempo
(La Ecuación de tu condena: tu tiempo no vale dinero)
    (2013, 11)

[You have nowhere to go,
you come from afar and there is no place for you in this city.
The day is infinite when the only thing you can do is
go round and round the streets
looking for something to help occupy your time
(The Equation of your condemnation: your time isn't worth money)]

Whereas consumer desires are the drive of agency (the desire to consume), the poem likewise proposes an image of the wanderer, of the unemployed searching for ways to fill their time. Is the verse speaking of an immigrant who comes from "far away"? Or an emigrant from Spain, in its reference to border crossings, that "inner European exile" for the unemployed seeking work? Much like the precariat referenced elsewhere (*los prescindibles*), the expendable are condemned to cyclical wandering without choice: "Se trata de un proceso inacabable de ida y vuelta, / un ir y volver de un sitio a otro, / en el que nunca llegamos a ser dueños de nuestro destino" [It is an endless process of back and forth / of going to and from place to place / in which we never become masters of our destiny], a *destino* that is less a destiny than the condition of never taking root in a fixed *destination* along this itinerary (2013, 15).

Estáis tú, y ese reducido espacio de almacenamiento con ruedas
que alberga el conjunto total de tus propiedades
en un país cualquiera en Europa,
una Europa a la que no se la ve especialmente preocupada por ti.
    (2013, 11)

[There you are, you and that little storage space on wheels
that holds the total sum of your property
in some country in Europe,
a Europe that does not look especially concerned about you.]

The transitory figure with the shopping cart, whose total wares fit inside this space, also lends itself to envision the homeless whose only belongings are contained within this wheeled basket. Who pushes the cart, specifically, remains unresolved and open, and possibly all of the above, as Apesteguía's verse pays attention to the movement of wandering as that of anyone, rather than that of a fixed subject, much less attributable to an identity. If readers interpret the spaces between each concept in the poem's title (agency, shopping cart, and the meaning of borders), then one might be further inclined to unfold this "unwilling wandering" into the question of money and goods in circulation across European borders, that is, the flows of capital according to which the unidentified wandering addressee of the poem, idle from work, is required to move.

What preconditions the act of wandering in this poem is made clear in the poetic "I's" second-person address, his/her unemployed status and (lack of) value in money. This lack of value, it conveys, has Europe looking like it is "not especially concerned about you." The adage that "time is money," here, is presented as a condemnation: the seemingly endless time of unemployment equivalent to no accrued capital in earnings, on the one hand, and due to it, the "self" that accrues no value in money, on the other. The value of the subject, suggests the verse, is measured by the purchasing power of the individual gripping tightly to the shopping cart. The accumulation of material goods between the shopper who *can* consume and the others who cannot, presents the dual image of wanderers trolling the cart who share in common, as two sides of the same coin, their subjecthood to an axiom of marketing logic. For, consumers with purchasing power are the sole agents who count in the markets as a potential source of profits in commercial address. The others without an expendable income, in other words, are unaccounted for, unprofitable, uncharted as an outlier to potential revenue. Or, to take up the nod to Descartes in Apesteguía's title *(Otras) Reglas para la dirección del espíritu* [(Other) Rules for the Direction of the Spirit (2012)], one might rephrase the ontology of marketing logic as, I (can) buy, therefore I am (countable).

The blunt tone of delivery ("No tienes donde estar," "no existe un lugar para ti en esta ciudad") bundles together the subject's lack of belonging in "money" and "worth," perhaps even self-worth, in this incisive second-person address. In light of the unidentifiable wanderer, the question of second-person address in the statement "you have nowhere to go" does not speak uniquely from the poetic "I" to the addressee (whether consumer, emigrant, unemployed, or homeless), but rather suggests, as in the colloquial use of second-person address, that this "you" describes a first-person situation, as much as it can be that of another ("en un país cualquiera de Europa"). The movement here, in circulation between the poetic "I," "you," and the third-person, tends to reinforce the fluidity with which this "anyone" who could be "anywhere" implies, at once, the poetic voice, the addressee, and the others in its very address. After all, statements like "your time isn't worth money" and "you've got nowhere to go" are transferrable to any one of the persons inferred in the enunciation. Together they configure an open, transferrable character: a wanderer in an inner exile through space—the city streets, the supermarket, and Europe—in which, perhaps, the employed who desire to shop, share a precarious transitory condition as susceptible to becoming the uncharted and the uncountable, those without purchasing power, as are "you," "I," and "they." Viewing in the "other" the possible condition of the "self," and vice versa, dissolves distinction between the three positions in address to reveal its collective character under the organizing principles of capital accumulation and consumerism.

For the poetic "I," the shopping cart is capable of capturing for posterity the "bleak existence of Europe's inner exile" and, in a verse echoing a poem discussed previously, the "humiliation and profitability of its borders" (2013, 11). In this manner, the shopping cart bears a cluster of immaterial attachments for the poetic voice that makes the object worthy of display in a future museum, "Historia Material de los Artefactos Humanos" [The Material History of Human Artifacts], so that one day its visitors will understand the ethos of the present time (2013, 11). The voice imagines the present bestowing the future anterior (this will-have-been) with an object of remembrance, specifically, one chosen for the feelings of precarity bundled metonymically into this material item—humiliation, detachment, transitoriness, anger, and so on—as well as, for those with capital, the consumer incentive substitutable for the very drive of one's will.

By situating readers in the future memory museum and amid imperial histories past, one gets the sense that Apesteguía's verse is produced, in part, by a desire to future remembrance on the financial crisis, its affects and otherwise immeasurable experience, written into poetry. As in other poems, the call to remembrance is vindicated in the elegy to the fallen construction workers so that they are not relegated to oblivion, unlike other commemorated heroes of imperial projects and wars past. Akin to Walter Benjamin's proposal to "brush history against the grain" by recuperating the oppressed and the vanquished excluded from historical account, Apesteguía's poetry invokes future remembrance of the current conjuncture in order to account for precarity under the rule of capital, of the uncharted, the unprofitable, the unemployed, the uncommemorated sacrifice of laborers, and so on (Benjamin, 1968, 257). The poetic voice projects the present radically into a post-crisis future in which the current economic model is no longer viable, having the poetic "I," in the words of Benjamin, "begin to recognize the monuments of the bourgeoisie as ruins even before they have crumbled," heard from the poetic voice's apartment late one evening (1999, 13).

Remembrance of the pre-crisis past has this voice recall those times of economic bonanza ("una oficina a pleno rendimiento / en la que hay personas con la camisa remangada / una vida estilo microondas" [a fully operational office / where people have their sleeves rolled up / a microwave-style life]), which results in the poet's hospitalization after the police take this delirium for madness (*Explicaciones*, 2013, 57). Notably, confinement ensues by the authorities who police *which* past must be remembered—that is, the policing of memory operates from the poem's inference that the economic boom has been forgotten in social memory and, thus, the "I's" remembrance is mistaken for delusion. Contrary to the critical activity of "distilling the present" practiced in verse, to forget the past is also to leave no record for posterity (the shopping cart exhibited in the memory museum) on the authors and social consequences of the financial collapse following this economic boom. Apesteguía's poetry, in other words, creates present-future worlds that necessitate remembrance of the crisis in experience in order to articulate critically the terms of collective subjugation to what the verse calls "El Gran Timo." For, if economic forecasts assert that the economy is cyclical, and hence that progressive growth will be seen in due time, then this poetry calls for remembrance of the present in an imagined future without recovery, one that, by communicating today's immeasurable social circumstance, strips bare the positive promise of return to precrisis times.

Distilling the present in verse, however, is not an exercise in self-loathing, nor does it construct a subject position that seeks validation in address. To this effect, the poetic voice calls for the creation of new songs, given that the others have been stolen by "multinational corporations and Europe": "¡A rapear y a construir teorías serias y nada de ir dando pena por ahí!" [Rap, build serious theories, and don't go around making people feel sorry!] (2013, 69). The imperative could be read as a caution to avoid falling into the trap of commiseration or seeking "pity" (*dar pena*) insofar as pity cannot induce desired change for the poetic voice. To this effect, the poetic "I" joins the precariat in the shanty-towns in the outskirts of Madrid. Passing the time with fellow "desamparados" the poetic voice reports a snippet of trailing conversation that has "I" reconsider why "I" clings to the present ways: " . . . pensar y hablar obedeciendo a algo que no le ayuda en su propio existir, que no le interesa ni a usted mismo. ¿No aspira a que se transparente en usted otra cosa? . . . " [to think and speak obeying something that won't help you in your own existence, that doesn't care about you. Don't you want something else to show through you?] (2013, 79). The realization that one has been duped by an illusion, so to speak, is taken in Apesteguía's verse as the basis for critical reflection and, indeed, lays the conditions for a potentially liberating transformation ("que se transparente en usted otra cosa") that constitutes the subject as an agent of change within its auspices for action. To restate the poetic "I"s conversation, why does "I" continue to obey the authority that has woven collective deception and subjugation? The question provides a critical instance in a movement toward *becoming-other* for this voice.

Marking a transformation in the series *Explicaciones*, the poetic "I" endeavors to pursue what the voice calls a "nueva fontanería," or a new hard-wiring (literally, plumbing) to "redefinir la trayectoria de las cañerías personales" [redirect the route for one's personal piping] (2013, 58). To presume complete autonomy in one's realm of action, however, would prove illusory (a present free of existing powers), thereby also negating the embedded relational character of the subject within, and to a degree a product of, its circumstance. Rather, it is the work of critical analysis in Apesteguía's verse, or his multiple critiques of the current times of crisis that ground what the poetic voice calls an "ética para desheredados valientes" [ethics for the brave disinherited] toward change. There are no specific measures to take, given that such promises would deliver a catch-all model, much like the self-help literature critiqued in the televised commercial advertisement. Rather, what the text does deliver is a mechanics of transformation in the abstract, in verse. Following the critical activity of "distilling the present" in verse, what are the operative elements of this transformation for the poetic "I"?

If the sense of progress has been shattered in the present—indeed, refused by the disinherited who claim *we don't like it, nor does it interest us*—then deception has resulted from the disintegration of the social pacts guaranteeing a better quality of life, and those of social and labor security, to expose their constructed character within this premise. The poem "Renuncia voluntaria a ser alguien en la sociedad" [Voluntary Relinquishment of Being Someone in Society] qualifies for readers in its subheading, that voluntary refusal of the self implies, better yet, "mejor no ser exactamente nadie: por un desarrollo de lo impersonal" [better not to be nobody, exactly: towards a development of the impersonal]

(2013, 54). De-individualization, or the development of the im-personal, takes shape in the poetic "I"s turn to alterity that sees in others the possible condition of the self, and vice versa, within a collective circumstance. To revisit the example explored previously, the circulating first, second, and third person in open address constructs an "anyone" who could be "anywhere" in a shared social condition governed by the same organizing principles under the rule of capital. Whether one calls it empathy, solidarity, or otherwise, what predominates in this turn to the other is the recognition of the damage incurred by clinging to the ways of life, like the affluent who continued to buy expensive chalets, that sustained the Great Fraud.

The precariat who can never take root by the imperative to search for work wherever it exists—that is, to follow the flows of capital beyond their control—chooses instead to refuse their indebtedness: "Pero nos basta con vivir / esta permanente mudanza, / perpetuamente incompleta, / con una alegría inalienable / aun sin tarjeta de débito" [But we simply live / this permanent relocation / perpetually incomplete, / with inalienable joy / even without a credit card] (2013, 15). "Inalienable happiness" linked to a life without credit, underscores the nonexchangeability of "inalienable" emotion, that is, one that cannot be sold or transferred in commerce after the refusal of its indebtedness to power. The figure provides a suggestive contrast in opposition to the false "promises" and "hope" sold in commercial advertising that are manufactured for consumers around the sale. Indeed, the refusal of indebtedness opens up to associations with credit and consumerism, and even to the poetic act itself. Poetry is the means through which the voice searches for a "new (nonexchangeable) verse" that can break away from "the standardized rhythm of compulsory competition-consumerism," in part, by refusing the poetic "I"s indebtedness to an automated life that had reappropriated the voice's very "song"; or, to return to Berardi's assessment, "Poetry is the language of the movement as it tries to deploy a new refrain" (2012, 151). But the specific measures to take in this new hard-wiring are never named explicitly, other than in the call to "posicionarse en una mutación favorecida de una otredad; / hay que vivir un desdoble" [put oneself in a favorable mutation of otherness / one must live an unfolding], an *unfolding* that abandons, in some sense, the former ways of the self (Apesteguía, 2013, 83). The poetic "I"s transformation begins, then, with the abandonment of the self as it is (was) constituted in its attachment to the illusory promise of a "society built for oneself" and others.

The first-person voice of the poem introduces the Great Fraud as a collective illusion inculcated from childhood:

Desde niño
me dirigieron hacia la sociedad,
de hecho, me dijeron:
"Mira Paquito, la sociedad está ahí para ti
y tú,
estás aquí para la sociedad"
    (2013, 55)

[Since childhood
they pointed me towards society,
in fact, they said,
"Look Paquito, society is there for you
and you,
you are here for society"]

In retrospect, the poetic "I" ("Paco") evaluates his solitude and discomfort felt "every morning" upon marching toward the future, or rather when reporting to work ("Cada mañana, / íbamos todos juntos hacia el Gran Timo / [...] yo me sentía solo, / solo e incómodo, acompañado por mi mente / quiero decir, / acompañado por la sociedad" [Every morning, / we all went together toward the Great Fraud /...I felt alone / alone and uncomfortable, accompanied by my mind / I mean, / accompanied by society]). Solitude, the "I" realizes, is due to the fact that all along the "I" was accompanied by an illusion, one that impelled daily routine for "I" and others (*nosotros*). Once this false appearance is signaled as a construct, feelings of deception bear an emancipatory character insofar as critical thought brings the poetic "I" to identify "I"s own participation in this premise: "¡Ay! / ¿Qué mejor legislador para mi propia estafa que yo mismo?" [Ay! / What better legislator of my own con than myself?]. The realization that the poetic voice has, to some degree, "legislated" its own deception and fraud begets a subsequent observation, articulated as a desirable change: "Mi única salida es desautorizarme, / poner en marcha mi propio descrédito / y perderme de vista a mí mismo" [My only way out is to deauthorize myself, / extend my own discredit / and lose sight of myself].

The self-legislation of one's own deceit, here, refers to the "I"s former belief in the Great Fraud, but also to a critical realization on one's own adherence to the ways of life and work that shaped it. That the stanza should turn from "self-legislation" as a technology of the self, to "self-discrediting" and thus the act of *des-autorizarme*, stages both the role of government ("legislature") and financial institutions (dis-"credit") within the constitution of the self desiring to delegitimize the formers' authority over the self's decisions and actions (*autorizar*). Viewed in this manner, the act of discrediting one's self—an emancipatory act, here, of articulating one's agency for change however small the scale—is entangled within the language of credit and indebtedness, as much as within the modalities of "legislative" self-controls over the subject. The verse makes allusion to specific powers (finance and the state) in the management of the self, not as power relations external to it, but as shaping the "I's" uncritical participation in the Great Fraud despite the damage it has done to the self and others.

Whereas the voice's proposed "development of the im-personal" entails a loss of the self as it was once constituted within predominant powers, this becoming-other also grapples with self de-*author*-ization (*des-autorizarme*) in the act of writing capable of de-individualizing this voice in its turn to alterity. Writing the self, and the (dis-)authority of writing, proves a transformative act for the poetic "I" that foresees the "I's" disappearance by the final poem of *Explicaciones*, leaving behind only these writings in an abandoned working-class apartment in Carabanchel, Madrid. This metaphorical disappearance of the "I," however, does not consist in dropping-out of society but rather in *becoming-other* in which the self dissolves in its turn to alterity in order to return with a new "hard-wiring": "tengo que dar pie a la aparición de otro Francisco. / [...] ahora puedo volver a la sociedad con la misma apariencia / pero jugando mis bazas de muy diferente manera..." [I have to bring about the appearance of another Francisco. /...now I can return to society appearing the same / but playing my cards very differently...] (2013, 81). The voice has joined the precariat, it is inferred, but has not done so alone, for this voice disappeared collectively with coed roommates who together formed a Theoretical Working Group, which beckons the narrator's final question: "¿Por qué no te llevaste tus escritos, Francisco? / Tu donación anónima / además de expresar tu idea sobre la propiedad intelectual / muestra tu interés por hablar en nombre de tu época / más que en el tuyo propio" [Why didn't you take your writings, Francisco? / Your anonymous donation / beyond expressing your thoughts on intellectual property / shows an interest in speaking in the name of your era / more than just your own] (2013, n.p.). These writings for posterity, notes the narrator of the find, are a useful analysis on the contemporary crisis and an antidote for those poisoned by "contacto prolongado con la cultura actual" [prolonged contact with the current culture] (2013, n.p.). Closure is positioned for readers, then, as the eventual disappearance of the fictional poet and his audience of roommates, whose work has been compiled in this volume—an open form of closure, of course, but one that brings the series to its end. The final invitation to read this collective vanishing of the poet and his audience (one might say, readers), stirs critical questioning on one's own participation in the Great Fraud.

Policing oneself need not be imposed by an authority but persists in the habits of an automated life. For, elsewhere, warns Apesteguía's verse, "tal vez se haya convertido en su propio sherrif y, consecuentemente, en su propio prisionero al mismo tiempo" [perhaps you have become your own sheriff and, thus, your own prisoner simultaneously] (2012, n.p.). To this effect, the repetitions of everyday routine are questioned for their controlled and self-controlling machinations. Apesteguía's writings articulate this point, notably, through the figure of the automaton in the post-crisis world who traverses times of hardship and scarcity ("Vale que tengamos que pasar por estrecheces / y que nos acompañe la escasez por donde vayamos / pero no queremos ser unos tristes autómatas" [Better that we go through hardships / and that scarcity finds us wherever we go / but we do not want to be sad automatons]; 2012, n.p.). In the poem "No nos quieren iguales, sino idénticos" [They Don't Want Us To Be Equal, But Identical], the poetic "I" warns that one day in the future, an unknown second-person singular (tú, perhaps the reader) must inevitably make an appearance, and participate in, this society. The poem constructs an image of a pedestrian ("you") traversing urban space with grocery bags in arm ("Tú también cruzarás la Gran Vía / Cargando con tus bolsas del supermercado" [You will also cross the Gran Vía / Carrying your shopping bags]; Manual, 2013, 39), who will pay careful attention to "your" own movement among the crowd as though being watched from the building rooftops: "Tú mismo te encargarás de tu propia vigilancia / (Moverás tu cuerpo como si hubiese gente / Con prismáticos en las azoteas)" [You will be in charge of your own surveillance / (You will move your body as if there were people / with binoculars on the rooftops)]. One might find this mechanical movement in space akin to Foucault's disciplinary panopticon or perhaps, to Lefebvre's dressage of rhythmic bodies moving through the city.[17] In either case, the verse suggests critical thought as a tool to change one's participation in this premise, for "no tendrás calma hasta que no consigas / permanecer dentro estando fuera a la vez" [you will not be calm until you manage to / remain inside while being outside at once]. The desire to seek a dual position at once within and outside this premise—a becoming-other capable of mitigating the self's subjecthood to existing powers—is one that has the poetic "I" search for possible practices capable of breaking from (and yet necessarily doing so from within) the automations of everyday life.

In everyday practice, the city must be returned to a space for desires and social engagement toward unknown others, his verse proposes at times. "Telepatía, sí; Internet, no": "Telepathy" refers humorously to social communication in public space in a mutual exchange of looks, "sin la intervención de medios físicos" [without physical intervention], one that can prove capable of shedding affective detachment from the world, as though seen through the window of public transit: "Nos irá mejor si basamos nuestros encuentros / en un código espontáneo de la mirada / con valor universal" [We will be better off if we base our encounters / on a spontaneous code of the gaze / with a universal meaning] (*Explicaciones*, 2013, 35). Apesteguía's poetry vies at different points for rejecting the social behaviors of technological dependency that would rather avoid human contact ("Internet, no"), in favor of an ethical model when faced with an "unavoidable attraction to the person sitting next to you" in any city space, in the terraces of ice cream parlors, bars, and cafes (2012, n.p.). Public space, contingency, and the possibilities of the chance encounter, suggests Apesteguía's writings, must be reinvested with the sensuousness lost amid the collective patterns of pedestrians who traverse the city as automatons—noted in the figure of "you" who carries "your" supermarket purchase from one point to another, that is, in the rhythms of city life organized largely by commerce and transit. This proposal, however, requires venturing outside the private space to reclaim the public, given that "no hay novedad posible en el telediario" [nothing new is possible in the TV news] (*Explicaciones*, 2013, 83). The chance encounter with unknown others in public space bears the possibilities of breaking away from an automated life, for Apesteguía, and of exploring new possible combinations as a social practice when engaging others.

To conclude with Berardi's reading of poetry and finance, the political act may be understood as one that pursues new conditions of possibility in a given system beyond the prevailing organizing principles and predominant patterns of behavior that tend toward limiting all possible combinations within it. Poetry can partake in this act as the language of nonexchangeability as it seeks a new refrain, new assemblages and terms for the possible (2012, 151). Since childhood, claims Apesteguía's verse, one has been taught that there exists a plane upon which all combinations have been given. Called "La Gran SuperFicie de todos los juegos posibles," *The Great SurFace* bears a double-meaning, or *The Great SuperStore of All Possible Games*, as a vast marketplace (2012, 5). The poetic voice speaks in the second-person plural (*vosotros*) to the painted figures in the illustration on the facing page, Bruegel's painting *Children's Games*, who are destined never to leave their canvas: "os habéis hecho mayores jugando siempre dentro de sus límites. Han conseguido que os creáis que es verdad lo que os decían" [you have grown up always playing within their limits. They have managed to make you believe that what they told you is true]. To believe that all possible combinations are already given on this plane, notes the voice, is to submit oneself uncritically as subject to the powers that govern the combinations within the closed system ("Han conseguido que seáis sus dóciles súbditos" [They have made you their docile subjects]). Practicing this suggestion in its form, the poem's repetition of the capital "F" throughout the typescript suggests that the author writes from a typewriter with a malfunctioning key. Not only does the repetitious error return readers to an analog world, of manual typing, but the frequency of the malfunctioning "F" stands to highlight words ("Fingir," "Falso"), or to give them to readers as assembled combinations that open up to other semantic fields: "superFicie," "deFinitivamente," "inFinitas posibilidades". The capital "F" highlights the "Ficie" as artifice, underscoring the constructed character of this surface-supermarket after all. The task at hand, in Apesteguía's invitation to readers, entails a collective creative action, or a leap—"Ahora, juntos, tenemos que dar el salto más allá de La Gran SuperFicie de todos los juegos posibles" [Now, together, we must take the leap beyond The SuperStore of all possible games]— toward a surface of other inexistent combinations. It is never a pure cleave from the existing plane, warns the voice, as "siempre se arrastra algo del fango en el que uno se cría" [you always drag behind you something of the sludge in which you were raised], but this *becoming* seeks to move beyond the existing organizing principles of the given system and its aggregates. In metaphor, it requires a collective leap toward shaping worlds that lend themselves to chance, error, or the encounter with an unexpected "other" by questioning critically the possibilities already given within the system, at least, as they are delivered to the "self."

CHAPTER 2

On Affect, Action, Urban Intervention

Desires can be changed because they are mediated by power: being mediated, they are subject to operations of appropriation and seduction—operations that are not exploitative or violent when... the deflation of desire results from a self-education, of the awareness of the damage done, to ourselves and to others, by the desires that are controlled by power.

—Ross Chambers, *Room for Maneuver*

Si no nos dejan soñar, no les dejaremos dormir.
(If they don't let us dream, we won't let them sleep.)

—Banner at the 15M Sol encampment

Practices of Oppositional Literacy in 15M

I.

In 2011, protest slogans and banners in Madrid's Sol encampment formulated plural responses to the circumstance of the crisis. On the one hand, these statements expressed the refusal of protesters to accept their constituent condition as *the represented* by government officials and policy makers making decisions against their interests and without their consent: "¡No somos mercancías en manos de banqueros y políticos!" [We're not goods in the hands of bankers and politicians!], "¡No pagaremos vuestras crisis!" [We won't pay for your crises!], and so on (Hardt and Negri, 2012, n.p.). On the other hand, and related to the former, the language of protest critiqued the growing social exclusions being forged amid the economic downturn and the dismantling of social welfare protections: "Violencia es cobrar 600 euros" [Earning 600 Euros is violence], "España, un país de gente sin casa y casas sin gente" [Spain, a country of people without houses and houses without people], and so forth. How do these statements identify and contest the standing political and economic powers for the ways in which they condition everyday life? What practices of opposition characterize the 15M protests and assemblies, in their multiple demands, areas of action, and desires for change?

Critical *readings* of Spain's crises in 15M can be understood as a form of *oppositional literacy* (or, knowledges and practices of reading) that bear a specific mechanics and have proved capable of fostering common production toward desirable change. First, in their oppositional readings, 15M protesters critique how predominant powers shape the world through which subjects move and, then, in assembly, pursue imagined alternatives that mitigate the authoritative effects of power wherever they bear a policing or repressive function—a dynamic comparable to oppositional narrative examined in Ross Chambers's *Room for Maneuver*. In certain contexts of storytelling, notes Robert C. Spires, "Chambers argues that oppositional reading consists of seducing the reading subject away from the subject position of narratee into that of interpretive subject" (1996, 208). The practices of protest, in the ways I address them here, are less concerned with narrative seduction, or the act of being drawn into the story, though they certainly may do so, than they are with the transformative *becoming* in this movement from addressee to interpretative subject that responds oppositionally to power (as addresser, in protest); that is, Chambers provides some analytical tools that can approach the mechanics of this productive drift in 15M from constructing the political as legible material for the ways in which it shapes everyday life, to diminishing its authoritative status through oppositional readings and practices that articulate desirable alternatives to, and within, the current conjuncture (Chambers, 1991, 179).

In his analysis on the politics of spectatorship, Ángel Luis Lara argues that 15M may be understood as a rebellion of the public from its constructed role as passive viewer (the "represented") whereby "los públicos ya no se contentan con la recepción de las narraciones y los contenidos culturales, ahora se los reapropian, los reescriben y resignifican" [publics are no longer satisfied with receiving narratives and cultural contents; now they reappropriate them, they rewrite and resignify them] (2012, 662). In the practices of the *indignadxs*, the activity of critical reading shifts from the "passive" reception of addressee (the "represented") to an "active" participant as addresser when interpreting the collective sources of perceived domination—indeed, even an active participant in mobilizing for change in opposition to them.

To understand the materialization of the 15M movement in 2011 is to explore, in part, the enunciations and actions of demonstrators in their context of production and address. This task involves analyzing the mechanics of the demonstrators' critical readings and voiced desires for change as a potentially transformative technology for political action and assembly, as they reappropriate, rewrite, and resignify meanings in the public square, reshaping the city all the while. Although the 15M demonstrators' claims register inequalities in their refusals and denouncements, both of which are strongly tied to (or, fuel and may be fueled by) political anger and outrage, protesters also assembled in public space to pursue alternatives through multiple actions and demands with great hope for change (Castells, 2009, 363; 2012, 110–55). If there is some character to "being drawn into" the narrative, it would possibly start with the plaza, which was a place that invited viewers to read its multiple statements and commentary on the recent aftermath of Spain's crises, and to do so among a growing plurality of readers who also participated in weaving the narrative through statements and actions.

Banners, slogans, and the language of protest tend to contest official state discourse on neoliberal policies in particular, and the ways in which these policies shape inequalities and exclusions from public access to an extensive range of issues in general (access to public education, free culture, the right to the city and housing, and so on). They are, in the words of protesters, struggles for "dignity" and the "quality of life." These are two interrelated types of critical reading, the former based in refusal, and the latter in observations on how inequalities and exclusions to access are shaped. Both are strongly associated with "anger," "outrage," and frustration, among others, notes Manuel Castells, from the sense that autonomous decision was usurped from the population in the Spanish State's management of *las crisis* (2012, 110–55). Democracy, to cite the words of the first demonstrations, had been "held hostage" by elite political and economic interests in which Spanish residents were targeted to repay the public debt funneled into private enterprise and rescued banks ("¡Manos arriba! ¡Esto es un atraco!" [Hands up! This is a robbery!]). The demands for "Real Democracy Now" captured the popular estrangement from democratic participation against those interests that protected financial and banking capital, the fiscal priorities of the European Union, and the existing partisan system at great costs to social rights.

As Chambers notes, "the very possibility of appropriation" of powerful discursive formations, much like the critical interpretations by protesters in 15M's speech acts, "is evidence that *no* meaning can be

'dictated' permanently and that change is therefore always possible"
(Chambers, 1991, 220). As political discourse attempted to legitimize
law and policy on austerity, speech acts also became fodder for demonstrators who read critically and opposed the official state discourse on
the crisis. On the whole, forms of protest and action challenged claims
from government officials and policy makers who in the neoliberal
rhetoric of 1980s Thatcherism, denied repeatedly the existence of any
alternative at all. The protesters' response, in opposition, is captured in
one slogan from the demonstrations, "¡Somos la alternativa!" [We are
the alternative!]. The assertion by government officials that "there is no
alternative" was contested directly by 15M Sol's open call for proposals
on change, as the very possibility from which to imagine alternative
models of direct democratic participation, constitutionalism, and inclusive social well-being.

As the demonstrators in Madrid's Sol encampment transformed
the public square into a space of reflection, action, and expression
for the movement's plural aims, the protesters' multiple statements—
their oppositional *readings* of the crisis—traveled beyond discontents
articulated against government officials and policy makers, into practices of collective action, captured in the Sol encampment's banner,
"Si no nos dejan soñar, no les dejaremos dormir" [If they won't let us
dream, we won't let them sleep]. By late June of 2011, 15M developed
into, and drew from, horizontal networks of working groups, commissions, neighborhood organizations, and an extensive list of platforms, which have operated through direct democratic participation in
assemblies. Among 15M's self-managed initiatives and the expertise of
its participants, these rhizomatic channels of democratic participation
have engaged in collective problem solving on complex issues through
deliberative process termed *cognitive democracy*—from the housing crisis and the protection of equal access to public services, to copyright
restrictions, and structural state and election law reforms, among many
others (Acampada Sol, *Propuestas*, 2011).[1] As Raúl Sánchez Cedillo
argues, the first mobilizations materialized quickly into what Félix
Guattari understood as, "una tensión afectiva y cognitiva que, por así
decirlo, pone en suspenso, tornándolo susceptible de cambio y mutación enriquecedora, el régimen normal de las funciones de trabajo-vida
sometidas a la movilización total" [an affective and cognitive tension,
so to speak, that suspends the normal regime of the functions of work-
life subjected to total mobilization, turning it into something susceptible to enriching change and mutation] (2012). Deserving greater
attention here, the mechanics of this transformation in the practices of

protest and informed public debate, shared a critical dynamics in common with the activity of interpretation among participants attempting to address these complex problems through coordinated, self-managed action. "If reading, then, is the mediation by which narrative discourse makes its impact on history," writes Chambers, "this impact depends on the fact [...] that reading is itself a realization of the implications [...] of the phenomenon of mediation," or the oppositional interpretation of power and collective subjugation constitutive of the multitude, a point explored in this chapter (1991, 18).

Oppositional literacy does not presume a body of literature per se, nor is this line of inquiry concerned with perceiving in social movements a form of literary practice that "reading literature" might imply from the privilege of an academic position. Rather, oppositional readings can be, and indeed have been, taught and learned from one another, even mimetically, in the experimental practices of assembly by *doing together* without the need for formal education (Corsín and Estalella, 2013, 73–88). Reading critically, in this sense, is one of self-education practiced collectively, which pays great attention to the cognitive process of analytical thought, on the one hand, and to the "contagious" character of emotions/affects that take shape around certain forms of reading, on the other ("Organiza tu rabia, pero no te olvides de defender la felicidad" [Organize your anger, but don't forget to defend your happiness]). As Judith Butler has noted on demonstrators in Tahrir Square in 2011, the language of protest is indissociable from what performative bodies do, and can prove capable of doing, when assembled in specific spaces and contexts, around specific issues; this returns us to the context of reading for the ways in which bodies perform interpretation through action, as well as situate and are situated by what they read, say, and do.[2] Transformation resides, in part, in the critical activity of reading and responding with oppositionality, or of identifying and contesting the existing structures of power for the ways in which they shape the possible (desires for alternatives) and, in turn, condition the real. In other words, the tools of interpretation already known at present, to draw from Chambers's argument, have been able to provide the necessary "room for maneuver" in order to pursue desired change through collective action. On the other hand, as all power is a paradox, oppositional "relations of power are not in a position of exteriority" to predominant relations decried by protesters (economic, state, and so on), and indeed always risk dissipation or absorption within the logics they oppose, which makes them precarious (Foucault, 1978, 94).

These are the three entrance points I take up when mapping 15M: the practices of oppositional readings in the enunciations of protesters; the roles of affect/emotion in mobilization; and the production of a space of articulation for the movement in the urban milieu, specifically, in the Sol encampment in 2011. These points of entry do not aim to be exhaustive, fixed, or total, nor do they pretend to stake a claim as the only critical concepts from which to approach 15M. Rather, in the practice proposed by Deleuze and Guattari, these points may be considered a map that is "detachable, connectable, reversible, modifiable, and has multiple entryways and exits" in the entanglements between these entryways or others (1987, 23).

II.

To understand what protesters *read* is to map out briefly the many groups comprising the first 15M demonstrations, not exhaustively—at least enough to grasp the questions binding them together from their plural set of common concerns. Notably, any register of these platforms and organizations appears as a series of conjunctions (in polysyndeton, "and...and...and"), or an assemblage of bodies for Deleuze and Guattari (1987, 23). In the multiple interstices among them, one can get a picture of 15M's plural demands for desirable change articulated in its assemblies. By winter of 2011, some organized causes and platforms had already established online social media, web pages, and working groups to plan actions and publish initiatives from user to user. Groups fostering international exchanges such as ATTAC and Universidad Nómada, counted on ample experience with conferences and publications within the alter-globalization movement. Whereas the Madrid Neighborhood Associations were actively involved in social struggles since the late years of the Franco dictatorship ("Memoria," n.d.), the recent local assemblies formed after the 2010 general strike continued to meet in preparation for a greater nationwide protest the following summer. Locations in Madrid such as the self-managed La Tabacalera cultural center, MediaLab Prado, and the Centro Social Casablanca from the *okupa* squatter movement served as meeting points to develop self-managed initiatives in defense of the commons, the right to housing, and free culture.

Many activist groups had organized independent actions by spring of 2011, which included platforms originating in university protests against the Bologna Plan (JuventudSinFuturo), others for copyleft and the protected online distribution of cultural material against the

"Sinde Law" (NoLesVotes), and others against the reported abuses of copyright fees collected by the Society of Authors and Editors—SGAE. Groups like Estado de Malestar protesting "social ills" and the corruption scandals of politicians had hosted periodic events in collaboration with other cities, Seville and Santander, for demonstrations, awareness campaigns, and debates. Other platforms included those in defense of LGBTQ rights and gender equality, eco-activism and renewable energy, and the constitutional right to decent housing (V de Vivienda). There were also those in solidarity with Judge Baltasar Garzón to try crimes committed under the Franco Regime, and others against the privatization of public services, to name a few. Although these and other groups were not in active coordinated communication with each other, their participants' critical responses and practices channeled some of those shaping the 15M movement in Madrid and would materialize later in the popular assemblies' first proposals seeking change through multiple actions. The endless conjunctions between their many areas of action, and still others that escape this list, provide some threads of the desirable changes debated in the assemblies (. . . and . . . and . . . and . . .).

In an action clamoring against the Spanish State's management of the crisis, reported corruption scandals, and so on, the platform Democracia Real Ya! (Real Democracy Now! – DRY) distributed an open call for a nationwide demonstration on 15 May 2011, which was seconded by numerous others. The protest #TomaLaCalle [Take the Streets] would be held "without ideologies" or adhesion to a specific political party, one week before the elections for municipalities and autonomous communities in Spain. The demonstration was articulated from a position of *refusal* itself: removed from any specific ideological banner, party, or labor union, the organizers rejected existing institutionalisms and partisan channels—that is, the refusal to be represented, or at least not in these ways (Hardt and Negri, 2012, n.p.). Therefore, one organizing principle for the first demonstrations was intimately related to the inclusive uses of public space as the locus of demonstration and assembly, which would transform with the practices of protest throughout the consolidation of the Sol encampment.

As Víctor Sampedro and José Manuel Sánchez have noted, these practices of "reappropriating space" for public usage were bound up in the discursive practices of "reappropriating political discourse" in cyber-culture already practiced at that time, whereby the network of "virtual" protest activities materialized in the public plaza and contributed to garnering support for assembly in urban space, in corelation with it (Sampedro and Sánchez, "Del 15M a la #acampadasol," 2011;

"La Red," 2011). The correlation between spatial and discursive reappropriation, following Sampedro and Sánchez, resided in the protesters' actions to retake urban space on the one hand and to sustain within them a space for deliberative discussion and debate in order to elaborate proposals, on the other. Both forms of reappropriation proved vital to the production of space through the protesters' practices:

> tras sucesivas reformas, la Plaza del Sol, como tantas otras, era un "no-lugar": un espacio de paso, sin bancos ni árboles, donde conversar o encontrarse resultaba casi imposible. Tomar las plazas no pretendía sólo visibilizar determinadas demandas. Implicaba detenerse y habitar los espacios colonizados por el tráfico y el capital. ("La Red," 2011, n.p.)
>
> [after successive renovations, the Plaza del Sol, like so many others, was a "non-place": a space of transit without benches or trees where it was nearly impossible to meet or talk. Taking the square not only aimed to make certain demands visible. It involved stopping and inhabiting spaces colonized by traffic and capital.]

Describing Sol as a space of transit and commerce alone, or a *non-place*, the authors make reference to Marc Augé's assessment of the kinds of spatial arrangements proliferating in advanced capitalism, which are dedicated to the priorities of the service industries, transit, entertainment, and flows of commerce and investment capital over those of public interest and collective use (1995, 94). For 15M demonstrators, the spatial practices of assembly and protest in the urban milieu arose together from the outset to articulate desirable change. The reterritorialization of public space and political discourse to which Sampedro and Sánchez refer is one that hinged upon the critical activity of refusal: "We're not goods in the hands of politicians and bankers," "They don't represent us," "We won't pay for your crisis," and so forth. Specifically, in space, the language of refusal also pointed to the demonstrators' participation in deliberative democracy and assembly as a struggle for the public, subtracted from the channels of popular sovereignty that had failed to represent them ("La lucha está en la calle, no en las urnas" [The struggle is in the streets, not in ballot boxes]). Practiced inseparably in language and space, then, was a refusal to concede a collective right to the city, as the host to inclusive democratic assembly in urban space, against the priorities of capital flows in everyday urban life.

To illustrate the authors' claim, one needs only to consider the ways in which the protesters and campers in Madrid's La Puerta del Sol had produced space *and* these oppositional readings together within some five days of May 15. Sol's buildings under renovation, covered by scaffolding, became motley collages where demonstrators pinned banners on the surfaces of walls, billboards, and facades. Their oppositional readings, which combined language and visual elements, pointed out the responsible parties for the crisis in the protesters' view, made appeals to readers in solidarity, and denounced the deteriorating conditions of life, often in English for a movement aware of its possible international projection: "Bankers, Robbers, responsible for the crisis"; "Working-class families demand a solution for our mortgages"; "People of Europe Rise Up!"; and so on. Wrapped around one scaffold was a commercial advertisement for L'OREAL shampoo, which demonstrators had cut and added words in order to form the demand, "REAL democracy now!" Such a reshaping of the commercial billboard, which nearly left the whole of its advertisement intact, stood as an exemplary form of "reappropriation" in the interpretive activities of the demonstrators through art and posters in which the original material of critique (here, consumer society) was layered with readings for viewers to see in slogans, banners, and calls to solidarity. As the Sol encampment reappropriated language and space together, the multiple responses to political and economic powers were not only captured in protest slogans used to redesign the "look" and "feel" of Sol but also formed an integral part in *producing* this space through resignifying practices.

In slogans, billboards, and chants, the language of protest was repeated and interpreted with difference, as it was online in coextension with the plaza, creating a sensible "volume of noise" about what was going on in Sol as elsewhere in Spain.[3] For brevity, I call this open series of statements circulating online and in the plaza the *multiplicity of refusals*,[4] which in the practices of the *indignadxs* made possible the assemblage of multitudes in Sol and may have reenergized mobilization with growing numbers. The multiplicity of refusals encompassed more than a series of outraged protest statements alone, but in repetition and social circulation articulated plural critical readings in open association with others who made likeminded claims. Here, the "volume of noise" about the protests and encampments plays an important role for its mobilizing potential, as one would sense the sheer magnitude of the refusals circulating online in images and statements. Concomitant to the reclaiming and rewriting of public space was Sol's generator-powered communication hub of tech teams who worked to distribute information online with growing visibility: to document events, communicate with other camps, and issue statements on Twitter, Facebook, Google Maps, its own webpage, and a "live TV" webcam broadcast online (Saleh and Pérez, 2011). This confluence between uses of public and virtual space sustained the autonomous, self-managed network of the encampments with growing sophistication and public visibility. By broadcasting itself live online, Sol circumvented the mainstream media through direct communication with potential sympathizers for the demonstrations, via alternative media sources online, as it transformed the public square. "Nos hemos enterado todos por internet" [We all learned about it on the Internet], stated a protester compelled to join the demonstrations in Sol ("Indignados," 2011). In effect, the intensity of this volume of activity, online and in the square, can be said to be sensed before it is articulated, as one might say "something is going on in Sol." This uncertain "something" is made perceptible by the buzz of activity surrounding it, due in part to the volume of noise generated in these plural critical readings and refusals. Noise, which contributed to the visible irruption of the protests in virtual and physical space, may have been a technology to mobilize sympathizers in great volume, though it cannot substitute for assembly or for the kinds of critical readings that brought protesters together.

Specifically, the multiplicity of refusals had a mechanics to them: they were spoken from the protesters' plural readings of social and political relationships between the technologies of government and the governed ("No to Bankers and Politicians") and what was inseparable from them, the ways in which these predominant power relations shape inequalities and limitations to access in everyday life, in sum, their biopolitical dimension ("Spain: A Land of People without Houses and Houses without People"). They are, in other words, critical readings that articulate political subjectification in great volume and difference, constitutive of the multitude. Stated in announcements for demonstrations and the slogans and signs used in them, these plural responses detected and refused the discursive formations of power in the everyday, even if their statements were not formed uniquely through negation alone ("Capitalism: System Error, Reboot"). As Eduardo Romanos and Ángel Luis Lara have noted, respectively, the 15M protest statements, banners, and slogans interpreted and re-appropriated the language of power, often with irony, in which oppositional practices can be said to form a part of a transformative process of critical interpretation in plural ways (Romanos, "Humor," 2013; Lara, 2012). Should visitors in Sol have any doubt about the occasional irony of these readings, a black-and-white portrait of SS officer Heinrich Himmler was depicted wearing a Mickey Mouse cap with the euro currency symbol centered between the ears. The use of metaphor, in this case, took the perceptible source of outrage and domination—confluent economic and political powers—and rendered them visually as a Disneyfied fascist regime under the rule of capital, the euro as the common currency. This visual troping of power in urban space indeed performed the *language* of statements refusing subjection to the perceptible source of domination, such as the statement issued later by the Economy Group from Sol that attributed the usurping of popular sovereignty to the Spanish state's complicity with the "dictatorship of the markets":

> Elevar a rango constitucional la limitación del déficit público no solamente es un atentado contra la vida de los habitantes de nuestro país, [...] es un golpe de Estado encubierto de los mercados, al que nuestro gobierno se somete de manera voluntaria. (Acampada Sol, "Grupo de Trabajo," 2011)
>
> [To raise the public spending cap on the deficit to a constitutional level is not only an attack against the lives of residents in our country...; it is an underhanded coup by the markets to which our government has submitted itself willingly.]

Although "noise" refers in certain contexts to intelligibility, of not being able to hear or discern what another is saying, in this case the volume of the refusals lend themselves, to the contrary, to be read in multiple ways from different subject positions. In this sense, in practice, the protests' subtraction from institutionalisms, parties, or ideological banners for the demonstrations may have played an effective role in mobilizing protesters, due to their openness *to be read*. On the one hand, these institutions were often the very subject of disenchantment and refusal in the context of Spain's crisis. And on the other, this plurality of protest statements likewise contributed to the multiplicity of readings, in difference, articulated across common concerns. Perhaps one of the technologies of mobilization was the openness of these statements in their difference and troping of each other, *to be read with difference* across segments of the population that found some form of agreement with the content of what they denounce or, as Manuel Castells (2009) notes in other social mobilizations, with the emotional attachments formed around the injustices they decried. Multiple refusals, in many senses, had an open character to them—in open circulation in physical and virtual circuits, and in open association with others who made likeminded claims. In this light, discourse, per Judith Butler, is not a simple expression in language but rather bears the potential to perform what it speaks, and its speakers, into material practice (2011). In circulation via social networks and other circuits, these series of statements comprised an open field of social contact and relational difference with new and repeated critical readings for other readers—not through accumulation (n+1), but through difference in their many enunciations repeated in other contexts: "Lo llaman democracia, pero no lo es" [They call it democracy but it's not], "Más educación, menos corrupción" [More education, less corruption], and so forth. The volume of noise generated by refusal, in other words, may also bear its own "riff," so to speak, in which statements can be read with multiple meanings while readers are invited to join in contributing their own note.

On the other hand, the content of what readers *read*, and reappropriate from the discourse of power, is an activity that involves critical thought and response to different forms of political subjectification, whether articulated as one's indebtedness to banking institutions on a subprime mortgage or as the conditions of precarity sustained by labor law, and so on. Official political and economic discourse on the crisis, in this light, provides one kind of material that protesters read. Reading the discourse of power literally, of course, presumes receiving the terms of an intended or implied message as it is dictated to the addressee, or to Spanish residents at large. But, as I mentioned earlier, in the practices of the *indignadxs*, statements by government officials and policy makers are not read literally as they are delivered to the general public. On the relations of power and authority in address, Chambers notes:

> If reading [...] is a technology of the self that is fostered in social formations [...], we can understand that fact in terms of an apparent paradox. Power depends on that which simultaneously opposes it, that is, on "reading" as a manifestation of mediation. If we need to *learn* to read—learn, that is, to oppose power in acquiring the techniques of interpretive reading [...]—it is because reading is *also*, and primarily, a condition of the production of authority, and "power" is a product of the same system as "opposition." Power is not given but a (produced) "effect of power," an allegory read as literal; and it depends therefore on being read, a by-product of that fact being that it is simultaneously vulnerable to oppositional (mis-)reading. And so the "effect of power," when it succeeds, is itself the product of a repression, since it is the inhibition of oppositional (mis-)reading through the ability to "forget" and to cause to "forget" the role of mediation. It is only as a result of that inhibition that the discourse of power comes to seem (to be read as) literal. (1991, 251)

Following Chambers, the refusals of protest statements in their many forms negate the assertions made by power, such as those on "No Alternative" by reinstating their mediated character, via interpretation, from these statements' literal address. Therefore, the interpretive character of protest language performs something else in its production of statements: it restores the possibility of reading the discourse of power wherever the latter asserts its authority at face value, "with no alternative" but to be read literally. If for Chambers, this form of oppositional reading rebukes the literal—and in the practices of 15M, reading tropes it in multiplicity (sometimes with irony)—then the repression emanating from the assertion of authority is one that hinges upon "denying" any room for interpretation, that is, repressing the mediated character of power upon which this authority depends. One might say that dictation, in this light, works to "naturalize" the authority of the power relationship over the addressee in the asserted speech act itself. It is in this way that speech acts can, in part, perform their authority. As Chambers reminds his readers, the activity of critical reading and response can likewise always destabilize the "naturalized" character of this authority by pointing out that powerful assertions are necessarily mediated within this dynamic, however imbalanced the strike between addresser and addressee. Such a power dynamic, stated otherwise, is at the heart of sovereignty, in which the sovereign's right to rule (authority) is dependent upon the willingness of his subjects to allow him to do so.

In 15M, oppositional literacy entails identifying the predominant powers that have woven a discourse and system of thought amid the crisis (government officials, media analysts, banking and financial institutions), one that operates from the dictation that "there is no alternative" to austerity. Official state discourse on austerity in Spain, from both the political left and right, has drawn from narratives on humility, the shames of excess and economic insolvency, and the honorability of sacrifice in attempts to identify Spanish residents as responsible parties for repaying the public debt funneled into private interests and rescued banks—one of several primary issues that sparked the 15M mobilizations. In oppositional practice, however, protesters read this pedagogical project critically in plural ways that identify this discourse and its "emotive" lessons dictated to Spanish residents as an assertion of authority attempting to conserve political and economic interests. That is, the *indignadxs* do not read this official discourse literally but interpret and re-appropriate its language in protest statements, providing one indication of opposition as a mediated, transformative process of interpretation. In this light, many slogans took aim at the channels through which this discourse reached residents at large, in the news media ("Televisión, Manipulación" [Television, Manipulation], "Apaga la tele, enciende tu mente" [Turn off the TV, turn on your mind], "El derecho a la Revolución no se puede callar con manipulación"

[The right to Revolution cannot be silenced by manipulation], and so on). In response, the language of protest answers to power with refusals and rebuttals, which suppose distinguishing between the (dictated) meaning of this official discourse on the crisis and a reality quite different from the picture being painted in literal address. The gulf between the two marks a specific space for *readability* in which the work of interpretation on the discourse of power locates its possibilities of opposition in the divide between "what one is told to believe as true" and "what one observes critically"—a mediated space of reception in address that allows for a plurality of interpretations. The many refusals by protesters negate the literal character of (dictated) truth in order to arrive, instead, at different conclusions. And in doing so, they point out to powers that their authority necessarily rests upon mediation, one that the official discourse on the crisis tends to deny ("there is no alternative").

This relational field of indirect address—for protesters, one of reading the discourse and everyday materiality of political subjectification—tends to suggest that outrage is not a purely emotional reaction but is necessarily seated in *readerly responses* as a basis for action and possible mobilizing potential. The activity of critical reading by protesters comes to light as a necessary condition to understand how "outrage" and its many forms arise as an affective critical response capable of compelling demonstrators to act, not only from specific social circumstances of economic hardship, but from the multitude's plural readings, for example, of how officials justify the adoption of economic policies that foster disparity. Or, of how media analysts attempt to recast citizens as irresponsible economic decision makers. When taking into account their mobilizing potential for action, emotions and affects can take shape around, and are reciprocally shaped by, critical responses to events, statements, and surroundings, as much as they are also formed by contexts, experiences, and systems of thought that inform interpretation. It is in this manner in which folded within so-called *indignación* in the 15M movement is the oppositional practice of reading critically and, inseparable from it, its affective potential to compel one another to take action from stasis. Affect is the nexus of intensity for action and critical response that are bound together, arising in the same way in which one who views a video of a policeman wielding the force of a truncheon upon an unarmed protester, recognizes "that's an injustice" without necessarily passing through the cognitive process to articulate the ideals informing this immediate response in this viewer's specific context. Or, far from any physical violence exerted upon the body, in the same way in which one would hear an analyst on television argue that Spanish residents have lived beyond their economic means irresponsibly, which stirs a critical response without thinking twice: "that's simply not true"; and then, "What about government officials' appropriation of public funds to benefit their own spheres of influence?" And yet, certainly not all viewers will respond similarly.

III.

On 15 May 2011, over one hundred thousand protesters marched in fifty cities across Spain, extending in Madrid alone from Cibeles to La Puerta del Sol. Despite the peaceful but tense nature of the march in Madrid, near its end, the anti-riot brigades charged to disperse protesters who had stopped traffic on Gran Vía, moving these demonstrators into side-streets where they were subject to police force—a violent policing strategy employed in other demonstrations in Madrid. In isolated incidents, property was defaced and trash bins burned. As many as 20 were arrested, several of them bystanders, charged with disrupting public order and undermining authority. In separate events, after the demonstration, some 20 protesters later joined by dozens others, gathered in Spain's kilometer zero and the symbolic center of the capital, La Puerta del Sol, where they discussed their determination to stay.

Arab Spring had sparked a series of revolutions against oppressive regimes, and protesters in Iceland had forced the ruling party's resignation for its management of the financial crisis, followed by a popular referendum on its sovereign debt and "crowdsourcing" to draft a new constitution (Castells, 2012, 31–52). Whether or not the protesters in Sol located in these events their inspiration to camp is perhaps less relevant than the irruption of a political instance that they together entailed by reconfiguring the sense that change is possible. It is an act of *dissensus* for Jacques Rancière, a "demonstration of a gap in the sensible itself," that is, one that "makes visible that which had no reason to be seen," here in public and virtual space, among those who "belong to a shared world that others do not see" (2010, 38). If this politics bears an affective intensity, it can perhaps be said to shape and take shape in the attachments forming around this collective reconfiguration of the possible, what Castells calls "hope," somewhat metonymically. Or, in one blogger's words, "INCREÍBLE AMANECER EN SOL. Abres los ojos y ves que no estás solo, cada vez somos más" [AN INCREDIBLE DAWN IN SOL. You open your eyes and see that you're not alone, there are more and more of us], in which the breakfast donated by local businesses, a form of care and solidarity, is perceived as "un síntoma más del incondicional apoyo popular que recibimos, al que los políticos hacen caso omiso, ¡que reaccionen!" [another symptom of the unconditional popular support we receive, which politicians ignore, Let them react!] (*Acampada Indefinida*, 2011).[5] Although this "unconditionality" may be an enthusiastic overstatement, it is noteworthy here that care and solidarity are formed in attachment to this "incredible," "unbelievable dawn" as one that shuttles between the collective "you" and "we" in opposition to "them" (politicians who ignore an elided "us"). Enthusiasm and the suspension of disbelief are attached to these acts of care, and shaped around them, to the articulation of a shared condition ("we" and "you") that "politicians ignore," or the irruption of the political for Rancière. Notably, the open call to government officials (*Let them react!*) lays bare the oppositional character of a protest action that seeks a re-action (by politicians).

Labors to make this configuration visible arose at once. Working quickly to launch Sol's first webpage, the demonstrators named the group @acampadasol on Twitter, announcing their intention to remain in Sol until Election Day on May 22, while calling for supporters to join them urgently. Protesters drafted their first declaration of intent, identifying themselves as persons unaffiliated with any political party or association, brought together by shared aims to advocate for social awareness, dignity, and uncertain change toward a "society that gives priority to life above all economic and political interests." These words were accompanied by an affirmation of the demonstrators' peaceful, nonviolent aims:

> Abogamos por un cambio en la sociedad y la conciencia social. Demostrar que la sociedad no se ha dormido y seguiremos luchando por lo que nos merecemos por la vía pacífica. (*Acampada Indefinida*, 2011)
>
> [We advocate for change in society and social awareness. In order to demonstrate that society is not asleep and that we will continue to fight in a peaceful way for what we deserve.]

Although subsequent declarations would see this language change over time, from the outset the Sol encampment was articulated as a biopolitical struggle in defense of "dignity" and the quality of life against the priorities of capital and political interests, on the one hand, and in the creation of alternatives through social change that had yet to be defined, on the other. On the first day of the encampment, the protesters established a live broadcast of Sol and published their declaration, schedule for assemblies, and links to a weblog on social media. Early in the morning on May 17, the local and national police dispersed more than 200 protesters from Sol, by force and arrest, among seated demonstrators chanting "¡No a la violencia!" [No to violence!]. When communicated through social networks, the incidents drew greater numbers to join them when retaking the public square. Citing Articles 20 and 21 of the Constitution on the freedom of speech and the right to demonstrate peacefully, the protesters returned to Sol to establish the beginnings of the first encampment seen in press images, where they held further assemblies on how to proceed.

As demonstrators in Sol were drafting their first public statement on May 15, incidents of police violence had continued in scattered points in downtown Madrid, in what became an important necessity for protesters to articulate a position, speaking from the particularity of this specific circumstance, to denounce all forms of violence, whether by security forces or other demonstrators. The incidents required them to enunciate publicly and collectively their defense of civil disobedience and passive resistance, which later proved a key action for numerous sympathizers to associate with the movement, granting legitimacy to its future lines of action. In Eduardo Serrano's analysis of discursive reappropriation in 15M, protesters uphold "no-violencia" as a value that grants legitimacy to their actions, while also demonstrating "ejemplaridad [y] autodefensa paradójica" [exemplarity (and) paradoxical self-defense] that delegitimize the "efficacy" of violence—hence, the paradox of nonviolence as an oppositional practice—when exerted by security forces or other demonstrators (E. Serrano, 2011). If the mass demonstration on May 15 and its offshoot in Sol constituted a multiplicity of critical responses addressed to politicians and the public at large, then the movement's constituent act was founded in the protesters' collective enunciation and public dissemination of a specific position of nonviolence before the state and its policing apparatus. In this manner, the generality of protest claims from the march acquired their status as singularities grounded in the physical encampment in space and in the positions spoken from a specific context in time, from that of nonviolence.

In the following weeks, as now, the legitimacy of demonstrations has indeed hinged upon the reenactment of this defining moment in practice whereby protesters distance their activities from engaging in, or associating with, violent forms of protest despite police repression. As government officials have attempted since to construct the multitude as the state's adversary in political rhetoric and law, the eruption of violence in protests only serves to benefit policing strategies within this dialectic: in the use of police force on demonstrators, in the campaign against demonstrations in public opinion, and in the engagement of multitudes within the friend/enemy binary constructed for the state's policing strategies. If considered from Deleuze and Guattari's notion of *affect*, of the ability to move and be moved, then these three strategies can be understood to generate an affective force aimed at decreasing a body's potential to act. Fear is deployed as a powerful emotive instrument, in this light, to deter further demonstrations through self-correction in Foucauldian terms, either to protect oneself from physical harm or to foster dissociation from demonstrators through social atomization. Played out in physical space, police violence is employed in order to disperse concentrations of protesters, which aims for a similar effect of stasis and atomization in social circuits. In the discourse of 15M, observes Eduardo Serrano, "fearlessness" (*sin miedo*) cancels this "fatality" and "paralysis" of inaction by upholding bonds of solidarity in which "together *we* can" and "*you* are not alone" in the political instance (2011). Therefore, the affects attached to collective action cannot be understood simply as "enthusiasm" for an "unbelievable dawn" but take shape in emergent "emotional power hierarchies that may emerge *within* activist groups" around specific valued practices such as nonviolence (Wilkinson, 2009, 40).

Civil disobedience and passive resistance reinforce the constituent practices of the movement to refuse the friend/enemy distinction through the protesters' reenactment of nonviolence. In this manner, when the police and anti-riot teams advance on peaceful demonstrators, the protesters reenact a declaration of nonviolence by practicing, time and again, the same gestures with an intensely affective force—by holding open-palmed hands in the air or by kneeling before the police while chanting, "No to violence!" and "¡Estas son nuestras armas!" [These are our weapons!]. This practice reenacts the oft-repeated slogan "No tenemos miedo" [We are not afraid] before the police, in what confronts the state's policing apparatus directly with the multitude's position of refusal (to engage violence), here against the potentially debilitating power of fear. It is a performative act, as Butler understands it, in the coordinated actions of bodies that bear an affective intensity in this confrontation, one in which the demonstrators' solidarity and corporal blockade (often, performed by sitting down together in numbers) are enacted repeatedly in different contexts as the practice of disengaging violence (2011).

These practices also provide a sense of security in numbers, in which their repetition—as Deleuze and Guattari would have it, in *habit*— cannot be teased apart from the performative practice and language of bodies, the affective force of the tense standoff before the police in space, and the habitual reenactment of the activist community's values in "nonviolence" and "fearlessness." More than habit alone, though, this knowledge has been cultivated in documentation. The labors of peer education among demonstrators (on the protesters' rights before the authorities, the legal uses of public space, and the norms of civil disobedience, as well as other educational and juridical issues) have since been developed extensively by legal experts and volunteers who distribute this information through the 15M network of legal commissions (*Comisión Legal Sol*, n.d.). Therefore, teaching and learning from one another on the legal rights to demonstrate and the practices to disengage violence have unfolded in 15M as a form of self-managed care for the movement's participants. If a "body of literature" for this oppositional practice exists, it is compiled in this documentation and is reenacted habitually in actions and speech that disengage violence in the standoff scenario before security forces.

In a defining moment of civil disobedience, some 200 protesters gathered again in Sol, determined to camp until Election Day ("Yes we camp!"). Different groups in cities across Spain quickly joined them by setting up simultaneous encampments in Barcelona, Seville, Valencia, Granada, Tenerife, Santiago de Compostela, among others, eventually totaling 58 reported encampments at that time, and over 100 documented later.[6] Communicating primarily through online social media and the web, the Sol encampment resisted in numbers, gaining thousands of supporters every day who responded to news of police repression in other encampments and, as oppositional practice would have it, to the Ministry of Interior's public order to disperse protesters in the event of disturbances. Others joined after hearing first word of the protests through the mainstream and social media, in association with the protests' multiple refusals, "They don't represent us" and others. When taking the public plazas, demonstrators in several cities renamed their place of encampment "Plaza May 15th" in Spain's co-official languages, highlighting the movement's constitution as a networked assemblage of multiplicities arising from the regional and local. Internationally, by May 18, the movement had stirred protests in solidarity in Amsterdam, Berlin, Rome, Mexico City, and New York, as elsewhere.

Against the extraordinary numbers of demonstrators and their growing visibility in the international press, the Ministry of Interior ordered the police not to intervene, justifiable only in the event of public disturbances. In separate incidents, video recordings and photography of police brutality, when distributed online, were a powerful tool to denounce violations against democratic rights, as well as to mobilize protesters in critical reaction to these abuses. In this sense, the free-lance and independent press played a fundamental role in defending the rights of protesters in Madrid, as did casual bystanders who recorded incidents of police violence with their mobile phones to distribute them online. As Manuel Castells argues on the simultaneity of digital media to potentialize mobilization, "A short SMS or a video uploaded on YouTube can touch a nerve in the sensitivity of certain people or of soci-ety at large by referring to the broader context of distrust and humilia-tion in which many people live" (2009, 348). Thus, it is not by chance that the state has attempted since to restrict the media's access to mass demonstrations before parliament and has outlawed photography and video recordings of on-duty security forces, as the public visibility of police repression has indeed fueled public outrage and, with it, greater numbers of demonstrators in defense of the right to assemble.[7]

The protesters' decision to broadcast the Sol encampment live effectively reappropriated one technique of state security for its own aim by transforming a powerful tool of surveillance into a protective measure to deter police intervention by force, which may have con-tributed to conserving the protesters' democratic right to demonstrate peacefully. One protest sign read: "Si viene la policía, sacad las uvas y disimular" [If the police come, take out grapes and pretend (it's New Year's Eve)], referring to the Spanish holiday tradition of eating grapes to ring in the New Year. What the sign points out humorously, however, are the "acceptable" practices of public space condoned by the authorities, for celebration and festivities, in contrast to a politi-cally motivated occupation that faced plausible police intervention. As labors for common production may be "closely interwoven with the themes of constituent power—adopting new media (cellular technolo-gies, Twitter, Facebook, and more generally the Internet) as vehicles of experimentation with democratic and multitudinary governance"—Hardt and Negri explain, so too was the technology of public sur-veillance made to work for the movement's own defense (*Declaration*, 2012). In this sense, oppositional practices demonstrate the paradox of power observed by Chambers, one that is necessarily mediated, not only in the content of its address but also in its form, here, as the very tools of constituent power can be harnessed and reappropriated toward oppositional ends.

Demonstrators in Sol held the first few assemblies addressed at collective needs and self-management (food provisions and supplies, camp maintenance and monitoring, peer education on protesters' rights, the prohibition of alcohol on site, and so on), at the same time as debates on its initial demands. Labor committed to these structural, logistic, and educational matters was, in part, the basis from which Sol could develop sustained actions and demands through deliberative process. An accessible sign-language was employed as a voting system for inclusive, horizontal participation in the popular assemblies (to express agreement, disagreement, continue to the next topic, and so on), in which administrative roles rotated among volunteers elected by the assembly (moderator, secretary, caller-of-turns, etcetera). It is noteworthy that the Madrid neighborhood assemblies modeled after Sol would also designate volunteers to care for the *ambiente* or atmosphere where the debates took place—particularly, in the distribution of water, spray bottles, fans, sunscreen, and so forth—calling attention to the situation of the debate in a hospitable environment. This arrangement and its attention to care, note Alberto Corsín and Gabriel Estalella, is one element that may contribute to making the assemblies "stick around" through the attachments developed in hospitality toward others:

> Like all experimental forms, however, the assembly and the neighbour share in the problem of duration. It remains unclear and uncertain how to make experiments last. Thus, an organisational problem for the assembly, common to squatting projects at large, is that people are known to come and go, only to eventually disappear forever. "People show up to help, work awhile, then disappear," Keith Gessen noted of Occupy Wall Street. Hence, perhaps, the practice of care: a technique for upholding hospitality under conditions of provisionality and adversity. Hence, too, the importance ascribed to the atmospheric, which performs the role of a political ambulatory. ("What Is a Neighbor?," 2013, 14–15)

Thus, care is not exclusively an oppositional practice for demonstrators faced with the task of disengaging violence, who must attend to each other and themselves, collectively, in the standoff scenario before the police. As Corsín and Estalella argue, an open disposition to others in hospitality and ambience may have contributed to the sustainability of the assemblies for the forms of care developed in these practices.[8] Attention to care in the assemblies and protests, as a practice of caring for the other, takes shape around the collective project at hand and toward others participating in it. The sustainability of activism, in this light, is one that depends, in part, upon "the emotional value of protest [as] continually *re-experienced* [...] to remain emotionally fulfilling to be sustainable" (Brown and Pickerill, 2009, 30). Or, as Eduardo

Romanos notes, the spatial arrangement of the assemblies was an *invitation* for participants to join in them:

> One of the novel aspects of the 15-M movement was the way it placed experiments with new forms of democracy in the centre of public space. In this way, the movement brought practices of deliberative democracy—previously confined to more or less limited spaces such as social forums, social movement headquarters, peace camps and social centres—out into public squares, where passers-by were invited to join in. ("Collective learning," 211)

There is something to be said, then, about the openness of the assemblies and this openness to others as part of the critical practices of opposition in 15M. It is, after all, a practice that is valued by protesters, named, and reenacted in procedure with political implications.

All participants, regardless of citizenship, had a voice and vote in the open-air assemblies in which long debates favored processual cognitive "synthesis" sustained by plural contributions among members, rather than an "outcome" by a given majority alone (E. Serrano, 2011). The question of reaching a plural "consensus of minimums," however, would become one contentious point that transformed over time in different assemblies and their debates on procedure.[9] In this manner, the assemblies' initial operative structure aimed to disable the potential concentration of power or cooptation of interests by specific platforms, partisan politics, or individuals among its participants, which when reenacted in practice contributed over time to defining another element of its self-managed care for the assembly: the defense of inclusive participation against potential concerted interests among its participants. The structuring of alternative modes of policing, those developed in order to defend the assemblies from cooption by specific interests, can be understood as a self-regulatory mechanism aiming to protect the open inclusiveness of the debates, while at the same time, they tend to articulate "social forces grounded in values and not merely organizations or networks" (Eyerman, 2005, 42).[10] The attitudes and practices of open engagement with others would be defined subsequently in the online 15M WikiLibro resource as the foundations from which to conserve the movement's horizontal, inclusive participation: "nonviolence, no-machismo, no-homophobia, no-racism, no-leadership, no-membership..." and so on, thereby giving names to a series of common values for engagement (a polysyndeton, as...and... and...and...) already in practice ("Descripción," n.d.).

Self-managed labor and deliberation were practiced through an open engagement with others, among participants familiar with assembly procedures who could teach and learn from one another by doing together, before procedure itself was a matter of contemplation. For Deleuze, these practices would constitute acquired *habits* or routine repetitions subject to change over time as they are practiced. "Repetition is a condition of action before it is a concept of reflection," Deleuze stresses. "We produce something new only on condition that we repeat—once in the mode which constitutes the past, and once more in the present of metamorphosis" (*Difference,* 1994, 90). As Jon Beasley-Murray takes this observation further in his work *Posthegemony*, repetition in the practice of "habit leads us to the multitude: a social subject that gains power as it contracts new habits, new modes of being in the world whose durability is secured precisely by the fact that they are embodied well beneath consciousness," that is, folded into action over time, as habit, before these actions are the subject of contemplation (2011, 178). Beasley-Murray's argument on the multitude here rings true, for self-managed labor and the open engagement of others were routine practices in the Sol encampment well before they were named, documented, or consciously contemplated for improvement. Stated otherwise, bodies came into contact with others by doing together, and their practices transformed into new habits and ways of doing together, in repetition. In this manner, the popular assemblies' guidelines for propositions, deliberation, and consensus would continue to change over time, developing into the movement's multiple lines of self-management and democratic process, compiled today on the Madrid Popular Assembly website ("Metodología asamblearia," n.d.). If reading is a social practice, to return to Chambers for a moment, then it should not go unstated that the forms of oppositional literacy outlined here (practices and knowledges of critical reading) have developed from contingent social relations, of being and doing together, and of teaching and learning from one another—or, for Corsín and Estalella, the politics of care in 15M—that have in common a hospitable disposition to alterity, to others, in these valued procedures for assembly and demonstration.

The generic structure for local working groups and commissions would be reproduced with growing complexity as the movement in Madrid expanded beyond Sol, which intended to "export" a form of deliberative democracy to Madrid's neighborhoods:

> De entre las diversas razones para continuar la acampada que han expresado los asistentes a la asamblea destaca la de exportar el modelo de trabajo a los barrios de Madrid. Se pretende que los vecinos y vecinas de la ciudad experimenten el sistema de participación directa que se vive en Sol. (Acampada Sol, "Acampada Sol continuará," 2011)

[Highlighted among the diverse reasons to continue the encampment expressed by the assembly's attendees is the exportation of the working model to Madrid neighborhoods. This aims for men and women neighbors of the city to experience the system of direct participation existing in Sol.]

When in contact with the nascent local assemblies and decision-making practices in activist groups and organizations—or, other bodies and habits of doing together—these channels developed in plural ways into the deliberative procedures employed by the 15M neighborhood assemblies in Madrid, which would become an extensive operative network by June 2011.

Within these rhizomatic channels at my time of writing, the commissions operate with horizontal interconnectivity, working to sustain the basic structural, communication, and informational needs of the local assemblies and their working groups. The *commissions* function as independent service providers, so to speak, and technical consultants with specialized knowledge whose activities are dispatched to support the self-managed working groups and assemblies that propose actions for specific causes from the local. Their coverage is extensive, worth repeating here. They include infrastructure, internal and external coordination-communication, analysis and documentation, legal advice and residents' rights, technical support for web design and audiovisuals, news feeds and 15M Ágora Sol Radio, information and recruitment, and arts initiatives and cultural activities, to name a few. Through similar channels, the *working groups* within a given assembly serve a dual purpose as both observatories and task forces that identify and address the neighborhood's needs. Their areas of action entail short- and long-term political initiatives, labor actions and strikes, the neighborhood economy, employment opportunities for residents, housing rights and evictions, services for small businesses and self-employed persons, international relations, the financial system, the environment, public education and the university, culture and thought, social cooperation and diversity, feminism and LGBTQ rights, ethical journalism, and so on.[11] Comprising volunteers, the self-managed working groups and commissions propose initiatives for the local assemblies and may be created, dissolved, or divided into subgroups on an ad hoc basis, as deemed fit by the collective decision of its participants. Informational sessions organized by 15M protesters, such as inviting guest speakers with specialized knowledge on economic and financial matters, on negotiating debt forgiveness, or the "alternative" State of the Nation debate held in the public square, articulate another value for the movement, one in which the bases for proposed actions must necessarily be critically informed.

As such, one of the 120 assemblies in the Autonomous Community of Madrid, the Chamberí Popular Assembly, has gathered petitions against the privatization of Madrid's public water supply in the past and has organized back-to-school events for parents and schoolchildren. It hosts repeated actions to halt forced evictions this week and to support the student and parent strike against cutbacks to public education. It will offer a seminar on constituent power in mobilizations next week and will develop further plans to install a new *okupa* social center in an abandoned building, to name only a few. That is, its channels of activities operate through diverse circuits across the local and regional, from which new initiatives may be proposed among different nodes of activity over time. As a decentered structure in constant flux, the so-called movement bears no static, polarized concentrations of activity or influence within it, rather giving the image of networked social relations. Within this rhizomatic fabric, initiatives may gain visibility across working groups, commissions, or other platforms, through online interfaces such as social media, listservs, and the N-1 web, and thereby may enact specific actions in solidarity with others. This is the tempo of adaptability with which participants can propose and carry out initiatives with apparent spontaneity.

In protest, when this incalculable "spontaneity" is practiced in physical space, demonstrators communicate, in part, through online social networks and mobile phones (particularly, WhatsApp and Twitter), reenacting the mobilizing capacity of the multitude to abandon the public square suddenly, which to the surprise of the police, migrates to Gran Vía where demonstrators stop traffic to seize the street in an unannounced march through Madrid. Together with the gestural reenactment of nonviolence in protests, this repeated practice—a sort of nomadism that requires active coordinated movement and the contingent flocking of other demonstrators—has become a habitual maneuver for protest in Madrid at my time of writing. This practice in public space, however, also illustrates a parallel to the networked operations of working groups and commissions in communication through online media: their short- and long-term initiatives rely on actions coordinated across networked channels and on involvement among supporters who join in their lines of action disseminated through social circuits.

In virtual and physical space, these oppositional practices overturn what Franco "Bifo" Berardi describes in the behavior of multitudes as both the *network*, "a plurality of [...] humans and machines who perform common actions thanks to procedures that make possible their interconnection and interoperation," and the *swarm*, "moving together in the same direction and performing actions in a coordinated way" (2012, 14–5). Whereas the *swarm*, for Berardi, describes the behavioral activity of individuals who assimilate the routine flows of traffic in city space—as automatons in transit—it would seem that, on the other side of the same coin, protesters who move through urban space in a *swarm* can also harness this maneuver to their advantage in oppositional practice. Such a swarm, then, refuses to engage the authorities suited in anti-riot gear, moving instead to reclaim an avenue of traffic in a performance that makes itself undeniably seen.

IV.

In the days before the regional and local elections, the Madrid Regional Election Board declared the Sol encampment an unauthorized demonstration that, in its view, could hinder the democratic freedom to vote, which in critical reaction drew thousands more to join the protests in Sol and to camp in Madrid and other cities (Barroso 2011). Supporting this decision, the National Election Board likewise interpreted the protests as potentially disruptive to the election process, thereby declaring all demonstrations illegal after midnight on May 20, within 48 hours to the end of Election Day.[12] With the successive prohibition of demonstrations throughout the week, the Sol encampment drew more protesters, as it drew supplies, materials to improve its infrastructure, and food donations from sympathizers and local businesses (the movement refused monetary donations), in tandem with growing visibility online and in the mainstream media.

Defying the Election Board's verdict, hundreds of thousands of demonstrators in public plazas across Spain participated in a synchronized "silent scream" at midnight on May 20. It was a definitive moment that strongly rebuked interpretation of the election law by defending the right to demonstration and public deliberation in democracy. For many, it constituted a kind of "political awakening" rife with an affective intensity for uncertain change. In Madrid, this coordinated action proved evocative of other mobilizations in recent memory, as the silent scream and the gesture of raised open palms had been practiced seven years earlier—at that time, in mass demonstrations on the eve of the 2004 general elections after the 11-M Atocha train bombings. In the 11-M bombings, specifically, mass protests responded to the ruling PP's assertion that the Basque separatist group ETA—not an

Al-Qaeda cell—was responsible for the attack, despite evidence to the contrary. The motives for these protests were worlds apart, yet both shared in common their circumstance as an outlawed demonstration before elections that refused the literal address of government officials. So too did both moments prove capable of mobilizing seemingly spontaneous multitudes through new technologies, as 15M's forms of cyberactivism echoed the *pásalo* ("pass it on") text messages disseminated seven years earlier. However, for many protesters, the crowds also paralleled Spain's mass demonstrations before 2004, when mobilizing against President Aznar's complicity in the Iraq War or, for some, even the mass protests against ETA's assassination of Miguel Ángel Blanco, both of which also drew record numbers (Fajardo, 2011). And again, the motivating reasons for these demonstrations are contradictory, far from what brought protesters together in 15M. For others, it was evocative of a peaceful 1968. And for yet others, the protesters' use of the hashtag #SpanishRevolution was only evocative in name, but not in similarity, to the 1936 Spanish Revolution in which workers collectivized businesses for self-management and defense after the Nationalist military coup that instigated the Spanish Civil War. Although the historical circumstances are worlds apart, the use of "#SpanishRevolution 2.0" to describe the 2011 protests, drove at the protesters' denouncement of the "concealed coup d'état by the markets." A sort of free radical capable of eliciting many pasts in association with the present, despite the evident political contradictions underpinning each event in time, this and the other mass demonstrations of 15M proved strongly evocative of unprecedented mobilizations in memory, even history.

To draw from Deleuze's argument on analytical method in *Difference and Repetition*, conclusions cannot be sketched out by any scrutiny of resemblance and difference across these demonstrations, or their contexts and many contingencies, as though to measure the singularities and divergences of each one in the shadow of the others. The search for identity in relation to each other, warns Deleuze, will tend to reproduce sameness in a reading that indeed locates the similarities being sought; that is, this method redistributes identity across temporal moments in order to have the pieces fall within existing knowledge about them. As such, any search for equivalence or identity among the contexts of each demonstration, or specifically in comparison to those of 15M, cannot explain precisely *what* returns in difference to the others across time (1994, 91). Rather, as the protest conjures up a catalog of cognitive associations in history and recent memory, in different ways for different subjects, it returns to itself and other moments in series, in a resonance of eternal return that "affirms difference, it affirms dissemblance and disparateness, chance, multiplicity, and becoming" in one moment from other moments (1994, 300).[13] Following Deleuze's problematic of method, the protest's strong evocation of repetition in history and memory can be understood, itself, as the cognitive activity of taking stock of the event's sensible magnitude, or its intensity.

This hopscotch of cognitive associations with past demonstrations provides its own map for the affective force of the 15M protests. Leaping from one moment and memory to another, the act of sense-making fails to locate specific referents and in failing to do so, instead draws out the immediacy of the demonstrations' intensity among some bodies desiring change. That these synchronized movements across multitudes stirred reflection in the search for comparable precedents in history and memory, strips away identity from the event as it is eclipsed by its sensible magnitude among protesters in the public square. What remains, in other words, is the sensed immensity of a present moment, or an *affective intensity*. Not the demonstration itself, but the affective potential implicit among bodies moved to action, is what Deleuze and Guattari call a *becoming* (1987, 283). And in Madrid this *becoming movement* proved to be forcefully evocative of return in difference to unprecedented demonstrations in recent collective memory. Its composite temporal dimension—having elicited many pasts within a present moment of *becoming* something else—confounds the logic of a linear timeline in which the past turns to the present to the future, in what Deleuze signaled before Derrida's reading of Hamlet in *Specters of Marx*, is a time of becoming that unfolds as out-of-joint, unequally distributed for measure along the empirical coordinates of a timeline (Deleuze, 1994, 88).

Here, it seems, affect is not a prepersonal intensity alone, but a corporal and cognitive activity that arises from a specific context. In *A Thousand Plateaus* the authors argue that the affective intensity that increases or decreases one's potential to act may "come from external parts or from the individual's own parts" in what is inherently made possible through assembly, in corporal and physical proximity in contact with others, here in the public square (1987, 283). The multitude in a given mass demonstration may lend itself to a certain affective potential in the proximity of assembled bodies, within the reach of others in a great crowd. But when reading the repetitions of demonstrators in protest—the reenactment of nonviolence in corporal blockade before the police, the nomadic movement of the swarm to occupy space, the mute scream and gesture of raised open palms—this affective force acquires heightened intensity in the coordinated movements of bodies performing the same gestures together in the multitude.

V.

In *Rebel Cities*, David Harvey defines the "right to the city" as more than a question of equal access to the public, alone:

> The question of what kind of city we want cannot be divorced from the question of what kind of people we want to be, what kinds of social relations we seek, what relations to nature we cherish, what style of life we desire, what aesthetic values we hold. The right to the city is, therefore, far more than a right of individual or group access to the resources that the city embodies: it is a right to change and reinvent the city more after our heart's desire. It is, moreover, a collective rather than an individual right, since reinventing the city inevitably depends upon the exercise of a collective power over the process of urbanization. (2005, 4)

For Harvey, the "right to the city" resides in how residents wish to imagine the city, to shape and reshape the urban milieu, collectively, amid the processes of urbanization that give priority to revenue and profits. It is, in the first instance, not only a question of counteracting efforts to privatize the public and common resources, as well as the restrictions to access that they produce or sustain over time (by socioeconomic status, citizenship, race, gender, or otherwise), but also of how to reinvent the city in different ways for it to become inclusively *desirable*. Such a right, notes Luis Moreno Caballud, is actively practiced in Spanish cities today among self-managed groups that organize in defense of inclusive access to common resources (*procomún*), which aim to forge a much-desired "sustainable imagination" for the future.[14] Considering Harvey's proposal, one might wonder if the forms of care produced in the Sol encampment were precisely the kind of collective labors concerned with imagining desirable alternatives to the current conjuncture. "If they won't let us dream, we won't let them sleep" read one prominent banner in Sol, in which the question of conceiving alternatives is also, like the right to the city, one that is motivated by collective desires to imagine other worlds. In what ways did the Sol encampment articulate desires for change?

If I have emphasized that synthesis in the assemblies and demonstrations takes the form of a polysyndeton (…and…and…and…), it is primarily because this construction can give readers a sense of the multiplicity of concerns among individuals and platforms in the mobilizations: gender equality, protections for undocumented immigrants, renewable sources of energy, election law reform, debt-forgiveness on foreclosure, precarious employment, political corruption, and so on. Nevertheless, it would also seem that the specific demands from the assemblies articulated desirable changes amid these conjunctions, in the relationships between them, which move into the question of *desire*. Here, I am not pretending to speak of any collective desire for the demonstrations or among demonstrators, but a multiplicity of desirable changes enunciated from the assemblies, or per Deleuze and Guattari, implicit in assembly-work itself (the "desiring-machine"). I read this synthesis as a "molecular chain" that signifies as it synthesizes connections among various disjunctions, which for Deleuze and Guattari, comprise the very interstices in which desires are produced across assembled parts (1983, 322–39). What strings the parts together, in other words, may be understood as the driving "motor" for a plural platform of change—or, in the words of protesters who renamed the public square, actions toward collectively desirable "Sol-utions" against claims that there is no alternative.

On May 20, the popular assembly in Sol approved 16 points of its first demands. The articulation of these proposals and demands comprised a subsequent constituent act—the first, a declaration on its position of nonviolence—collected in a press release addressed to the Spanish state and the public at large (Acampada Sol, "Propuestas aprobadas," 2011).

1. Modify the Election Law to allow for open lists with a single constituency in which the number of elected seats is proportional to the number of votes.
2. Attend to the basic, fundamental rights in the Constitution of 1978, such as the right to decent housing by reforming the Law of Mortgages to allow for debt cancellation in cases of foreclosure; universal and free public healthcare; the free movement of persons; and support of a secular public education.
3. Abolish discriminatory and unjust laws and measures in the Bologna Plan and the European Space for Higher Education; the Immigration Law; and the "Sinde Law."
4. Fiscal reform favorable to persons with the lowest incomes, including a reform of property and inheritance tax laws. Implementation of the Tobin Tax on international financial transactions and the abolition of tax havens.
5. Reform the working conditions for the political class to eliminate salaries for life, as well as to make political programs and election promises binding.

6. Reject and condemn corruption. Make it a requirement by Election Law to present lists free of candidates charged or condemned in corruption cases.
7. Adopt plural measures regarding public savings banks and the financial markets in compliance with Art. 128 of the Constitution ("The entire wealth of the country in its different forms, irrespective of ownership, shall be subordinated to the general interest"). Reduce the IMF and ECB's power. Nationalize immediately all banking entities that have been rescued by the State. Harden controls on financial entities and operations to avoid any possible abuses.
8. True separation between the Catholic Church and State, as established in Art. 16 of the Constitution.
9. Direct, participatory democracy in which citizens have an active role. The people's access to the media must be ethical and true.
10. True regularization of labor conditions in compliance with the law, overseen by the powers of the State.
11. Close all nuclear power plants and promote free renewable energy sources.
12. Nationalize privatized public companies.
13. Effective separation of executive, legislative, and judicial powers.
14. Reduce spending on the military, the immediate closure of weapons factories, and greater control of the State's security forces and organizations.
15. Recuperation of Historical Memory and the founding principles of the struggle for Democracy in the State.
16. Total transparency of political parties' accounts and financing as a measure against corruption.

Within this extensive list, some statements propose specific measures ("modify the election law..., nationalize rescued banks..., promote free renewable energy sources..."), which range in content from specific proposed actions to rather vague effects ("reduce the IMF and ECB's power"). Notably, the other kind of statements in this list relates to the latter. This second type of statement does not outline specific measures, at least not at this stage, but the *desirable* outcomes for future lines of action ("true separation between Church and State..., effective separation of powers..., total transparency of political parties' financing..."). Once the demands were articulated, they became interpretable material on what plural actions to take.

One year after the first Sol encampment, protesters assembled again to reclaim the public square, as they documented accumulative desires for change written on notes, categorized by theme, and released for publication in the mainstream press (Comisión de Información, 2012; García de Blas, 2012). Aside from organizational recommendations on assembly procedure, the top 20 most-cited issues could be grouped into at least four main categories:

(1) State and partisan politics: the abolition of political privileges; open election lists and election law reform (opposed to the current d'Hondt Law); measures to prevent political corruption, including greater controls on donations and harsher criminal sentences; direct democratic participation of the citizenry, including constituent referendums and Popular Legislative Initiatives; measures to guarantee political responsibility for government officials; the separation of state powers; transparency in administration; the implementation of requirements for public office; and the elimination of the monarchy.

(2) Education and Social Rights: the right to a public secular education; the right to public healthcare; the right to accessible housing; and the improvement of labor conditions for workers.

(3) Regulations for the banking and financial sector: the regulation of nationalized banks and the adoption of debt forgiveness for homeowners after foreclosure; measures to favor public companies, including placing a halt to privatization and the nationalization of privatized businesses; the regulation of caps on the highest salaries.

(4) Strategies for sustainable public energy sources and transportation, the defense of free culture (opposed to the Sinde Law and copyright restrictions), and the protection of animal rights.

Although any summary of these points risks reductionism, which tends to collapse their series of conjunctions into a general schematic, one can also note a set of organizing principles shaped around these desirable outcomes. In the interstices between conjunctions, one can locate the desirable effects of future actions: to recuperate state decision making before economic and financial interests in a more equitable management and distribution of common resources and wealth; to guarantee egalitarian access to public services, common resources, and the uses of public space; and to secure the protection of residents from confluent interests of state powers among them and in concert with external (largely, private) institutional arrangements. The alternatives proposed in the assemblies, and at once practiced in them, likewise demanded some form of direct democratic participation in the decision-making powers of the state. On the whole, these desirable outcomes and their effects tended to articulate, with oppositionality, the very conditions of political subjectification that had constituted the multitude in its multiplicity of refusals. Nevertheless, there exists a *productive drift* or becoming that moves beyond the latter to articulate (future) desirable outcomes imagined collectively from the cognitive process of democratic assembly.

Chambers reminds his readers that desire is a mediated affair, subject to change in the shifting power relations of its circumstance; conversely, desire can beget change (1991, 232). Whereas these desirable outcomes were articulated about, and in critical opposition to, the prevailing structures of power, they likewise partook in imagining the future effects of limitations placed on these powers wherever their relations worked (at present) to repress or police these material possibilities. One needs only to remember the protest banner in Sol ("If they won't let us dream...") to understand that the demonstrators made this point themselves: the possibility of imagining futures (*soñar*) is articulated directly as one that is perceptibly conditioned by the prevailing structures of power (*si no nos dejan*). This temporal dimension, in relay between the current conjuncture and future actions imagined for their capability to *mitigate* these forms of repression at present, appears as a mediated space of desires that opens up radically to imagined possibilities. Within it, the articulation of desirable outcomes can be sensed as emancipatory, with affective force, ensuing from "the deflation of desire [that] results from a self-education, of the awareness of the damage done, to ourselves and to others, by the desires that are controlled by power" and their repressive limitations shaping the real (Chambers, 1991, 232).

It is this instance in which I would like to underscore that the critical practices and knowledges of opposition among demonstrators (their oppositional literacy) have been capable, in part, of calling attention to the ways in which power is necessarily mediated, despite and due to authoritative claims that there exists no alternative. It is what happens in-between, however, in the mediated scenario of imagining desirable outcomes capable of mitigating forms of repression, where the authoritative status of power is seemingly displaced, if only momentarily, that is, until it comes to bear again upon subjects in whatever the form (the eviction notice, the charge of the anti-riot brigade, the idle time of unemployment, and so on). For Rancière, the partitioning of this space of mediation is precarious, "always on the shore of its own disappearance," threatened by being subsumed into the very logics, if not powers, that it opposes (2010, 39). However, in 15M, it is also this room for maneuver that works toward producing desirable changes, which, once articulated in speech, can be conceived as conscious changes in desire, in a productive movement from the perceived forms of domination to coordinated actions that pursue alternative futures. In this scenario, nevertheless, there is no emancipating line of flight, as Deleuze and Guattari would have it, which escapes repression completely as it mitigates the authoritative status of prevailing powers. Nor does it suppose an ideological fantasy, as it would for Žižek, in which revolutionary change requires the castration of power.[15] Rather, change can be hatched *within* the prevailing structures of domination, but it would presume in the first instance, as Harvey suggests, a collective critical questioning, "What is desirable and why?" And following Chambers, then, "In what ways are desires shaped by the prevailing relations of power?"

Any endeavor to describe the developments of Sol fails to grasp the reasons why it drew thousands of visitors, which had moved quickly from the supposed "outrage" that brought demonstrators together, to assemblies articulating desirable change. As Amador Fernández-Savater notes, "no estábamos allí para gritar nuestra indignación contra nadie, sino por la belleza y la potencia de estar juntos, ensayando modos de participación común en las cosas comunes. Por lo tanto, redefiniendo y reinventando lo político" [we weren't there to shout our outrage against anyone, but for the beauty and power of being together, practicing ways of common participation in common things, thereby redefining and reinventing the political] (2012, 677). Astonishment might best describe the Sol encampment's achievements in its seemingly unbelievable self-management. Like its computer hub, Sol's operations were staffed by volunteers, which included security teams and first-aid personnel, a day-care with activities for children, a portable library of donated books and educational materials, and programmed cultural events, theater, and concerts. The encampment received infrastructural support through donations of supplies like tarps, tents, hygiene products, portable water closets, and reported in the media, a solar-powered shower. Campers planted small gardens in the plaza's only green zones surrounding the fountains, christened "La Huerta del Sol" in a play-on-words for the square's proper name, and regulated waste disposal, recycling, and collective cleaning duties among occupants. Perhaps surprisingly, an unannounced health and safety inspection by the municipal government reported that the site complied with standard regulations, including the open-air kitchen where food was prepared collectively (García Gallo, 2011). Presumably, these labors required expert knowledge on the legality of the encampment's operations coordinated among the protesters and likewise stands as one example, to my mind, of the suspension of disbelief about 15M's accomplishments.

Inseparable from the encampment's organizational practices and structure were its activist centers arranged along passageways through the plaza where visitors could be informed of an array of issues, sign petitions, and create signs for the demonstrations. Tents provided materials to create artwork assembled from scrap materials (often, recovered from trash bins), a telling expression of the movement's claims by protesters who vindicated their status as jettisoned expendables to political leadership. In this manner, the encampment served as an information point on the legal rights of protesters and undocumented immigrants; on actions developed in defense of equal rights and gender equality; and for the circulation of petitions for causes against privatization, international human rights offenses, business practices harmful to the environment (and ... and ... and). As the site outgrew its physical boundaries haphazardly, campers restructured Sol by redistributing its points and passageways to facilitate pedestrian traffic. Once redrawn, space was organized around the equestrian statue of "Enlightened King" Carlos III, which was reduced schematically (and synecdochically) on the encampment's maps to simply "the horse."

Because the large-scale cohabitation among strangers did not ensue without reported social tensions—and, for some, would mark a cleave among demonstrators who claimed that the encampment was not synonymous with the 15M "movement"—the campers restructured the stands and assemblies to include specific working groups on "respect" in defense of the norms of engagement, difference, and dialog in the popular assemblies.[16] Wherever language, attitudes, or practices were considered disrespectful or exclusionary to its participants, the assemblies addressed these issues by generating peer education initiatives in defense of the common values described earlier (nonviolence, no-machismo, no-discrimination, respect ...). Montserrat Galcerán reports, for example, that some participants were reluctant at first to include feminist commissions, for a movement skeptical of identity positions as potentially divisive to collective aims; once reassessed, however, feminist commissions were successfully incorporated after peer education, outlined in Galcerán's proposals and excellent documentation (2012, 31–6). In electronic communications, attention was drawn to the use of the plural masculine *indignados*, replaced by the gender-inclusive, *indignad@s* or *indignadxs*. Although the use of inclusive language alone cannot guarantee nondiscrimination, and indeed can give the false appearance of equality, the participants understood the forms of communication as vital to their practices, as inextricably bound together—that is, as *desirable* for the movement's aims.

Such a case is evident in the open invitation for a "bike criticism," an event to meet others and discuss common concerns, culminating in a performative parade of cyclists, banners, and flags through the city streets. The public invitation to the "Bici-crítica Trans-mari-bollo-bi-queer-feminista" takes derogatory slurs for LGBTQ identities (*trans, mari, bollo*) and in this well-established formula, reappropriates them to the empowerment of the collective by affirming them as one's own ("tranny," "fag," "dyke"). It provides an example of what Luis Martín Cabrera calls "queering the commons," that is, of deconstructing existing forms of oppression, whether racialized, gendered, or sexualized, so that they are prevented from "endangering the very same project of living in common," here, through the oppositional practice of reappropriation-as-empowerment itself (2012, 602–3). In the invitation to the bike criticism, the string of hyphenations tends to exceed naming difference in its many identitarian constructions of gender and sexuality, in an attempt not to leave anyone out. As it does so, the conjunctions among them (polysyndeton) replicates one of 15M's organizing principles in the assemblies and assemblage-work—the desire for inclusiveness, or the hospitable invitation to join the assembly, in the turn to others.

For Amador Fernández-Savater, "Una de las mayores potencias éticas y políticas del 15M es la pregunta y la preocupación constante por el otro, el que no está ya aquí, *entre nosotros*" [One of the greatest ethical and political potentials of 15M is the question and constant concern for the other, those who are not here and now *among us*] (2012, 677). Such a turn to alterity and concern for *those who are not present*, much like the invitation to join the open-air assemblies in the public square, is one of the defining oppositional politics of 15M. In this disposition to inclusiveness and to "Others," these forms of opposition and their reappropriating, resignifying practices tend to engage what Deleuze and Guattari called a minoritarian politics.

Minoritarian politics "is concerned less with the political status or rights of minority groups than with the degree to which minorities [as a segmented partition of the represented] embody a distinct power or capacity to transform majorities," writes Paul Patton. The minoritarian embodies a form of political engagement in *becoming*, for Deleuze and

Guattari, as it can work to secure "the general conditions that ensure the emergence of new forms and new systems of right" from the unrepresented and oppressed subjects who share in common their subjugation (Patton, 2005, 67). Following this line of thought, a majority is a form conceived for group decision making, and thereby a "majority" in this abstract form cannot be desired, per se, but is rather a means to arrive at desirable outcomes among decision makers. Minorities, in the plural, then, are segmented and partitioned by their subjugation to the rule of the majority without part in it (they are, after all, "represented"). Conceived abstractly as the determinate legitimacy of sovereignty in democratic procedure, the majority must be forged between decision makers and is never given.

> For Deleuze and Guattari, it is precisely those excluded from the majority as defined by a given set of axioms who are the potential bearers of the power to transform that set, whether in the direction of a new set of axioms or an altogether new axiomatic. These are the source of minoritarian becomings that carry the potential for new earths and peoples unlike those found in existing democracies. (Patton, 2005, 408)

Shadowing the definition of the "political" for Rancière, a minoritarian politics is practiced when subjects "inscribe, in the form of a supplement to every count of the parts of society, a specific figure of *the count of the uncounted* or of *the part of those without part*"—a "part of those without part" or the unrepresented, one might say, whose subjection to the prevailing system of "who counts" (the majority) irrupts with visibility and voice (2010, 35). Turning to alterity in 15M's practices of cognitive democracy is one in which the supplement ensues from the desire for inclusiveness, appearing in language as the string of conjunctions (polysyndeton), so as not to leave anyone uncounted.

The minoritarian politics of 15M do not suppose the celebratory ethos of multiculturalism or diversity given that, in practice, demonstrators actively problematize existing inequalities in ways that flee from any presumed ignorance about them, noted above by Martín Cabrera. Nor can the desires to inclusiveness that undergird these practices be construed as a form of "representation of the excluded" in the ways in which the standing partisan system can be said to "take up the interests" of its constituents or, say, "the poor." Finally, this turn to alterity cannot be claimed as any desire to surrender to, or to be swept up by the "Other" ("state" or "movement") that Rancière notes in the totalitarianisms of twentieth-century regimes, which to the contrary, constructed minority others with culpability and squelched minoritarian politics altogether (2010, 45–61). What minoritarian politics involves in the practices of care in the assemblies and demonstrations is rather closer to what Rancière describes as "democracy" in the "infinite openness to that which comes [future possibilities]—which also means, an infinite openness to the Other or the newcomer" in the forms of hospitality that practice "many ways of inscribing the part of the other" in collective conversation (2010, 59–60). Or, as Patton explains, "the power of minoritarian becomings, whether borne by minorities excluded from the majority or by subjects of the majority who no longer coincide with its norms [...] carry the potential for new assemblages of affect, belief, and opinion that [...] thereby transform existing systems of governance, recognition, and rights" (2005, 71).

The Sol encampment was a self-managed "city within a city" (Lara, 2012, 652), described by the journalist Joseba Elola as a kind of utopian "mini-republic" ("El 15M sacude," 2011). Reporting from Sol throughout the week, Elola's news coverage attempted to portray, in his words, the unique "euphoria," "magic," and "feeling" of the plaza, far from the reported outrage that had presumably brought protesters together. In the peaceful communal nature of the encampment, Elola reports, some protesters wore flowers and hugged policemen, offering strangers water and food. It seemed to conjure up the "feeling of 1968" according to his article, in the encampment's "love" and "promise of hope" for change that had moved one interviewee to tears in Elola's interview.[17] Indeed, these sentimentalisms in retrospect, warns Jakob Tanner in his analysis of 1968, can have the events slip dangerously into a "nostalgic artifact" thereby ignoring the mechanics of how protesters came together and what they achieved (2008, 78). The affective intensity of common production in Sol found one form of expression through social networks, as visitors tagged public photographs and commented on their own presence in the encampment. On the evening of Election Day, Cadena Ser radio played selections from the late 1960s and early 1970s, including "Imagine" by John Lennon, interspersed with the radio announcer's narration of a "new dawn" in Sol, the so-called Spanish Revolution. Clearly, Sol conjured up associations with the return to a more peaceful 1968, given that there were no barricades being built in Sol or elsewhere in Spain, unlike Paris of 1968 (Townson, 2011). After all, demonstrators in 2011 had not only resisted police repression through civil disobedience, but there seemed to be no reasonable explanation to account for this suspension of disbelief, other than Sol's "look and feel" of change.

On the other hand, another sign of the "feel-good" happening in Sol was the criticism it drew for its "hippie utopianism," language circulating online in social networks and the conservative press, and by rightwing media commentators who criticized protesters as *perroflautas*, a derogatory term that describes dog-owning, street panhandlers who play the flute for money (Díaz Villanueva, 2011). When used pejoratively, the term marks a definitive class distinction as the very reason for which to ignore the encampment's proposals or activities, as it attempts to recast the heterogeneous makeup of the protesters in the public eye into a lumpen social category of "indigents and derelicts." True to the mechanics of oppositional readings that characterize 15M, however, its use was captured, reappropriated, and vindicated with irony by the protesters themselves, who would later coin terms such as *yayoflauta*, or the older grandparent generation of protesters, and *poliflauta*, or protesters and sympathizers who belong to the police corps.

On the other hand, throughout these weeks the news media emphasized almost exclusively the economic losses for businesses near Sol and the tourism sector at large (M. Serrano, 2011)—a sign that the encampment had indeed produced its own spatial arrangements that disrupted the usual rhythms of everyday traffic and commerce. Business was the priority, above all else. Yet, sensitive to the encampment's coexistence with local businesses, protesters in Sol voted to stay intact through the end of May and then to leave voluntarily in mid-June, turning the site into an information point and meeting space for organizational activities, while strengthening its online infrastructure and the network of neighborhood assemblies. Even though the encampment's durability was a contentious point among protesters, another of the movement's strengths resided in the awareness of and responsiveness to discrediting attempts to undermine support for its initiatives in the public eye, which developed in tandem with the decentralization of Sol into popular assemblies, working groups, and commissions in Madrid neighborhoods (Elola, "La silenciosa expansión," 2012).

But, the paradox of power in oppositional practice means that it is always precarious. On May 27, security forces in Barcelona charged and fired rubber bullets to disperse protesters from #acampadabcn in Plaça Catalunya, citing "hygienic reasons" to clean the plaza, in the event of a victory that evening by Barcelona Football Club and the ensuing celebrations in the streets. The images of police brutality circulating online outraged and further fueled massive protests across Spain in solidarity with the Barcelona 15M encampment. Protesters demanded the immediate resignation of Conseller of Interior Felipe Puig who insisted that the police force was justified. Tens of thousands of protesters join the *indignadxs* in Madrid and Barcelona, as the Community of Madrid urged the Ministry of the Interior to clean Sol in the same manner, citing it as a *chabola* (shantytown) of unhygienic conditions. The following day, 15M hosted the first Popular Assemblies in over 40 neighborhood associations in Madrid, which since then, have shared a part in the many "mutations, effects, and convergences" to mobilize protesters since the first demonstrations of May 2011.[18]

Afterword

The election results from May 22, 2011 (for all municipal governments and 13 of Spain's 17 autonomous communities) showed only slightly higher rates of voter participation overall, with significant losses for the Socialist party (PSOE) and a boost in representation for minority parties, mainly for the United Left (IU) and the right-of-center Union, Progress, and Democracy (UPyD).[19] As Hardt and Negri observe in *Declaration*, following their conversations with 15M protesters:

> The *indignados* did not participate in the 2011 elections, then, in part because they refused to reward a socialist party that had continued neoliberal policies and betrayed them during its first years in office, but also and more importantly because they now have larger battles to fight, in particular one aimed at the structures of representation and the constitutional order itself—a fight whose Spanish roots reach back to the tradition of antifascist struggles and throw a new and critical light on the so-called transition to democracy that followed the end of the Franco regime. The *indignados* think of this as a *destituent* rather than a *constituent* process, a kind of exodus from the existing political structures, but it is necessary to prepare the bases for a new constituent power. (2012, n.p.)

Later that year, in the General Elections of November 2011, the conservative PP secured an absolute majority in Parliament, which consolidated its pursuit of sharpened austerity measures after PSOE's tenure. Mariano Rajoy, who had been the PP's presidential candidate in 2004 and 2008, lost both of these general elections and then was voted into office in 2011. The total number of abstentions and null or blank votes rounded out to some 10.4 million (31.0 percent) in 2011, or higher in comparison to over 9.6 million (27.9 percent) in 2008. The margin of difference for the PP, nevertheless, meant that it gained half a million votes from 2008 to 2011. How were these half a million votes (about 2.2 percent of the total ballots cast) enough to usher the party from the minority opposition in 2008 to an absolute majority in 2011? In Raúl Sánchez Cedillo's assessment, "El PSOE ha encajado los peores resultados de su historia en unas elecciones generales: ha perdido 4 millones y medio de votos respecto a las generales de 2008" [The PSOE matched the worst results in its history of general elections: it lost 4.5 million votes with respect to the general elections in 2008]; while, on the other hand, the "PP tan solo ha recibido medio millón de votos más respecto a 2008. Así pues, su mayoría absoluta sólo se explica por el completo hundimiento de la base electoral del PSOE" [PP only received half a million more votes with respect to 2008. In this manner, then, its absolute majority can only be explained by the complete fallout of the PSOE's electoral base], coupled with an increase in the numbers of voters who refused to cast a ballot for any party, at all ("Las elecciones," 2012, 72). Barring the PSOE's fallout for the role it may have played to secure an absolute majority for its opposition, one should not underestimate the PP's general election campaign, crafted to convey positive emotions and attitudes toward "change," among them "hope."

"Súmate al cambio" [Join the Change], announces the PP's television spot, which begins with a close-up shot of a contemplative man looking upward at an unseen sky (Partido Popular, 2011). The profile of his upward-looking gaze transmits a sense of hope and observance in this establishing shot, which persists throughout the elevated mood of the music and the narrator's confident delivery of the script. "Saldremos adelante" [we will move forward], the narrator repeats throughout. A cinematic orchestra provides the score, which builds in intensity from the opening shot's soft piano melody of high notes and then swells dramatically into a full instrumental accompaniment by the final scene. The narrative arch of the audiovisuals follows this trajectory from the individual to the collective, from the first shot of the lone man (scored to the soft single keys on the piano) to the final panorama of a packed stadium where the party's members vigorously wave flags with the PP's logo (accentuated by the sounds of a full orchestra). The sense of strength and solidarity in numbers, then, is transmitted by recruiting viewers to "Join the Change" through inspired feelings of belonging and its opposite, of not being alone. "Never give up hope," to paraphrase the narrator, and "think positively" are the initial messages that take shape in image, score, and narration. Some actors pictured in subsequent shots look up from their activities—whether sports or work—to smile at the camera directly in its appeal to positivity. However, the transmission of positivity in the audiovisual sequence is also constructed around emotions attached to specific values.

First, the sequence conveys perseverance in spite of all obstacles ("saldremos adelante"), as the camera shows a fit woman scaling a rock-climbing wall at the gym. As she falls to the padded mat below, the narrator states, "cada vez que un golpe nos tire a la lona, nos levantaremos" [for every time we get knocked down, we will get up again], an action reinforced by a camera-cut to a young man on a volley-ball court who reaches out to his game partner, lifting him up from the ground. The images, in this sense, tend to work with idioms on economic recovery, such as "getting back on one's feet" after a hard fall, which mix gestures of solidarity (helping one another to "get back up") with those of individual determination, particularly in sport. In this light, viewers see a shot of a mountain climber clinging to a sharp cliff; a surfer who falls mid-air from his board in the curl of a wave; a pole-vaulter seen from below, clearing the bar; and an amateur soccer team celebrating a goal, among others. These values of solidarity and self-determination, spoken in the first-person plural "we," are likewise associated with character traits such as the "resilience" of Spanish citizens who "never lose hope" despite difficult times: "Porque nunca perdemos la esperanza. Porque no nos resignamos fácilmente. Porque no somos de los que abandonan la tarea" [Because we never lose hope. Because we don't give up easily. Because we're not like those who abandon the task at hand].

As this brief narrative develops, repeating the confident "saldremos adelante" throughout, its positive appeal to voters constructs value in, and thereby recognition of, the many sacrifices made by Spanish citizens without needing to name them directly. They are conveyed, instead, through the emotions shaped around idioms and metaphors of perseverance, positivity, and the power to overcome challenges together ("porque si los españoles no se rinden, nosotros tampoco" [because if the Spanish don't give up, neither do we]). For, when it seems there is "no future," "we will find a way out" ("si el futuro se hace estrecho, haremos un agujero para ver el horizonte"), in what highlights the industrious character to create solutions and to adapt to difficult times. The announcement conveys an uplifting sense of agency and empowerment in this statement, in the possibility of shaping an undefined future, "a pesar de los fríos números, de las estadísticas y las cifras del paro" [despite the cold numbers of statistics and unemployment rates], as numeric figures race across the screen in an abstractly digital ("dehumanized") space. In contrast to the "cold" markets, the warm values and personable smiles in the announcement construct "hope" as a test of endurance against challenges and the overcoming of "fear" that may accompany them ("si la desconfianza nos invade, volaremos por encima de los miedos"). Just "getting by" in difficult times, then, is compressed metonymically into the positive emotion "hope" for change, but it is also attached to a set of values in self-determination, perseverance, and industriousness. One might call them a work ethic or, returning to the establishing shot of the individual looking skyward, perhaps even a faith in economic recovery.

These are values in the whole of society, the narrative suggests, as the different camera shots depict women and men working in various labor segments: tailors, fishermen, construction workers, a welder, farmers, surgeons, a bartender, workmen loading a plane, and so on. Employed and visibly happy on the job, the camera shows some of these figures smiling directly at the viewing audience. In this idyllic image of work and happiness, one might read self-fulfillment, the advertisement shows a representative whole of the country's working population employed and productive, which constructs the only inferred campaign promise to viewers (employment), given that the advertisement lacks all mention of an electoral program or platform. Finally, the announcement draws to its close by revealing the stuff of determination—something "that no one has, but us," that is, "our will" ("contamos con algo con lo que nadie cuenta: nuestra voluntad"). Volition, or the autonomous power of control over action, returns viewers to agency as an uplifting sense of empowerment, at least for those who have the right stuff. Then, the camera cuts to the final panoramic shot of the stadium as the narrator invokes the present, the past under PP rule, and the future, defining itself by one specific attribute: "Porque sabemos hacerlo. Porque ya lo demostramos. Porque hicimos de España un país de oportunidades. Y lo volveremos a hacer" [Because we know how to do it. Because we've already shown it. Because we made Spain a country of opportunities. And we will do it again]. The campaign ad's emotive appeal to viewers tends to evoke feelings of hope for change and self-empowerment, and it does so around specific values of self-determination, perseverance, and industriousness despite all obstacles. In this manner, the "land of opportunity" attributed to the PP's former rule under Aznar's administration, tends to show itself comprising ideally productive, even enterprising individuals adaptable to change and resilient to hard times.

If I have paid great attention to the way in which this campaign constructs its electoral promises purely around "hope" and a specific work ethic, it is because election propaganda demonstrates a sophisticated understanding of how emotional appeals to viewing audiences (voters) are made even in the absence of an election platform, on the one hand,

and yet bear their own politics for the ways in which they associate emotions with certain values, on the other. In the context of the 2011 general elections, the campaign spot draws from the "great hope for change" that was already in currency some six months earlier during the mass demonstrations. The advertisement stands as an illustrative example, to my mind, of how an emotional appeal in a given address to viewers can be formed around a set of ideal values that the addresser (the party) deems to be desirable *for* the population. This point might be obvious and could be said to apply to almost any political campaign. However, what seems most striking to me is the campaign's ability to shape positive emotions—and thereby possibly generate votes—around values that are desirable, in this view, for greater economic autonomy (self-determination) and adaptability to market conditions (industriousness), among a population adjusting to austerity measures (perseverance). Neoliberalism, despite the "coldness" of market indicators recognized in the ad, might find its warm cultural values in the attachments that foster self-empowerment as a novel kind of hope.

City, Interrupted: Sierra and Galindo's Performance *Los encargados*

15M has drawn significant public attention to the pacts and consensual agreements from Spain's democratic *Transición* to its membership in the European Union. In the wake of the global crisis, so too have mobilizations called into question the undifferentiation between the fiscal and economic policies of Spain's main parties on the political left (PSOE) and right (PP). Consensus, however, is more than the consensual agreement among government officials on policy and law alone. The culture of consensus since the *Transición*, observes Víctor Sampedro, is made perceptible in its rupture, particularly, by the visible *appearance* of social mobilizations such as 15M, which challenge the institutional and media discourses prevalent since the *Transición*:

> [El 15M] significa pues una reapropiación discursiva, ya no de espacios públicos, de espacios de debate...Y esta reapropiación parte de la impugnación de la Cultura de la Transición, es decir, de los vetos y de los consensos que pesaban, de los vetos y de la correlación de fuerzas que imponían una serie de consensos de facto que bloquean una serie de debates, que bloquean una serie de políticas públicas, que bloquean una serie de políticas expresivas y simbólicas, y que está siendo impugnada en toda regla...No sólo el 15M es una impugnación a las tramas

clientelares de práctica política—corrupción, cleptocracia, pseudocracia, es decir, el gobierno de la mentira, de la mentira institucionalizada, de los silencios mediáticos sobre realidades sociales, etc.—sino que es cuando [...] te das cuenta de que se está concretando en medidas políticas e institucionales que literalmente desarmarían el sistema de representación político e informativo tal y como lo conocemos ahora. ("Del 15M a la #acampadasol," 2011)

[(15M) signifies a discursive reappropriation, no longer only in public space, in spaces for debate...And this reappropriation stems from its challenge to the Culture of the Transition, that is, the vetoes and consensuses hanging over it, the vetoes and the correlation of forces that imposed de facto a series of consensuses blocking a series of debates, blocking a series of public policies, blocking a series of expressive and symbolic politics, and that is being fully contested...15M is not only a challenge to the cases of cronyism in political practice—corruption, kleptocracy, pseudocracy, that is, a government of lies, of institutionalized lying, of silences in the media about social realities, etc.—but it's when...you realize that it's taking specific political and institutional measures that would literally dismantle the system of political representation and information as we know it today.]

The abdication of King Juan Carlos I in June 2014 can illustrate Sampedro's claim on the series of vetoes exercised, which do not correspond exclusively to state powers. In the afternoon following the king's speech, protesters assembled in Spanish cities, demanding a constituent process to decide on the continuation of the monarchy, while many politicians, media analysts, and prominent figures from the culture industry closed rank and file in public support of the institution, if not directly opposed to consulting Spanish citizens by popular referendum. Leading government officials from the PP and PSOE agreed that an initiative for a referendum should be blocked from materializing in parliament, as PSOE Secretary-General Alfredo Pérez Rubalcaba delayed his planned resignation in order to usher through the coronation of the king's successor Felipe VI. Rubalcaba expressed a debt of gratitude to the Crown in his parliamentary address, stating that socialism is compatible with the monarchy, while the PSOE invoked *disciplina de voto* with maximum fines for any Socialist representative who should vote against the party whip to ratify the succession, despite vocal opposition within the party ("Rubalcaba," 2014). The publishing group RBA Revistas censored the cover of its satirical magazine *El Jueves*, which was set to print a comic of Juan Carlos I holding a crown with flies swarming around it—a "rotten inheritance" was its inferred message—resulting in 18 resignations by workers who denounced censorship ("Los dibujantes," 2014). Spain's news media, both television and the press, introduced the public to the future royal family before the succession was voted into law, while news coverage gave priority to commemorations attributing the consolidation of democracy to Juan Carlos's figure in the *Transición*—an "official" memory. Amid an ongoing judicial investigation into Juan Carlos's daughter Cristina de Borbón and son-in-law Iñaki Urdangarín on allegations of fraud, tax evasion, and embezzlement, the monarchy held the lowest approval ratings in democratic history at that time, and yet, media analysts construed favorable results from public opinion polls in creative ways. In sum, the discursive space on the continuation of the monarchy tended to monopolize the media, whereas, overall, the mass demonstrations in Spanish cities were relegated to a smaller corner of coverage and visibility that seemingly did not correspond to the popular clamor for a constituent process. None of these agents alone can be signaled as responsible for the tacit consensus forged across them, which rather has the effect of producing a blanket of silence and invisibility over the popular demand for a constituent process.

Consensus, in the notion approximated by Sampedro, relates to what issues *can be said* and *made visible* (in the media, in the state, in society at large), and by whom. To elaborate on Sampedro's observation, a sphere of consensus is shaped by the criteria that determine what debates, public policies, and symbolic expressions are regarded "properly" political, or in the case of the news media, worthy of coverage.[20] He calls these practices the "Culture of the Transition," sharing the views of Guillem Martínez and his contributors who define *Cultura de la Transición* (CT) as the predominant culture of consensus in Spain's democratic present, one that tends to depoliticize issues, practices, and thought from within rigid frameworks designating the limited terrain of proper questions to be asked, by whom, and about what issues. As Guillem Martínez notes, "En un sistema democrático, los límites a la libertad de expresión no son las leyes. Son límites culturales" [In a democratic system, the limits to the freedom of expression are not in law. They are cultural limits] of the permissibly sayable and the doable: "solo es posible escribir determinadas novelas, discursos, artículos, canciones, programas, películas, declaraciones, sin salirse de la página" [it is only possible to write certain novels, speeches, articles, songs, programs, films, declarations, without straying from the page], all of which bear restrictions that result in "que la cultura española realizara pocas formulaciones" [having Spanish culture create few formulations] (Acevedo et al., 2012, 14).[21] The operative mechanisms of consensus hinge upon a tacit axiomatic of selection, according to which issues are considered legitimate or not; that is, consensus is a legitimating practice of distinction and selection based necessarily on veridiction. In institutional arrangements, the criteria of consensus can contribute to blocking certain discussions from taking place—such as a popular referendum on the monarchy—or they can halt certain proposals from consideration for decision, not only in state politics, but across the media and the culture industries (in publishing, literary criticism, film, music, art, and so on):

> [La CT] aseguró durante tres décadas el control de la realidad mediante el monopolio de las palabras, los temas y la memoria. Cómo debe circular la palabra y qué debe significar cada una. En torno a qué debemos pensar y en qué términos. Qué debemos recordar y en función *de qué presente* debemos hacerlo. Durante años, ese monopolio del sentido se ejerció sobre todo a través de un sistema de información centralizado y unidireccional al que solo las voces mediáticas tenían acceso, mientras que el público jugaba el papel de audiencia pasiva y existían temas intocables. (2012, 668)

> [For three decades, the CT assured the control of reality through the monopoly of words, subject matters, and memory. How words should circulate and what each one should mean. Surrounding what we should think and on what terms. How we should remember and in function of *what present* we should do so. For years, that monopoly of meaning was exerted, above all, through a centralized, unilateral system of information to which only media voices had access, while the public played the role of a passive audience and there existed untouchable subject matters.]

Evidence of consensus is made conspicuous, in part, by its discursive absences, by its spaces of silence and invisibility. It is this point on silence and invisibility which I should like to emphasize here for the analysis to follow. Notably, for Sampedro, this consensus is *made visible* by the resignifying practices of protest, assembly, and digital media (reappropriated discourse, occupied space) that disrupt consensual silences and spaces of invisibility. His is a definition that resonates with Jacques Rancière's notion of *dissensus*, which is "not a conflict of interests, values, or opinions, [but a] dispute over what is given and about the frame within which we see something as given," that is, as a political act that makes visible at least "two worlds in one and the same world," each with its own organizing principles (2010, 69). The tacit presumptions and agreements working to secure consensus resemble a policing function, notes Rancière, as they have the effect of dispersing public attention as though to say, "Move along! There is nothing to see here!" (2010, 71–2; 37).

In August 2012, the artists Santiago Sierra and Jorge Galindo staged their performance *Los encargados* [The Ones in Charge] recorded in downtown Madrid, which simulates a presidential motorcade to denounce the complicity of state politics and capital interests in the production of Spain's recent crises as the very result of the *Transición* (Sierra and Galindo, 2012). The urban intervention stages a performance in city space—indeed interrupts everyday routine in it—that makes its political statement undeniably visible. Staged provocatively to command the attention of pedestrians in the city, the intervention equates Spain's history of democratic leaders, with great pageantry, to the authoritarian rule of dictatorship. Or, in the artists' words, due to the priorities of capital and political interests, "hay gente muriendo y otros miles robados y echados de sus casas" [there are people dying (amid the crisis) and thousands others robbed or thrown out of their homes], which they attribute to an origin, "el tocomocho de la Transición, dirigida por las élites políticas del franquismo para perdurar hasta nuestros días" [the scam of the *Transición*, directed by Francoist political elites to last until our time] (García, "Arte para denunciar," 2013). In this light, Sierra and Galindo's performance challenges the consensual "official" regard of the *Transición* as a model democratic achievement, and it does so by articulating this position, without nuance or subtlety, in urban space. The performance takes up the object of criticism, CT or the *Transición* writ large, and presents it as a kind of operative machine in relation to what is seen and goes unseen in the parade.

The video recording of the intervention situates viewers in Madrid's most emblematic boulevard, La Gran Vía. The black-and-white recording opens with an establishing shot of the Carrión Building in Plaza Callao, recognizable for its sleek architectural curves and neon Schweppes billboard. Then, the camera cuts to another shot of Gran Vía, framed above street level, providing the image of an abandoned, silent city. In the opening sequence, viewers are shown the monumental architectures along the capital's signature avenue, from the Press Building with its cinemas and dance hall, to the crowning statue of La Unión y el Fénix insurance company. These establishing shots set the urban stage of performance against the cultural icons of (the) Capital: the monumental grandeur of Gran Vía in its offices of investment and banking capital, its advertising images, its theaters and spaces for entertainment. Shown from the outset, in other words, are the representative pillars of advanced capitalism in the postindustrial era of services, consumerism, and financial services and securities. However,

Gran Vía also holds the cultural status of a colossal icon for early twentieth-century modernization, the time when these buildings were constructed.[22] The black-and-white video recording provides a split vision, at once, of its referents to the modern and to the contemporary, past and present folded within the same sequence of images. The video offers a double image, one of economic and financial activities in which material and monetary exchange (the era of industrial production) is eclipsed today by consumer culture, immaterial investments and securities, and the service industries of hospitality and entertainment (the era of the production of production itself), as two times folded into one image.

The camera cuts to a motorcade of black limousines, each one equipped with a large-scale portrait, displayed upside down, of every head of state from the *Transición* to the present. Appearing in order, viewers see King Juan Carlos I wearing a military hat, followed by Presidents Adolfo Suárez, Leopoldo Calvo Sotelo, Felipe González, José María Aznar, José Luis Rodríguez Zapatero, and the recently elected Mariano Rajoy. Their stateliness is augmented by the gray backdrop of Gran Vía's towering architectures. As this parade travels solemnly past bystanders on the streets of Madrid, who are now within view, its resemblance to a motorcade of official state vehicles conveys the public appearance of authority implicit in the protections of state security. Indeed, one might say that it *commands* its authority over viewers. The camera provides a traveling shot of the sky and towering buildings above as the score "Warszawianka" interpreted by the Alexandrov Ensemble (Red Army Choir, 1993), marks a snare drum beat to the military march. The musical score builds its narrative crescendo from the singing chorus, first softly and then in full volume, cueing to the viewer a musical climax accentuated by its cut to a spliced frame. The screen splits into two, then three, consecutive frames (figure 2.1). In some, the portraits are displayed at a 180 degree turn, right-side up, which shows the heads of state advance in several sequences of close-up and distant shots.

The measured cadence of the military march and the solemnity of the motorcade in moving image together contribute to the authoritarian prowess of the intervention's aesthetics, evocative of the spectacles of state power in twentieth-century regimes. The oversized scale of the portraits, the pageantry of their public display, and their marked separation from pedestrian traffic, configure the parade's spectacular character as a simulated demonstration of state power constructed relationally in sight and distance from onlookers.

Figure 2.1 Still image from the urban intervention *Los encargados* by Santiago Sierra and Jorge Galindo.

This is one feature of the parade's humor, residing in part in its interruption of the everyday occurrence (its surprise, perhaps) with a very serious political denouncement and, vital to this message, the lack of subtlety in its mediated delivery to viewers. Its humorous irreverence rests upon simulating the visible signs and symbols of "authentic" state authority (the iconic portraits of heads of state, motorcade security, the parade), to the extent that the performance surpasses its object of imitation while overturning it (literally, upside down like the portraits) in a comparison to their dictatorial character. Oversized and prominently displayed, the portraits of *Los encargados* invert the command of state authority, of course, by commanding public attention to their literal inversion, which is part of the irreverent character of the artists' critique. But they also do so with public visibility by detaining, even briefly, the everyday rhythms of traffic in downtown Madrid through an unusual interruption that bears a humorous element of surprise. As a device that defamiliarizes everyday routine in the city, the parade performs a similar task to that of divulging an open secret, one that is sensed as known but that goes unstated directly in public speech. That is, if the act of disclosing a generally accepted but unspoken secret may transgresses social proprieties (of the "properly" sayable in public speech), then the parade transgresses a form of political propriety (relating to "officialdom") by speaking the unsaid in public, with great visibility. In this manner, the performance is not only a representation, but it performs an interruption in the urban rhythms and flows of traffic and pedestrians, that is, it articulates "a situation" in practice by staging visibly what should otherwise remain publicly unspoken and unseen.

That this public performance uses the street as its stage to interpellate bystanders with a political denouncement, certainly folds back onto a tradition of Situationist urban interventions in the 1960s. Participating in the events of 1968 in Paris, the members of the Situationist International, eventually led by Guy Debord, developed their critique of contemporary capitalism and its media culture, as they observed that spectacle and consumerism had increasingly become the organizing principle for social relations and urban planning.[23] It was from this basis that its members held that "a society organized as appearance can be disrupted on the field of appearance," particularly, through ephemeral actions that can resignify and make new meanings of urban space (Marcus, 2002, 8). The site for these actions was necessarily the city, according to one member, the Dutch architect Constant Nieuwenhuys, the locus where social atomization and alienation took root in the practices of everyday life vis-à-vis urbanism:

> The crisis of urbanism is worsening. [...] In old neighborhoods, the streets have degenerated into highways, and leisure is commercialized and adulterated by tourism. Newly built neighborhoods have only two themes, which govern everything: traffic circulation and household comfort. They are the meager expressions of bourgeois happiness and lack of any concern for play. [...] We opt first to create situations here, new situations. We intend to break the laws that prevent the development of meaningful activities in life and culture. (2002, 95)

Among the many experimental practices of the Situationists, the creation of "situations" in the urban milieu would have spectators reflect, in part, on their prescribed (passive) roles as potential (active) agents of action and change. In the words of Guy Debord in the Situationist critique, the spectacle of democracy is driven by "the dictatorial freedom of the Market, as tempered by the recognition of the rights of Homo Spectator" whose alienation calls into question the impetus of entwined economic and political powers that produce estrangement and social atomization writ large (1995, 9).

To create a situation, then, is also to situate viewers critically in relation to the performance at hand, one that commands viewer attention in Sierra and Galindo's parade. In the audiovisual sequence, a mix of street level, angled, and rooftop shots assemble composite viewpoints from which to observe the motorcade's journey down Gran Vía, whether from the various perspectives of viewers traveling along with the motor-cade or observing as a bystander from the sidewalk. Space is constructed in the visual sequence from the many camera angles that add depth to the urban setting, from different perspectives and frames. In this man-ner, the camera takes up a specific, established mode of looking: that of the multiple bystanders who observe the parade from different angles, and who do so from a distance. State security, here, marks a specific dis-tance between spectators and the passageway of the motorcade through traffic. Not only does its slow pace disrupt the normal circulation for drivers and call attention to itself for pedestrians, but the sense of dis-ruption that it creates also reiterates the motorcade's (security) distance from the onlookers traversing the city at that moment. Even as the video ends, while the screen fades to black, the final sound that can be heard is the siren from an emergency vehicle among the traffic. Keeping in mind the multiple perspectives filmed, here we are not dealing with one spectator but with composite viewpoints, one might say a viewing public. This spectatorship is folded within two defining characteristics at once, for onlookers who view the motorcade are situated as both the *represented* (by "the Ones in Charge") and the *securitized* (in the distance from its security apparatus) (Hardt and Negri, 2012). In this crafted situation, state leaders are conveyed as untouchable, unreach-able, and indeed immune from the interests of pedestrians and drivers, as they parade along.

Now, at the musical climax, the split-frame sequence displays the heads of state upright, framing them in such a way that as they advance to the tempo of the military march, they give the impression that each one dangles in the air as though propelled from above by a mechanical conveyer belt just beyond the frame. Nevertheless, the mechanism of propulsion remains unseen. That is, the sequence resembles assembly-line production in the factory, a linear and mechanical process that, here, seems to produce each Head of State. It is a linear march of assembly-line production that reduces the portraits of these government officials into a mere industrial byproduct of processes unseen here, pictured against the backdrop of Madrid's emblematic symbols of (the) capital. Unseen beyond the frame is the mechanical ensemble of working parts that keep on producing the same product in succession (the portraits of political leaders), propelling them along this time- and assembly line as they scroll across the screen. In this manner, the video-editing work on the performance alludes to a field of possible associations with all that is modern in production: the punch-card temporality of the factory, mea-sured and tightly regulated like the tempo of the audiovisual sequence;

the factory's linear mode of assembly by rhythmic measure to produce a given product; and, indeed, the over-determined conception of a linear historical time that regiments and orders, and as it orders, produces the self-same product along a timeline, *los encargados*. This situation again positions viewers within the double-vision of past and present crafted in the video's establishing shots. In Sierra and Galindo's performance, the modern mechanical time of the factory-state (the parade) lends itself to an open series of associations with regimes (past and present) assembled from "back stage" mechanisms that produce this linear military parade, or the heads of state in Spain's democratic history.

The parade calls attention to itself, indeed situates itself forcefully in its tightly organized and codified regimes of signs, as a kind of machine. The modern factory, the state, and the temporal cadence of history are collapsed into one and the same overstated gesture—and yet, paradoxically, they are propelled by operative parts excluded from view, beyond the camera's frame. This invisibility is precisely where the artists stake their claim that the *Transición* to democracy was hatched in continuation with the Franco dictatorship, and consistent with it, notably, the *Caudillo*'s portrait is nowhere to be seen among the other officials in the military parade. So too does the space created by the performance make reference to alternative spaces along Gran Vía that remain largely invisible to spectators.

In the opening sequence, the camera travels twice past the boarded-up Edificio España located in Plaza de España. Traces of graffiti are marked visibly on the wooden slats that cover the ground-floor windows. Although the camera does not show viewers much more, Madrid residents will recognize this square as replete with empty buildings today due to property speculation and investment losses, some of them occupied by squatters. Despite the monumental stateliness of the avenue's buildings, the shot of Plaza España serves as a subtle reminder that behind and along the façade of Gran Vía lie the ruins of property speculation. In them, the abstract calculus of invisible market forces is made material in Madrid's cityscape and the social effects of its economic downturn. If one returns to the split vision of the establishing sequence, this relay between two times situates viewers between Gran Vía's inception in the early twentieth century—the modern image of burgeoning financial capital, services, and consumerism—and one hundred years later in the wake of the global crisis, its decadence and decline in advanced capitalism. The product of what viewers see in the video, then, may be understood to both show and conceal what is only peripherally pictured in these shots. It is as if to say, following the camera that travels along with the motorcade before the boarded-up building, "Move along, there is nothing to see here." By the artists' suggestion, the spectacle of democracy parades along the measured march of history, and as it does so, it positions itself as an empty product of mechanical processes and operations concealed from view that produce *Los encargados*. In other words, the portraits come to light as the sublimated byproduct within a mechanical configuration of (political, capital, historical) forces unseen.

It is worth noting here that the *encargados*, this self-same product in state leadership, are portrayed as constant, static, and unchanging, in a Benjaminian suggestion on the illusion of difference and novelty that provides the perpetual return of the same. Taken literally, these political leaders of different partisan colors are shown as substitutable, the one exchangeable for any other, regardless of their political leanings. Their equivalence, which erases political ideology from this association, might seem overstated for some viewers, if not problematic. After all, certainly not all of them can be construed to share the same political and economic agendas, can they? There exists here, in other words, a question of ideological contradiction that, at first sight, beckons clarification and yet remains unresolved in the parade itself. This apparent contradiction is at work, most notably, in the assemblage of the audiovisual narrative, particularly in the artists' choice to score the final recording to a Soviet march. As the military parade pairs these audiovisual components to address its viewers in the likeness of a regime, the regimented cadence of "Warszawianka" contributes to this perceptible totalitarianism of the *encargados*, in which the form and address of the parade are inseparable for viewers to decode its cultural and historical allusions to regimes past. For, even as the lyrics speak to proletarian empowerment and revolution ("Let's tear down the czars' crown . . . " "Today when the working people are starving / To indulge in luxury is a crime"), the choice of song, with its regimented cadence and chorus of voices, provides the visual sequence with coherent readability *as* a totalitarian construct, independently of its message. On the other hand, it seems not to bear a form of revolutionary nostalgia that Rancière observes in late Situationist performances, nor is it a call to insurrection as the Situationists upheld in some militant actions of 1968.[24] An ironic choice, the military march at once conveys this demonstration of power as a regime, as much as it contradicts its readable effect. Or, perhaps then, if viewers take up the split-vision noted earlier, this contradiction between the ideological position of the critique and its Soviet song can provide a reminder to viewers on the experience of twentieth-century history in which revolutionary struggles, when successful at consolidating a position of power within the state, have also reproduced the (totalitarian) forms of subjugation and violence that propelled them to power from insurrection.

What is conveyed to viewers is not the ideological position of the march gathered in the lyrics on the proletarian struggle against an oppressive state. Rather, it is the steady, driving tempo of the parade and its augmenting chorus of voices that provide a totalitarian figuration independently of political ideology—as viewers are invited to read all *encargados as* an authoritarian construct. If I read the parade in terms of ideology, however, this contradiction, and the attempt to resolve it by differentiating between ideological partisan positions, takes precedence over any of intervention's other features—the linear production of state leaders, the icons of advanced capitalism along Gran Vía, the continuity it suggests between dictatorship and democracy, and so on—and thus privileges the question of ideology over them. Rather, it is this possibility of "neither and both" (ideological) positions that coexist at once in the address of its message and its form. Instead, the performance provides a critique of "democracy-as-dictatorship," leaving spectators with few guesses on the explicit aim of its criticism in which the invitation to read the parade ends up "dictating" its intentions to viewers. And, nevertheless, this straightforward critique is obscured if read through the lens of political ideology, which cannot reconcile easily the historical production of the political right and left in democracy, nor that of fascism and communism in the twentieth century, as "one and the same." Thinking about the performance along ideological lines requires falling back on critical operations that draw distinctions between these positions, in a form of partitioning that the parade itself rejects. Rather, the Grand Master Narratives of history, or the experience in twentieth-century history with ideological narratives, are rendered conceptually as producing a similar totalitarian effect—a machinic output, like that of the assembly line, that produces identity, similarity, and the ready-made head of state. If taken as a kind of machine, the ways of reading this address are only for viewers to recognize, in part, by interrogating the critical operations that would rather endow its address and delivery with interior unity.

Sierra and Galindo's "situation" portrays the security state, and indeed the history of the *Transición*, as a construct materializing from an ensemble of different unseen forces—taken up together, a certain consensual machinery—that work in concert to produce the Ones in Charge. The performance does not grapple with how this might be, of course, and rather interpellates viewers to have them perceive *Los encargados* as marching forth from the factory assembly line. But viewers are situated before a spectacle that creates its own space, rhythm, and security in distance, inviting onlookers to take pause for a moment, whatever their interpretation, and contemplate the viewer's role before this authoritarian apparatus. In the recorded performance, as a device itself, what goes largely unseen is made conspicuous, not by its total absence, but by the marginal traces that disrupt its totality and in the assertion of authority by what can be, peripherally, seen. Given that the artists' intervention collapses the machine-factory-state-history into the same modernist gesture, thus making it readable in its exaggeration, the question that this configuration proposes in its reductive equivalence is also one of readability. Beyond the intervention, how might one approach reading the authoritarian configuration denounced in the performance, of the political and capital powers made largely visible and yet also obscured from view? How might one read the operative parts of manufactured consensuses, made legible and illegible at once?

CHAPTER 3

The Biopolitics of Neoliberal Governance

Our work will be guided by a shared belief that market principles, open trade and investment regimes, and effectively regulated financial markets foster the dynamism, innovation, and entrepreneurship that are essential for economic growth, employment, and poverty reduction. [. . .] We recognize that these reforms will only be successful if grounded in a commitment to free market principles, including the rule of law, respect for private property, open trade and investment, competitive markets, and efficient, effectively regulated financial systems. These principles are essential to economic growth and prosperity and have lifted millions out of poverty, and have significantly raised the global standard of living. Recognizing the necessity to improve financial sector regulation, we must avoid over-regulation that would hamper economic growth and exacerbate the contraction of capital flows, including to developing countries. We underscore the critical importance of rejecting protectionism and not turning inward in times of financial uncertainty.
—Declaration from the G-20 Washington Summit 2008

Violencia es cobrar 600€ al mes
(Earning 600€ a month is violence)

—15M protest banner

Neoliberal Myth

I.

Amid the burgeoning financial crisis, the Group of Twenty (G-20) met for the 2008 Washington Summit, attended by President Zapatero of the ruling Socialist party (PSOE), where the world's wealthiest nations called for concerted international cooperation to reform the financial sector favorable to reviving global flows of capital. The many points identified in the declaration may have been a legible indicator that the world's leading economic powers were coming to terms with the responsibility of unethical business practices and systemic flaws, among other factors, in the successive tumbling of international markets in a domino effect (*Declaration of the Summit*, 2008). Yet, despite the nuances of different policy positions in the European Union at large, political and financial powers have interpreted the need for "structural reform" as the basis from which to pursue deeper austerity measures and labor laws favoring precarity, thereby dismantling the welfare state and social rights in Spain under the aegis of neoliberal reform. According to this logic, as the G-20 declaration asserts, greater competition, private investments, and the surveillance and tempered regulation of the free market—in sum, free market activity with minimal state intervention, as deemed necessary—equate directly to greater opportunity, entrepreneurship, and prosperity that deliver poverty reduction and a higher standard of living on a global scale. Yet, in extensive literature on the effects of neoliberal policies in general and of austerity in particular, nothing could be further from the social reality experienced by world populations, as these reforms have correlated to greater inequality, unrest, disease, and mortality (Basu and Stuckler, 2013; Blyth, 2013; Harvey, 2005; Lustig, 1995; Navarro, 2013).[1]

Myth, writes Roland Barthes, bears an ideological mechanics that "naturalizes" its constructed character in order to legitimize its claims as truth. Exemplified in Barthes's reading of a magazine photograph in which a soldier of African descent salutes the French flag, myth produces a sleight of hand—here, forged from an image of colonial subservience to the French Empire—that collapses the signified into a signifier by reducing its connotative meaning into a "self-evident" truth: "that France is a great Empire, that all her sons, without any color discrimination, faithfully serve under her flag, and that there is no better answer to the detractors of an alleged colonialism than the zeal shown by this Negro [*sic*] in serving his so-called oppressors" (1972, 116). As myth naturalizes its constructed character, its significations can become an accomplice to the act of legitimizing power relations and, at once, their alibi. In Barthes's critique, myth legitimizes the "natural order" of the cultural (and ethnic) "superiority" of the metropolis and its right to military rule over the colonial subject, demonstrated gesturally in the subordinate's salute of allegiance to the empire. In this sense, myth may adopt or invert the arguments of its opposition, despite the lack of veracity in its production of meanings or claims. "Myth is a *value*, truth is no guarantee for it; nothing prevents it from being a perpetual alibi: it is enough that its signifier has two sides for it always to have an 'elsewhere' at its disposal"—an *elsewhere* which Barthes locates in the empire's benevolent intentions as its alibi to implicit racial subordination and colonial oppression (1972, 123). Thereby myth becomes indisputable material if its nature is taken literally, at once passing itself off as the preexisting order of things while bearing a malleable disposition to be appropriated in further myth-making, say, at the service of imperial power and its legitimacy of rule.

Considerable myth-making ensues from the related claims, and their mechanics of production, that assert that neoliberal policy delivers wholesale prosperity. In practice, neoliberal reforms assiduously reorganize state expenditures, sovereign debt, and public common resources to the benefit of private profits. In the arguments of supply-side economics, all things public are claimed to "crowd out" opportunities for private enterprise, hampering market competition, which often serves in turn to justify privatization initiatives—particularly, in the urban milieu (Observatorio Metropolitano, 2013, 46). Where state expenditures are concerned, neoliberal reforms do not aim to eliminate *all* public spending, as Pablo Carmona Pascual and his co-authors note in Spain, but rather to reduce expenditures for social welfare programs while bolstering forms of aid, contracts, and financial exemptions for private enterprise, on the one hand, and expenditures for the military and domestic security, on the other (Carmona, 2012, 135–50). In what David Harvey calls the *accumulation by dispossession* of capital, these measures entail the "reversion to the private domain of common property rights won through past class struggles (the right to a state pension, to welfare, or to national health care)," which often, if not exclusively, benefit the greatest fortunes through privatization ("The 'New' Imperialism," 2004, 75). That is, where the private accumulation of capital reaches its limits of projected growth, the sustainability of a given enterprise must be secured through dispossession, or through takeovers, expropriation, the payment of private debts from public funds, the privatization of public space and common resources, and so on. Here, neoliberal myth weaves its own alibi, asserting that wealth eventually "trickles down" the socioeconomic ladder or is redistributed "naturally" by market forces, despite evidence of the social disparity left in its wake.[2] Nevertheless, the fail-safe benevolence of neoliberal governmentality resides in its myth and the impervious alibi it asserts, noted in the G-20 declaration. Neoliberal policies provide the *essential* legitimate measures for "economic growth and prosperity" today; second, in the inseparable suture between policy and prosperity, they have "lifted millions out of poverty" and "significantly raised the global standard of living," in a grammatical string of causalities in which legitimacy is spun—indeed naturalized—from the premise of a greater quality of life for all (G-20, 2008, n.p.).

In Spain, the myth that neoliberalism produces poverty reduction and social well-being for all has become an alibi to dismantle the welfare state and social rights, on the one hand, and an accomplice to channel state coffers into private interests to the benefit of banks, financial institutions, and private enterprise, on the other. Amid the crisis, such a polemic has been flagged by the economist Vicenç Navarro, who noted that the European Central Bank (ECB) and the International Monetary Fund (IMF) have placed conditions on Spain's eligibility to receive financial rescue by urging the government to pursue measures that would increase the flexibility of labor, reduce public expenditures on pensions, and privatize the welfare state—in sum, neoliberal reforms ("The Euro," 2013). This circumstance is not new, however, nor is it unique to Spain. In the 1970s, foreign credit-lending from financial institutions in the United States would wield powerful leverage to reshape strategically the economic and social policies of indebted countries. After Mexico was pushed into default on its debt to New York financial institutions in 1982–84, the IMF and United States government would work in concert to demand neoliberal reforms of Mexico toward greater labor "flexibility" (deregulation and the dismantling of labor protections for workers), free market laws, and privatization (Harvey, 2005, 28–31). Echoing the test case of Mexico, today the European Commission (EC), the IMF, and the ECB, known as the Troika, have urged the European member states of intervened economies to pursue further neoliberal "structural adjustments," called "shocks" in the IMF's literature, met with reduced public spending and deficit controls, in order for these countries to be eligible for sovereign credit lending and assistance in other forms (*Poverty and Social Impact*, 2008; *World Economic Outlook*, 2012). One should not presume that these measures are adopted coercively, however, as government officials in Spain's predominant left and right parties (PSOE and PP, respectively) have historically pursued likeminded policies, voluntarily and in part, to meet the accords for Spain's adhesion to the European Union after the 1992 Maastricht Treaty.

Even so, a great pitfall exists in criticism wherever it views neoliberalism, conceived abstractly, as a culpable agent for disparity, which tends to sidestep a critical examination into how its myth is reproduced in systems of thought and pervasive social attitudes, with material consequences. Across heterogeneous sectors and institutions, the weft and weave of neoliberal thought concerns what Michel Foucault understood as a *dispositif*, a discursive and nondiscursive ensemble of mechanisms and institutional arrangements across the breadth and depth of the social fabric that secures its own veridiction, that is, its own worldview as truth in the exercise of predominant powers (2008, 19).[3] In his lectures *Birth of Biopolitics* delivered at the Collège de France in 1979, Michel Foucault continued to develop his analysis on the exercise of sovereign rule through technologies of government that surpass the competencies of the state in liberal democracies into the biopolitical administration of all spheres of life. Broadly, he defines neoliberalism as an art of government that seeks out "a general regulation of society by the market," one that has historically bundled together democratic freedoms as synonymous with tempered free-market economics (2008, 145). In the lectures, Foucault provides some foundational antecedents from which to question the biopolitics of neoliberalism in his time, on the eve of its consolidation in state administration in the 1980s Thatcher and Reagan era, which I would like to revisit since then as a possible tool for critique, particularly, for the ways in which economic self-sufficiency and welfare are sutured together with policy aims in the neoliberal imaginary.

Whereas the advent of the state's calculation and management of birthrates illustrates one clear case of biopolitical governmentality for Foucault (state planning on the projected growth, productivity, and wealth of its citizens, and so on), the biopolitics of *neo*liberalism ensue from the state's self-imposed limitations in liberal democracy to secure its citizens' "freedoms" through the protection of certain private rights, private property, and the pursuit of private enterprise. According to Wendy Brown, "the withdrawal of the state from certain domains, followed by the privatization of certain state functions, does not amount to the dismantling of government but rather constitutes a technique of governing; indeed, it is this signature technique of neoliberal governance, in which rational economic action suffused throughout society replaces express state rule or provision" (2005, 44). In the *dispositif*, thus, we are no longer dealing uniquely with the top-down implementation of policies by the state, urban planners, transnational institutions, or corporate brokering alone, but rather the reproduction of statements, social attitudes, and (dis-)affections formed in everyday life, between policy and the social, and the relationships forged among them in governance—those that call for economic self-sufficiency, self-responsibility, and self-care of the population through each individual's private investments. This movement between government and governance, between the logics of neoliberal policy and the onus of individual self-autonomy, organize my analytical drift in the following pages.

II.

Neoliberalism, in the first instance, has a history. New liberal technologies of government develop from a specific political climate around the time of WWII and during the Cold War era, marked by the twentieth-century crises of liberal democracy and the breakdown in its *dispositif* of governmentality. The material reconstruction of Europe after WWII, specifically the German case, hinged upon rebuilding and modernizing projects that could secure economic recovery in order to deter the outbreak of another war, which included the concerted planning of transnational reconstruction efforts and sources of aid (the Marshall Plan) and the enforcement of social objectives to hinder the return of fascisms, implemented together with the eventual deregulation of price controls in occupied West Germany. This model would become the new liberal (de-nationalized) formula for social and economic policies that could bolster the legitimacy of state sovereignty in Germany after the crisis of the war, especially as the call for unity and individualist freedoms through the markets, it was believed, could impede the potential rise of social cohesion to nationalisms (Foucault, 2008, 75–100). It is a formula seen again, beyond the German case.

In the United States context, new liberal discourse in the Chicago School as early as the 1930s (and later, by the father of neoliberal economics Milton Friedman, author of *Capitalism and Freedom*) targeted its criticisms on Roosevelt's New Deal that had vigorously pursued Keynesian interventionist policies and greater public expenditures largely on social welfare to overcome the Great Depression. In the United States, Foucault views the social pacts of economic security guaranteed to the postwar society at large (or, the promise of state and labor security in exchange for military service and domestic war efforts), as well as the expansion of federal administration (management of poverty, education, segregation programs, and so on), as the primary targets of criticism from neoliberal advocates in the Chicago School (2008, 215–37). That is, throughout the Cold War era, a new generation of economists and political theorists alike viewed "free market liberal democracy" as a formula to enhance the security of individual freedoms and to reduce statism, both of which were conceived in economic terms as the remedy to the danger of totalitarianisms, whether fascism (in the reconstruction of Germany for the Ordoliberals) or communism (in the postwar hegemony of the United States for the Chicago School) (2008, 69). Minimizing the state's role in providing social services, it was believed, could provide at once a safeguard against the rise of a powerful state (communism, socialism, national-socialism, fascism), on the one hand, and likewise the necessary leverage to reformulate Keynesian policies consolidated from the 1930s to the 60s, on the other. Even today, some proponents of neoliberal orthodoxy purport that its policies are a cure to the "evils of a strong state," whether socialism, communism, or fascism, terms that are sometimes used interchangeably, and fallaciously, in the triumphalist rhetoric of neoliberalism and free-market capitalism. In the words of the former director of Spain's most influential neoliberal think tank, the Real Instituto Elcano, "no había ni hay alternativa, ni a la democracia ni al mercado" [there wasn't, nor is there any alternative to democracy and the market], that is, a democracy defined in the final instance as a liberal democracy for the markets (Lamo de Espinosa, 2007, 16–7). Or, restated in former President Aznar's call for proposals on a "National Reform Agenda" founded in austerity, privatization, and market liberalization (*apertura*), "Ése es el camino de la libertad económica que tantos frutos ha dado siempre en la historia de la humanidad" [That is the road to economic freedom that has always given so many fruits in the history of humanity] (Aznar, 2009, 8, 12). Mythology, after all, lays its own kind of timeless roots to explain the order of things as wholly natural.

The suture between "free-market policies" and "democratic freedoms" is not casually connected; for orthodox neoliberal reforms, in practice, seek to roll back the remaining Keynesian interventionist policies and to curtail public spending on social welfare programs (the neoliberal call for market deregulation and reductions in state expenditures) while, at the same time, neoliberal proponents often preach against "big government" in tandem with the benefits of opportunity and market freedoms. According to this logic, to foster unfettered market activity with minimal state intervention as necessary is to beget greater individual freedoms in liberal democracy. This equivalence is one myth asserted as truth, which engenders further myth-making in neoliberal discourse—a point I return to—often through a metonymic slide from one side of the equation to the other, and vice versa, in an attempt to pin the two together. From free-market laws to privatization, from cutbacks on public expenditures to regressive tax breaks, these positively valued measures take shape around individual "freedoms," and conversely give positively valued notions of individualism as the natural outcome of the former. In neoliberal rhetoric, so too does the political mentality upholding the claim "freedom = free-market" carve out its own adversaries in diametric opposition to it, whether big government, to be feared, or all things public, to be disparaged.

Free-market policies in general and neoliberal reforms in particular have been instrumentalized as a powerful political tool. During the Cold War, the United States' interest in securing other countries' participation in free-market capitalism, as well as its covert intelligence operations abroad, would serve as a political instrument deployed within this *dispositif*, which correlated policy aims with the feared spread of communism in the United States popular imaginary amid the nuclear arms race. In the Cold War climate, United States foreign policy sought alliances with rightwing dictatorships toward joint political and economic ends, such as the exemplary case of the so-called Chicago Boys in the 1970s and their role in securing the economic solvency and political stability of the Pinochet Regime in Chile through neoliberal reforms. In Spain, the Franco Regime was no exception to these alliances, though it remained staunchly isolationist by comparison, as the 1953 Pacts of Madrid would consolidate financial and military aid for the dictatorship in exchange for United States military bases for a country otherwise excluded from the Marshall Plan due to the regime's ties to fascisms in Germany and Italy.

In the 1980s and 90s, similarly, free-market policies would become synonymous with the promise of democracy and the newfound individual freedoms in societies undergoing transitions from dictatorial regimes, akin to what Foucault observes in the democratizing social objectives of early neoliberal thought in occupied Germany (2008, 79–80). For Latin America and Spain, a swift entrance into the global market often went hand-in-hand with a newfound sense of "freedom" after dictatorial repression. As Susana Draper has noted on postdictatorship societies in Latin America, "forgetting" the dictatorial past and the possibility of future (economic and social) progress in democracy shaped the conditions through which free-market activity and consumerism were conflated with individual freedoms (2012, 31–46). Joan Ramon Resina and Cristina Moreiras-Menor, respectively, have noted likeminded attitudes in the *Transición* to democracy in 1980s Spain, in which desires to embrace the intensely individualist and consumerist tenets of the "new" democratic (free-market) era were motivated, in part, by the promise of laying to rest the dictatorial past.[4] As Foucault outlines the earliest developments of neoliberal policy in occupied Germany, "Economic freedom is jointly produced through growth, well-being, the state, and the forgetting of history," in which the realization of social and political objectives through private enterprise and tempered market deregulation should not be underestimated for their correlation to a temporality of market presentism that turns away from, if not works to disavow, the past in the social imaginary (2008, 86). Consolidated in the fall of the Berlin Wall in 1989 and the disintegration of the Soviet Union in 1991, then, was a new world order of democracy and free-market capitalism without alternative, the celebrated and falsely conceived "end of history," or the subject of Jacques Derrida's *Specters of Marx* (1994, 49–75). The development of the neoliberal way throughout these years would mark a turn in the Cold War in which the future of liberal democracy, international trade and investment, and the financialization of the world economy would prevail. That is, neoliberal orthodoxy has become everywhere, in one form or another, the predominant order of the present time (Harvey, 2005).

Within the decade after Foucault's lectures, the Reagan and Thatcher administrations of the 1980s would consolidate neoliberal practices in state government through the continued minimization of social protections from the Keynesian era, hand-in-hand with the dismantling of labor protections for workers, the pursuit of privatization, and deregulation writ large, as the emergent practice of the world's wealthiest powers. It is during this time that Jamie Peck and Adam Tickell note a shift in the 1980s *roll-back* neoliberalism "preoccupied with the active *destruction and discreditation* of Keynesian-welfarist and social-collectivist institutions (broadly defined)," to a *roll-out* neoliberalism "focused on the purposeful *construction and consolidation* of neoliberalized state reforms, modes of governance, and regulatory relations," or the deterritorializing and reterritorializing double-movement I described earlier (2002, 384). In this manner, neoliberal policies seek out new forms of social governance while redefining the state's relationship to the markets and sovereign debt, instead of the outright minimization of the state per se; they constitute an art of government that delimits the state's terrain of activity to an economic one that has, in consequence, the divestment of the standing social contracts with the population.

As has been noted previously, however, neoliberal "structural readjustments" are not simply imposed coercively in all cases, as they have been very much welcomed from both the political left and right. In the post-Cold War era, European socialist projects would adopt policies in a form of neoliberal economics adherent to a social program called the Third Way, but not without compromising labor security by introducing flexibility (part-time contracts, temporary employment, legal restrictions on labor strikes, and so forth) and by pursuing greater market competition through privatization. Socialism withered to neoliberal technologies of government, which European socialist parties increasingly had to mitigate with constituents against the abandonment of the social and labor issues that these parties were supposedly committed to (Albarracín et al., 1994, 8).[5] In Spain, for example, the first wave of labor reforms and privatizations from 1984 to 1996 was undertaken during Socialist rule, which cleaved the political relations between the PSOE and the labor unions CCOO and UGT, one motivation for three countrywide strikes on labor issues during González's tenure (Encarnación, 2008, 119; SEPI, n.d.).[6] During this time, in turn, the Spanish government also built the foundations for the welfare state, one that in democratic Spain never reached the European average of public expenditures by comparison, following the inheritance of minimalist social welfare provisions under the Franco Regime (Navarro and Shi, 2001, 488–90; Navarro et al., 2011, 44–5). Subsequently, after Socialist rule, a second wave of continued privatizations under President Aznar's tenure (PP) was pursued under the Programa de Modernización del Sector Público Empresarial [Modernization Program for the Public Business Sector], the hallmark for Spain's full adoption of deregulatory neoliberal policies that established a global framework for privatization and competition (Ortega and Sánchez, 2002, 34–5).

Neoliberal practice is transformative over time and, today in the wake of the global crisis, malleable in its local, regional, and transnational implementation, which gives rise to internal contradictions in governance from the experimental *ad hoc* instruments employed as corrective measures for the markets at a given time (Peck and Tickell, 2002, 388). Such contradictions can be observed, say, in the deregulatory neoliberal reforms pursued under Zapatero's administration (PSOE), which were mixed with weak Keynesian initiatives in increased public spending (the "Plan E" Economic Stimulus Package in 2009), or Rajoy's administration (PP), which aggressively sought out, at once, roll-back and roll-out neoliberalism, or system "shocks" in acute austerity and labor reforms, but also raised taxes and nationalized rescued banks. Although the applications of neoliberal policies vary in circumstance, region, and administration—and in their resilience, allow corporate and political decision making to seek out and adapt to new opportunities for profitable gains—the heterogeneity of practices and contradictions in neoliberalisms bears a general schematic that favors private enterprise and tempered market intervention. Though the policies may be mixed in practice, the arguments that uphold neoliberal orthodoxy in political discourse tend to be more formulaic, following the praises of competition, incentive, entrepreneurship, and private investment against the "wrongs" of almost all things public.

III.

What governing logics define neoliberal policy whereby "markets" and "democratic freedoms" become stitched together? The neoliberal rationale is not attributable simply to an accelerated continuation of liberalism in advanced capitalism, nor is it, in practice, synonymous with laissez-faire or noninterventionist market policies. The Ordoliberals and Chicago School of "new" liberal theory elaborated different approaches to the state's "permanent vigilance, activity, and intervention" in the markets through specific *corrective instruments* that aim to sustain competition as any healthy economy's self-regulating motor (Foucault, 2008, 132). States and transnational financial institutions today are required to decide the time and measure for market intervention through specific instruments that aim to produce secondary, corrective effects on market systems in order to foster greater competitive activity within them. Competition drives the baseline rationale to pursue private economic activity in neoliberalism. As such, neoliberal thought is predominated by the criteria of selection that validates these corrective instruments if they can be argued to foster greater competition, capital flows, private enterprise, or the "liberalization" of markets. In order to maximize on competition, the privatization of public services is pursued in public companies or sectors that receive state subsidies, freeing them of bureaucracy, theoretically, in favor of business (Harvey, 2005, 65). In this light, privatization serves a dual purpose as it reduces the state's role in providing public services in healthcare and education, pensions and social security, infrastructure and energy, and so on, while neoliberal policy releases these sectors to market competition for profit-seeking ventures. Competition becomes naturalized mythically as an organizing behavior of the social, as it is for the markets, whereby incentives are praised as the guarantor of market competition, claimed to increase productivity through profits, bonuses, payoffs, and other rewards based on the corporate management model. One returns, then, to the neoliberal orthodoxy of the G-20 declaration, drafted thirty years after Foucault's lectures, which upholds the legitimating criteria of state instruments for market intervention through "a commitment to free market principles, including [...] respect for private property, open trade and investment, competitive markets, and efficient, effectively regulated financial systems," without isolation or "overregulation that would hamper economic growth."

Not all forms of market intervention are permissible in neoliberal practice, however. Neoliberal economic policies are shaped by specific mechanisms and instruments aimed at regulating market prices and purchasing power, such as monetary policy (printing less money to reduce inflation) and adjustments to taxation (lowering taxes to increase purchasing power), never intervening directly in the markets through price-fixing or, say, mandates to regulate unemployment. Proponents of neoliberal policy defend the use of "instruments" and deregulation as operational tools in lieu of direct state intervention, which aim to induce secondhand effects in the markets conceived as a complex operative system whose calculation can never be grasped in totality (Foucault, 2008, 139). As such, one of the tenets of neoliberal policy is to achieve greater "flexibility" in the labor market through legal deregulations that minimize corporate employers' fiscal responsibility for its employees, while introducing temporary employment, new hiring practices for pluri-employment (part-time and micro-jobs), legal controls on strikes, and greater ease for employers to hire and fire at will. Whether in the labor or other markets, this rationale seeks to "free" market activity from stops or controls that would otherwise hinder its operations, but not without favoring corporate enterprise, in the case of labor, at the expense of job security, living wages, and labor rights for workers. In practice, observes Maurizio Lazzarato, "the specific role of government is then, on the one hand, to detect the 'differences' of status, incomes, education, social insurances, etc., and to set these inequalities to act effectively one against the other," which in neoliberal rhetoric sustains competition as the stimulus for greater efficiency and productivity; on the other hand, "it is a question of amplifying the politics of individualization—of salaries, of careers, of the monitoring of the unemployed—inside each segment, each situation, as a way of inciting competition" among actors within them (2009, 119).

Consider, for example, the arguments by conservative neoliberal proponents in Spain, who contend that state subsidies for the culture and the arts should be minimized, leaving this sector to finance itself through sales revenue and sponsorship. Such is the argument made by economists Rocío Albert and Rogelio Biazzi (and later, by Finance Minister Cristóbal Montoro), who advocate for the elimination of state subsidies for Spanish cinema as a measure to *incentivize* the industry "to stop making auteur film to make films for viewers" profitable by ticket sales revenue and corporate sponsorship (2009, 8).[7] The subjective judgment of "good" versus "bad" cinema is representative of neoliberal arguments unrelated to the culture industry in that it mimes the justifications to promote incentive-based reforms elsewhere, whether to pull state funding or to privatize the public, by discrediting the alleged quality of an output or outcome (public television and radio, state museums, government bureaus and agencies, state-owned property and parks, and so forth). This is another important mechanics to myth-making in neoliberal discourse in which a specific axiomatic governed by the praises of incentive, competition, quality output, autonomous productivity, entrepreneurialism, and so forth, tend to provide (rather formulaic) justifications to pursue neoliberal policies. As they do so, they likewise attach positive values to policy aims that benefit private enterprise, while recasting others negatively, in the case of state subsidies for film, as lacking incentive, gusto, or initiative.

Amid deregulation and privatization, administration in public and private hospitals, schools and universities, social services and pensions programs, among others, must justify decision making based on profitability, competitiveness, and incentive. The private firm, in this sense, becomes the management model (Rose, 1999, 142) and the "business culture" for almost all institutional arrangements, from the university to the clinic. In this light, the market logic of competition and incentive extends vastly from workers' social interactions on the job, to market forces on the whole. One might be led to wonder in consequence whether the management model that seeks greater competition within a given institutional hierarchy is likewise prone to reinforcing the prevailing power relations of its tiered structure, due to the competitive practices that it aims to raise among "incentivized" subordinates. Nevertheless, as corporatization becomes more commonplace in the media, schools, hospitals, prisons, and so on, it presents unethical conflicts of interest among government officials and policy makers, private endeavors, and corporate ownership. Take, for example, the cases in Spain, among many, in which privatization initiatives have served the business interests of government officials who, if not reaping the benefits of privatization and private investment directly, then enjoy the protections of a "revolving door" to hold influential positions in corporations and advisory boards once they finish their tenure in the public service.

Together with the development of neoliberalism's instruments of market correction and competition (different from the noninterventionist, free-market practices of liberalism), Foucault identifies another significant, and social, attribute to twentieth-century *neo*liberal governance. Liberal economists shifted their theorization of rational economic activity, which in any complex system cannot be fully calculated, toward the accountable domain of the individual who is presumed to make private decisions out of self-interest (Foucault, 2008, 267–313). Following Foucault, one observes that this accountable, nontransferrable atom of economic and social activity is likewise *held accountable* for private investments and securities on his private earnings. Whereas in liberalism this individual, the *homo oeconomicus*, was conceived as the irreducible, rationalized "unit" of labor and social production quantifiable by census statistics, the new abstracted form of neoliberal economic man endows him with a novel characteristic. "The *homo oeconomicus* [...] is not the man of exchange or man the consumer" alone, as in liberalism; rather, he becomes "the man of enterprise and production" out of self-interest, resilient to adversity and adaptive to market variables in his environment in order to become self-sufficient, whatever the context of his making (Foucault, 2008, 147).

The *homo oeconomicus* is imagined as an enterprising, self-sustained unit capable of maximizing his own productivity, economic autonomy, and independent responsibility for self-care through private investments and securities. This envisaged individual autonomy, which presumes a surplus in one's income for private investments, extends to conjectural economic behavior and choices on one's risk, future dependency, prudent spending and saving, and so on. Economic growth becomes a social policy allowing an individual to acquire an income that maximizes his capital in order to realize fully his enterprising possibility for production and investment. Therefore, private insurance, access to private property, and individual capitalization are achieved through privatization itself, which aims to minimize the state's hand in social protections and public services (Foucault, 2008, 144). After all, the *homo oeconomicus* can only realize his fullest productive potential as an autonomous, enterprising unit if he benefits from the minimum possible tax withholdings on his income and acquires the maximum possible capital to finance his own endeavors, independently of the state. Effactually, argues Jason Read, "the discourse of the economy becomes an entire way of life, a common sense in which every action—crime, marriage, higher education, and so on—can be charted according to a calculus of maximum output for minimum expenditure; it can be seen as an in-vestment," contemplated from a market logic that views positively the competitive private gains of the enterprising individuals comprising the population (2009, 31). For its proponents, neoliberal policy thus significantly curtails welfare provisions, of course, but it also counts in tandem on institutional arrangements developing beyond the state in *civil society*, which are charged with "awakening responsibility" and "solidarity" from NGOs, private initiatives, social volunteers, and so forth, to substitute, if at all, for a languishing or absent security net (Muñoz-Alonso, 1995, 27–8). In the current conjuncture of Spain's crisis, this civil society has been increasingly called upon to absorb the social costs and provisions (medicines and treatments, insurance, education, legal assistance, housing and food, and so on) for segments of the population left without coverage (Fundación Foessa, 2013).

As the development of neoliberal governmentality has taken shape around certain *corrective instruments* to foster market competition, neoliberal governance tends to entail corrective instruments of a socially competitive character forged around economic and fiscal priorities. Examined in chapter 1 and above, the justifications for neoliberal policy aims tend to scuttle from economic circumstance to personalized attribute, from labor market to individual motivation for the unemployed, and back again. In doing so, as Carmona et al. observe in Spain, the policies and discourses that propose minimizing social welfare often slip into moral arguments, among them, that welfare is "degrading" and demoralizing for its recipients, as the other side of this individuation (2012, 135–9). As do claims that the unemployed or disadvantaged should be incentivized to "pick themselves up by the bootstraps" toward the model of self-sufficiency that the economic man requires. Echoing this model, the political scientist Alejandro Muñoz-Alonso writes that welfare provisions "hacen crónica a la pobreza, creando un sector que se instala al amparo de las ayudas sociales y abandona toda voluntad de asumir los compromisos de la responsabilidad individual" [make poverty chronic, creating a sector that settles into the shelters of social aid and abandons all will to assume the commitments of individual responsibility] (1995, 26). In the metonymic slide from the welfare state to the individual, one observes how "lack of incentive" (notably, an adversary to the logic of market competition) becomes a moral question of self-responsibility, one that is pinned together with the "chronic ills" of poverty attributed to welfare dependency, and vice versa. As such, in the most neoconservative stripe of neoliberal discourse, socialism, social welfare, and metaphors of disease are pinned together (metonymically) as responsible for the "moral relativism" and "illness" of Spanish society in its alleged crisis of morals and values (Mayor Oreja, 2010, 6).

Notably, the Welfare State, which includes an extensive range of social expenditures on state provisions, is reduced in neoliberal rhetoric to *only* the recipients of unemployment pensions and aid (the welfare check), which come under attack through disparaging character traits (irresponsible, lacking incentive, even criminal) as a metonymic stand in for the state itself. In neoliberal governance, social attitudes towards unemployment and poverty form around this presumption, leading to contradictions from segments of the population that may receive benefits from the welfare state (say, in the United States context, Medicare) but, at the same time, adamantly support the minimization or elimination of welfare services to their own detriment. In this light, socially corrective instruments can be deployed as forms of judgment toward segments of the population or entire socioeconomic classes, as in the case of recasting the unemployed and welfare recipients as "slackers," which can potentially strengthen class-based antagonisms and competition through individuation. Such is the case, for example, in the complaint that welfare recipients are a tax burden on one's own private profits, as "productive society" pays for the "free ride" of the nonproductive (Carmona et al., 2012, 139).

To recast the unemployed as receiving a "free ride" from tax contributors, it can be said, is likewise to seek a popular distinction between the "productive" and "enterprising" (an upstanding model for society) in binary opposition to its others. Seated in an economic rationale, competition can therefore operate as a regulatory measure for social interactions. As David Harvey notes, "Individual success or failure are interpreted in terms of entrepreneurial virtues or personal failings (such as not investing significantly enough in one's own human capital through education)," which form judgments and attributions blind to class difference and preexisting social disadvantages (2005, 65). This is the stuff of the social production of class difference in neoliberal thought, which not only reaffirms the fully autonomous economic actor as the ideal model for productive society, but furthermore contributes to justifying—if not naturalizing—the inequalities of socioeconomic status as properties of the "self." The predominant economic paradigm and its practice become the lens through which political and social relations are explained and organized, indeed personalized.

Among the rhetorical strategies deployed toward policy aims, to stigmatize the poor shares its place within the justifications to dismantle social welfare services, benefits, or compensation paid to individuals (unemployment, social security, retirement pensions, worker's compensation, disability and aid) by constructing the poor in the social imaginary as lacking self-responsibility (Carmona et al., 2012, 139). Individuation, note Carmona and his co-authors, upholds "un discurso de culpabilización de los pobres que, a fin de cuentas, son señalados como los únicos responsables de su situación" [a discourse of blame for the poor who, in the end, are flagged as the only ones responsible for their circumstance], thereby shifting attention from the labor market to individual actions, behaviors, and attitudes (2012, 139). In the slippage between the two, welfare provisions are believed to be an intrusion of the state into the private lives of individuals, which "adormece[n] los espíritus y aplaca los impulsos de superación' [numb the spirit and placate the drive to overcome (adversity)], on the one hand, while these assertions uphold empowered "self-initiative" as the solution to economic dependency rather than an equitable distribution of wealth, on the other (2012, 136). To remember Barthes, myth always has an elsewhere at its disposal, located here in the virtuous model of an autonomous economic man, fashioned positively with self-empowering attributes to overcome his economic circumstance on his own accord. And *homo oeconomicus* cuts a curious figure, given that his subjectivity is constituted by the very economic circumstances and market conditions that go ignored altogether in his condition *as subject* to them. Nevertheless, the figure of *homo oeconomicus* as a theoretical model can shed some light on the mechanisms at work in neoliberal governance, in the relationships forged among the markets, the state, and the social, from the very domain in which this "ideal" subject is imagined, individualized, and personalized with attributes at the service of private enterprise.

In Spain, the political rhetoric that assigns blame to Spanish residents for having lived beyond their means tout court, echoed in the discourse of government officials, media analysts, and economists, ignores the endogamous mix of private gains and political interests that ushered unbridled construction from boom to bust in recent years. This argument likewise serves in turn to justify austerity measures in the language on government cutbacks, and as it does so, targets residents as responsible parties for paying the sovereign debt "dispossessed" from state funds, to use Harvey's term. Fiscal policy, in other words, or specifically the management of state expenditures and public debt, is recast in social and, particularly, moral terms on prudent spending and the private investments of the population. The message to be read is one of shame, moral judgment, and irresponsibility for one's own circumstance. This is another nexus at work in neoliberal myth-making after the global crisis, in which social judgments on autonomy and self-responsibility are recast as an accomplice to the ends and aims of austerity. As Nikolas Rose argues, "We have seen the birth of political mentalities and governmental practices which have served to sharpen and neutralize the divisions between the autonomous and the dependent, the contented and the discontented, the haves and the have-nots" in decisive divisions that outcast society's "unproductive" others as second-class citizens (1999, 254).

What lies beyond the imagined model for the *homo oeconomicus* are its many exclusions, defined loosely as "non-productive individuals" (un-incentivized) in society for different reasons and at different stages of life. Among Spain's cutbacks to its social welfare programs, these exclusions in practice encompass the unemployed, the dependent, the elderly, the disabled, and so on, as well as those who cannot accumulate private capital to pursue private investments in insurances, healthcare, education, and so forth. As such, an unemployed person is presumed to be in a transient position on her way to future employment, regardless of the circumstances of the labor market that might impede the realization of this naturalized assumption (Foucault, 2008, 139). If this person cannot secure work over time, however, then she suffers from "chronic unemployment," which ignores the very market conditions that might make this so. External forces and conditions, in other words, are personalized as properties of the individual and her choices. If classical liberalism may be understood as the political doctrine of the bourgeoisie, which the ruling classes presumed to be universal, then in neoliberalism this political-economic doctrine presumes that a specific segment of the population (or, the "productive" with a surplus of capital for private investment, insurance, property, and so forth) is naturally representative of the whole of society. Cultural narratives of upward mobility, self-empowerment, and equal opportunity, which often ignore social disadvantage or privilege, are evidence of the rationalizing suture required to justify the myth that hard work and perseverance equate to a better quality of life, attainable for all.

In this manner, one should also temper Foucault's concept of "society" in the neoliberal regime, which is not a homogeneous entity, of course, but instead shows itself as both a dynamic meshwork of institutional arrangements (state, civil society, corporations, and so on) and a hierarchical structuring of certain actors and institutions among and within them. Consider, for example, that those who are excluded from the ideal subject envisaged as the self-sufficient *homo oeconomicus* are increasingly held to bear the burdens that limit an individual's possibilities, paradoxically, to become self-sufficient. As such, risk of economic insolvency is a more tangible threat to the precariously employed and the "non-productive" who find themselves increasingly unprotected, than to certain areas of corporate activity and private ownership freed of risk by protectionist benefits. As Lazzarato notes on the financialization of the economy since the time of Foucault's lectures, the onus of risk has come to bear unevenly upon the vulnerable rather than the well-to-do.

> Contemporary capitalism has overturned this relation of relative risks, for, as we have seen from the new strategies introduced to insecuritize or make precarious the condition of wage-earners, contract no longer provides the guarantees and securities once prevailing; the opposite movement has seen the introduction of stock options, golden handshakes and so on to protect management as well as shareholders from risk. This is a qualitative shift—it prompts us to temper the comments of Foucault on liberalism and competition by taking account of the asymmetrical effects of financialization for, on one side, "non-owners" and, on the other side, shareholders and holders of savings. The former must rely on their earnings alone, often blocked or eroded because of the systematic reduction in social expenditures, whilst the latter can shift risks onto the stock market or insurances. (2009, 124)

It would seem, then, that the intangible "socio-cultural" factors forming around neoliberal policy aims, such as values, attitudes, affects, and so on, are produced as inscriptions within the neoliberal regime as they work to legitimate a socioeconomic structuring and, within this hierarchy, its many exclusions.

On the other side of an upstanding civil society, however, alternative community formations develop with force, which David Harvey notes, provide a sense of belonging, affiliation, and stability.

> Stripped of the protective cover of lively democratic institutions and threatened with all manner of social dislocations, a disposable workforce inevitably turns to other institutional forms through which to construct social solidarities and express a collective will. Everything from gangs and criminal cartels, narco-trafficking networks, mini-mafias and favela bosses, through community, grassroots and non-governmental organizations, to secular cults and religious sects proliferate. These are the alternative social forms that fill the void left behind as state powers, political parties, or other institutional forms are actively dismantled or simply wither away as centers of collective endeavor and of social bonding. (2005, 171)

Among them, the alternative modes of socialization, often entangled within the necessity of securing economic subsistence, constitute an antagonism to the upstanding civil society that perceives them as a dangerous threat. Their collectives comprise a lumpen category of second-rate citizens excluded from certain privileges, protections, and even basic rights. As some social attitudes would have it, writes Nikolas Rose, they are civil society's "abject others" existing "outside the communities of inclusion": "an array of micro-sectors, micro-cultures of non-citizens, failed citizens, anti-citizens, consisting of those who are unable or unwilling to enterprise their lives or manage their own risk, incapable of exercising responsible self-government, attached whether to no moral community or to a community of anti-morality" (1999, 259). Their abjection is a powerful case of how a society's marginalized are constituted within the neoliberal imaginary through the reification of class difference, one that rests upon the moralizing criteria formed around (economic) subsistence and social modes of being in the world.

Undoubtedly, some of the most visible effects of neoliberal policy and its socioeconomic structuring are located in the urban milieu, where the rights to public access erode to the priorities of privatization initiatives, traffic and commerce, property speculation and investments, and so on. As the urban commons are refurbished or released to private investors, often to re-suit them for profitability—via tourism, commerce, property speculation, and so forth—so too do these reforms have a hand in fostering gentrification by making the cost of living in these neighborhoods inaccessible to the current residents, which rather displaces them for others with a higher income in order to see returns on investments and rent (both property and taxed income) (Observatorio Metropolitano, 2013, 59).[8] Although these material and social effects have been signaled by David Harvey as a territorializing feature of advanced capitalism (its predatory activity), the neoliberal character of these urban reforms resides in part in the logic (and myth) that all things public, once "freed" to market forces and competition, shall deliver greater returns for the common good. Implicit within this turn to the private, moreover, is the *demographic sorting* in urban space of those segments of the population displaced elsewhere due to their own socioeconomic status (for Rose, their "abjection" or casting out), in which the affluent no longer necessarily come into contact with other social classes, or their everyday realities. If the security cameras keeping watch over the gated communities in the Madrid suburbs have become a fixture installed into the habits of the affluent classes, then this desire for self-security can be said to share its logic, as two sides of the same coin, with the surveillance cameras fixed in public space to police the working-class multicultural neighborhood of Lavapiés. Across the great distance between the two in the urban landscape, perhaps more palatable to the imagination is the myth that the pursuit of enterprise and private investments guarantees prosperity for all, even for those who paradoxically under surveillance, remain largely invisible and unseen.

Sensing the Crisis in Nophoto's *El último verano*

Spain's many contemporary crises, folded into the catch-all term *crisis*—a financial crisis, a housing crisis, a political crisis of governance, a crisis of the state, a crisis of survival for many, and so on—tend to organize everyday conversations in Spain, from social encounters to broadcast debates.[9] This observation raises the question of how subjects traverse the everyday structured in part by ongoing crises in which, perceptibly, life is somehow no longer as it was. Here, I am particularly interested in the plural, contradictory modes of perception imbued by crisis when social mobilizations and oppositional practices, such as those in the unprecedented demonstrations of 15M, are not alone in question. That is, what happens in everyday life unsettled by change when it seems that, generally, not much is happening at all? To address the reshaping of ordinary life amid the crisis, I turn to photography and narrative captions as one medium that in its possibilities to construct and frame images, privileges relational ways of looking from subject positions toward the photographed milieu.

In their group project *El último verano*, nine artists of the Madrid-based Nophoto photography collective provide some one hundred photographs and videos that aim to document everyday life in summer of 2012 in response to the government's most aggressive labor reforms and cutbacks to social programs in Spain's democratic history.[10] Captured in their suggestive title for the project, the artists assemble a collective document on *last summer* in 2012, or the previous season's vacation, and *the last summer* as the photographers have known it, in the perceptibly deteriorating conditions of life in times of austerity.[11] In difference to Barthes's assessment that the noeme of photography resides in its evidence of the *this-has-been*, however, *El último verano* gathers perceptions in the "future anterior," or the *this-will-have-been*, which strongly conditions the temporalities of memory and projection in the images as they draw from the direct experience and anticipation of personal losses amid Spain's plural *crisis* (Barthes, 1972, 77, 96). Even so, the realism of economic hardship and social exclusion, in a similar vein to what Germán Labrador Méndez calls *subprime life histories* (2012, 557–81), are only the subject of select images, as in Jonás Bel's portrait of a worried construction worker foregrounding the record unemployment rate ("27 de julio, Madrid. 5.693.100") or the growing numbers of homeless ("26 de julio, Madrid. 1.863"). Still, other photographs imagine the future for youth today and depict the experience of the elderly in reflections on the passing of one generation to the next. In them, future prospects are often pessimistic, captured in Paco Gómez's photograph of a white flag flying over a castle and in the caption, a father's explanation to his son that "Spain has surrendered" ("11 de agosto, Antequera. Málaga. Rendición"), while others bristle against any predictions about an uncertain future at all ("27 de agosto, Rishikesh. Pasado-presente-futuro"). Together, they provide a collective, contradictory reflection on the structure and sense of fragility, precarity, and the retreat from social well-being in ways that are irreducible to a uniform approach to the photographed content across the images.

El último verano evokes many times, memories, and predictions with such variety that Eduardo Nave's sad remembrance of his grandmother's choice to retire from splashing in the pool at age 88 (figure 3.1) shares its place in perceptible symbiosis with Jonás Bel's spliced image of "property for sale" signs in Madrid (figure 3.2).

This unlikely comparison, as any other in the project, works to remind viewers that its exploration of the subjective experience of the crisis extends well beyond losses attributable directly to the markets and government expenditures alone. Rather, what structures the sense of fragility in the photographs, I propose, are the subject's affective ties to disappearing ways of life, in sadness and disillusionment, in the joys of escape, and in appreciation for what one still has. Thereby the project

Figure 3.1 Eduardo Nave, "23 de agosto, Cheste. El verano pasado".
Photo: © Eduardo Nave / NOPHOTO.

Figure 3.2 Jonás Bel, "21 de agosto, Madrid. Se vende".
Photo: © Jonás Bel / NOPHOTO.

brings together subtle moments from the sensory pleasures of summer, in Eva Sala's untitled photograph of a napkin from an ice cream parlor ("19 de julio, Gandía"), to uneasy moments of concern for others, in Paco Gómez's empathetic encounter with a kind man who suffers a psychotic episode moments later ("30 de julio. Rascafría. Madrid. Desesperación"). Viewed in its entirety, *El último verano* is an estranged and estranging collective portrait of the historical present in waiting, a kind of impasse framed as the doldrums of summer in times of crisis.

An impasse, writes Lauren Berlant in *Cruel Optimism*, consists in a present of the ordinary, everyday occurrences "shaped by crisis in which people find themselves developing skills for adjusting to newly proliferating pressures [and] scramble for modes of living on" (2011, 8). Unlike an event punctuated by transcendental importance, the impasse for Berlant comprises the usual, sometimes banal, happenings of everyday life experienced as a perpetual crisis in which subjects find themselves adapting to new circumstances as best as they can, aiming to get by. In its imaginative stories and socially committed documentary portraits, among others, *El último verano* sketches out the vulnerability of an impasse due to "social catastrophe, when one no longer knows what to do or how to live and yet, while unknowing, must adjust" to new terms of daily life (Berlant, 2011, 200). The photographs portray the burdensome ethos of a crisis underway in which minor daily occurrences prove largely significant for the ways in which they are mediated by subtle maneuvers for survival, perceptible losses, and the remaining attachments to the world through which subjects move.

Summer itself is a kind of impasse, not simply of escape from daily routine and work, which often involves travel, as it did for the photographers. The summer of 2012 also marks a specific historical present in which this hiatus coincides with the government's announcement before adjourning for vacation that it will pursue further austerity measures, which anticipates that the fall season will bring more "bad news"; it is the sensible structure of the moment's unshaped present, of a burgeoning crisis with more to come. Juan Valbuena provides a poignant observation on how the long duration of the summer months resembled a cyclical holding pattern as Spain faced a potential bailout from the European Central Bank (ECB). The photographer comments on the fluctuations of interest rates in his image of a laptop computer screen displaying headline news from *El País* on the rising risk premium, which has served as one thermometer for the crisis. In the caption, viewers learn that another Dark Friday is the product of the weekly rhythms of state administration:

Llevamos meses igual: el fin de semana los tipos más listos de Europa se reúnen para salvar el euro, el lunes y el martes la cosa se tranquiliza... el miércoles y el jueves no saben si rescatarnos o ahogarnos y el viernes parece el apocalipsis... ("20 de julio, Madrid. Otro viernes negro")

[This has gone on for months: on the weekend the smartest guys in Europe meet to save the Euro, on Monday and Tuesday things calm down...on Wednesday and Thursday they don't know if they should bail us out or drown us, and Friday looks like the apocalypse...]

The administrative time-cycle of state and European government produces the sensible burden of the crisis in weekly repetition, which amounts to yet another Dark Friday from speculations about a grim forecast for the future. In Valbuena's photograph, news of the ECB's power of decision to intervene with bailout loans for Spain is responsible in part for conjugating the temporal outlook for the immediate future in which the sensible mood of the photographed present—or, the micro experience of an impasse marked by crisis—is inflected by macro processes, reported news of market forecasts, and economic policies emanating from boardrooms in European administration. The cyclical temporality of the impasse in Valbuena's photo commentary is sensed first as an anxiety for a present that perpetually hedges on the brink of disaster against the risk of sovereign insolvency. The financial and political crisis of state sovereignty here, in indebtedness and democratic representation usurped from the power of autonomous decision making, is relayed as one mediated by impotence and the anxieties it provokes when reading the morning news.

Far from the markets, the mood of perpetual crisis resides in the most imaginative narratives. In *El último verano*, viewers discover ironic plans on how to prepare for an apocalypse, just in case, by buying less at back-to-school sales or by escaping to a paradise island until heavenly bureaucrats manage to sort out "all hell breaking loose" (Gómez, "3 de agosto, La Isla. Apocalipsis"). For even consumerism and bureaucracy will survive the end of the world in this eschatological imaginary. Among moments of dark irony such as these, the project includes accounts on the inflection of the crisis in everyday perception, in Jonás Bel's uncanny encounter with a taxidermic, extinct species that seems to laugh cynically at humankind ("2 de septiembre, Madrid. Extinción"). So too does Paco Gómez perceive the present as an estranging time that has met its end in his lighthearted account on training his family to live on Mars as a more inhabitable planet than Earth. The science-fiction fantasy, told with doses of humor and nostalgia, recalls the photographer's fond memories playing at the beach, as his children do now, in what collapses futurist fantasy and memory into a narrative of difference and nostalgic loss from one generation to the next, against the impossibility of returning to more comforting times. Inspired by news coverage of the first landscape images from the NASA rover Curiosity, Gómez's recollection of his childhood suggests a form of time travel away from the foreignness of the present as an uneasy, inhospitable time to be living in; he proposes escape, shared in his children's fantastic expedition. But the unsettling photograph of innocent child's play, their mouths covered at the risk of "ingesta de líquidos" [fluid intake], and staged in suffocating "condiciones de calor extremo y ausencia de oxígeno" [conditions with extreme heat and a lack of oxygen], bears the qualities of a hostile Martian terrain that speaks more to a manner of perceiving the present time and photographed place than to the imagination ("18 de agosto, Embalse del Burguillo, Ávila. Curiosity").

In other entries, stories of downward mobility are not simple grievances on the deteriorating conditions of material comforts, as one might expect. Rather, they expose the remains of a naturalized belief in forms of historical progress, understood here as the expected improvement in the quality of life from one generation to the next. Jorquera names seven differences between his father's circumstance and his own through a double image of a photograph taken of his father before the Twin Towers in the Manhattan skyline in 1974. Faded in yellow and cyan colors that visibly mark the passing of time, the double image places into evidence, too, a doubling of the photographer's circumstance and his father's at the same age. An unstable job market, uncertain retirement plans, and paying rent for life instead of owning one's home are underscored among the seven contrasts in the quality of life between two generations, past and present. Underpinning this comparison is the lack of means for the present generation to secure economic self-sufficiency, in the wake of disintegrated social pacts that once guaranteed job security for life for the father's generation. The image's relay between two times is marked by the caption's concluding point on the presence and absence of the World Trade Center, the only historical referent mentioned in these seven points, as the foremost symbol of American capital now disappeared. Whereas Jorquera's father had his photograph taken in front of the towers as a souvenir for his travels to New York, the photographer himself "h[a] visto caer esas mismas torres en directo por televisión" [saw those same towers fall, live on television], in what relates the passing of one generation to the next through the televised event in which the absence of the towers today, in retrospect, is relationally invested with a disappearing way of life ("12 de agosto, Nueva York. Las siete diferencias").

In Jorquera's photograph, precarity is anchored in the mediated simultaneity of the broadcast event. It is a moment sensed as historical before it can be processed, as it is (was) experienced in two times: in the collapse of the towers that marked the so-called war on terrorism, and in the conditions of a crisis underway that also (as then) has yet to become history. The experience of the subject in Jorquera's photograph, related in terms of the quality of life, becomes grafted within a macro narrative of economic dominance and its decline in both times. The biopolitical dimension of this double history, recapitulated in the seven differences between the experience of father and son, resides within the photographer's cognitive association to the macro history of monumental political power and capital that once reassured a sustained belief in better times to come. Jorquera's photograph and text suggest provocatively in this doubling of image and tower that the decaying remains of a historical narrative on capitalist-driven progress are embedded within this intergenerational inheritance. In it, the loss of great expectations for better times is sensed first with disillusionment while it also remains open, unshaped by the meaning that will come to bear upon it, despite its perceptible significance as a present destabilized by historic change.

As viewers may begin to see, several images speak of an intergenerational inheritance, whether from the experience of the elderly, children today, or uncertain speculations about the future. Such is the case in Paco Gómez's photograph of his father picking tomatoes from his oversized garden. Gómez remarks that his father's childhood experiences "le han generado un miedo al hambre" [created a fear of hunger], which persists today as his father tends his garden that could easily feed over ten families ("30 de julio. Navaluenga, Ávila. Los tomates"). In a clear allusion to the years of dictatorship, the caption relates the disproportionate size of this land to its owner's childhood experience marked by hardship and scarce food. As such, the photographer observes that his father has started to teach his grandson how to care for the garden, which, with upkeep, could provide them with a source of food and the pleasures of "calabacines y unos pepinos que están de llorar" [zucchini and cucumbers so good they make you cry]. Teaching care in this tender narrative at once underpins an intergenerational handing-down of knowledge in a return to rural ways of life while it responds to unsettling projections about the future conditioned by the subject's experience in the past. In this sense, the crisis may evoke a perceptible return to the historical past, in hunger or economic strife, as the conditions from which to prepare for the perceived future, even if the precautions seem disproportionate, like the dimensions of the father's garden in the photographer's view. The knowledge taught from grandfather to grandson prompts memory in storytelling and sharing; it is, in effect, a productive care for the inheritance of the past here. Viewers are invited to reflect, then, on the photographs' contemplation of vulnerability for subjects who perceive in the future the partial replaying of the past and whether despite it or in preparation for it, develop forms of care in the transfer of knowledge that adjusts to projected needs.

In its reflections on the ECB, NASA, price fluctuations, and other newsworthy stories, *El último verano* often takes up the news media as its plural account of the crisis in everyday life. As summer unfolds, some photographs are grounded in specific events reported in the newspapers like the seasonal wildfires in Spain's arid inland, the deaths of Neil Armstrong and Santiago Carrillo, and even relevant debates in daily sports news. For the exhibition "El último verano" held the following fall season at CentroCentro Madrid, Nophoto issued a lengthy newspaper compiling select images in a printed catalog that presents itself as an alternative news source on the collective experience of the crisis, not least the relation of this experience in tension with that of the daily news (Nophoto, 2012). Nearly six million unemployed. A 15 percent increase in prostitution. A 62 percent increase in services provided for the needy. These quantified rates and figures cited in *El último verano* prove insufficient to convey the true social impact of the crisis, which is where the images do their interpretive work. Yet, these data are often presented to viewers as though borrowing from the reporting function of the news media, as endowed with an instrumental ability to convey the urgency of their personal stakes in resonance with the global crisis as a media event (Banet-Weiser, 2012, 111). In them, the simultaneity of reporting in the news media bears a similar immediacy with which affective attachments and emotions are mediated for viewers as information in the images. The catalog-newspaper provides viewers, then, with forms translated from one genre rewritten into another, or from a genre founded in its claims to objectivity (the news media) against another that privileges the experience and reception of the subject (art).

For example, Eduardo Nave recounts the pessimistic outlook for the arts and culture sector in "16 de julio, Madrid. 53 fotografías" in which the closing of the gallery where he exhibited his work amounts to much more than the cited value of his 53 photographs held in temporary storage. These photographs have nowhere to go for the moment, he acknowledges discouragingly, not a warehouse, much less another gallery. Similarly, Juan Valbuena's caption to his photograph of an abandoned movie theater comments on the impact of the VAT tax increase from 8 to 21 percent on cinema ticket sales, which anticipates the closing of movie theaters in downtown Madrid, except for perhaps the commercial cineplexes in shopping malls accessible by car ("13 de julio, Madrid. Sueño de una noche de verano"). The percentage increase frames the pessimistic outlook for film under the aegis of market competition, which Valbuena laments as an expected loss for the city's cultural offering if one compares the revenues from blockbuster theaters to those of independent film houses. Told through his desire to live one day within walking distance from a theater in downtown Madrid, Valbuena's reflection frames his own expected loss, and the disappointment it evokes, in relation to that of Madrid's cultural landscape. With a separate measure, in Nave's black-and-white portrait of a traveler with his suitcases in Barajas Airport, the photographer quantifies the distance of his brother's separation from his wife and son—precisely 8,003 km—before a flight to the Americas where he has been relocated for work ("11 de septiembre, T4 Barajas. Muy lejos"). The growing phenomenon of emigration is captured here as an intimate story in which quantified distance indicates but cannot adequately describe the emotions and uncertainties of separation. All three narrate some form of personal loss in the present and immediate future, reported in percentages and numbers, and the photographers' affective ties or emotional responses to them.

These images find their particularity of the quantifiable in economic losses, percentage tax increases, or kilometric distance, and their immeasurable effects: in the unsettling doubt about whether one can continue making a living from a current profession; in truncated desires interwoven with the expected denuding of Madrid's cultural scene; and in missing a loved one far away. These and other images provide a portrait of the fragility of vulnerable states in which the "structure of an affect has no inevitable relation to the penumbra of emotions that may cluster in the wake of its activity," as these perceptions of loss suppose forms of rationalization, disappointment, coping, and so on (Berlant, 2008, 4). In them, viewers are reminded that micro narratives comprise intimate portraits of a greater history that cannot be quantified or measured in the data reported in the rise and fall of markets. And, yet, the abstractions of numeric figures in these works indeed provide some index of lived experience as they are invested with feelings of loss, separation, and speculation about the future. Nowhere more prevalent is this economic inflection observed than in the framing of moments of friendship and enjoyment presented in calculable terms. In a piece that captures an afternoon spent with a gathering of friends, Nave provides a lively, accelerated stop-shot video of a paella cooking on a wood stove, with itemized prices for each ingredient to serve fifteen people, totaling 21.68 euros ("24 de agosto, Cheste. Paella para 15"). Contrary to austerity measures, he comments, this is the price of one day of happiness with others. In the inverse of previous entries, in which the measureable is presented as quantifiable evidence, here Nave quantifies leisure in calculable terms, territorialized into an economic logic, in the language of Deleuze and Guattari, that reports expenditures amid austerity and as it does so, fails to account for the value of joy in a community of friends.

Beyond mere news data, some images offer critical, oppositional readings of the government's discourse on sacrifice in its austerity program circulating ad nauseum in the mainstream media. Eva Sala provides a photograph of a statue in India in which the sculpture's textured hands peel apart the skin of a trap door opening to the heart ("23 de agosto. Rishikesh. Sacrificio"). The caption, which compiles many news headlines with the word "sacrifice" echoes a similar repetition in the statue whose red door is designed to open and close, exposing the heart time and again. It is a form of repetition that draws from the redundant talk of sacrifice in the media as one measure of the government's battery of cutbacks to social programs, and the choice of language to explain them to the general public, over an extended period of time. The predominant discourse that demands self-sacrifice is addressed as well in Juan Santos's photograph of an anonymous subject wearing a T-shirt that critiques the political rhetoric in the media alleging that Spanish

residents have outlived their means: "Vivo por encima de mis posibilidades, pero muy por debajo de mi nivel" [I live beyond my means, but
very much below my level] ("25 de agosto. Casillas de Coria, Cáceres.
Posibilidades"). In it, the photographer uses the camera as a critical
tool to reject the government's justification for an austerity program
that preserves the greatest fortunes, which lacks "respeto a la inteligen-
cia" [respect for intelligence]. That is, both photographs posit a critique
of the government's discursive strategies to rationalize austerity in its
address to citizens, an implicit exacerbation with the saturation of this
discourse on sacrifice in the news media (troped in the photos with critique and, in Santos's case, irony), and the chasm existing between this
official language and the lived experience of being "bled dry," to draw
from the language of sacrifice.

Perceptions of the present, past, and future often coexist in the
impasse of the crisis as it is experienced in the first person, taken up
through the camera lens. Different senses of time, taken with specificity
for the visual and narrative framing of each image, serve to structure
the precarity of the present impasse in these photographs, whether in
teachings on care, disillusionment for the loss of better times, fantasy
in escape, or the sensed unending repetition of disaster. Similarly to
market projections that convey anxious speculations about no eventual
end to a perpetual crisis in reported news of interest rates and sovereign
debt. Similarly to Gómez's father who perceives his grandson's future
as an echo of his own childhood experience under dictatorship. And,
following the growing phenomenon of emigration, similarly to Jonás
Bel's wonder about whether the granddaughter pictured in his photograph, accompanied by her grandfather peering through binoculars at
the horizon, will one day move to the Americas and remember these
moments fondly from across an ocean ("10 de agosto, Cabo Sardão
(Portugal). Porvenir"). For, the circumstance of the crisis unsettles the
present in anticipation for an uncertain future that often establishes the
tone of perception from immediacy, urgency, release, concern, and so
on. The senses of time imbued within these modes of perception on the
becoming-past of certain terms of life, configure in part the basis for
adaptation as subjects modify their practices, routines, and plans, making adjustments for survival as fit.

As these relational temporalities and their moods mediate perception, viewers are reminded that the consequences of the crisis today
are also material and corporeal, modifying everyday practices. In his
play on the genre of advertising, Juan Valbuena turns the camera lens
toward himself for an ironic announcement written in the third person,

which sells the photographer as both a service provider with experience in "viajes, álbumes familiares y proyectos colectivos" [travels, family albums, and group projects] and an appealing object of consumption with qualifications and references ("13 de septiembre, Madrid. Hombre anuncio"). His shirtless self-portrait mimics the *selfie* genre of self-snapshots circulating primarily on the web and social networks—often, as is the case here, taken of one's own reflection in the mirror—in which self-image is constructed for public consumption. Valbuena stresses this comparison humorously in a description of his youthful tastes (who still "prefiere el cola-cao al café" [prefers cola-coa to coffee], and rub-on decals to tattoos, pictured on his shoulder). Here, however, the construction of self is quite literally a product for sale. Valbuena's announcement for the artist-for-rent calls attention to the logic of market value in which the photographer's work to produce an album for a client is more profitable than the same photographer's artistic production, a point reiterated in a separate image in which he reports feeling "welcomed and well paid" as a wedding photographer ("3 de agosto, Bilbao. Bienvenido y bienpagao"). In this manner, and in the suggestive popular reference to prostitution in the term *bienpagao*, the personal details included in this announcement on the subject-for-rent underscore the objectifying character of the markets, or bodies and services trafficked as merchandise. So too does Valbuena's self-portrait augment marketability, with irony, to the extent that it brings to the fore self-objectification as valuable know-how in a competitive market. This point on the knowledge of selling oneself brings me to another image in comparison.

Eva Sala publishes a photograph and text of a house for sale in rural Asturias, which in its straightforward visual framing of the property and its descriptive language draws from the genre of advertisements to sell real estate. True to this model, the ad highlights the uniqueness and advantages of the property in a succinct economy of words: "Vistas al mar. Cocina de carbón. Taller de trabajo' [Views of the sea. Coal stove. Workshop], including an orchard ("22 de julio, Godina"). Sala twists this genre, however, by personalizing information otherwise excluded from an advertisement, on the current homeowners (her aunt Ana Mari, uncle Manolo, and their dog Ringo) and her positive experience picking plums from the orchard. If Sala's photograph seems misplaced within this project, I believe it is because it reminds viewers of the unclear distinction between the prescribed role of the artist as author of artistic production and, in contrast, the photograph's mimicry of an advertising genre in which the traces of artistic authorship are largely erased.

In this sense, Valbuena and Sala's advertisements, respectively, shuttle between the signature of the photographer as artist and the use-value of photography on the market, to sell and make a living from production. Whereas Valbuena's announcement moves toward self-objectification for marketable value, Sala's advertisement takes the object for sale and personalizes its competitive features by appealing to experiences and feelings associated with it. Both images highlight, in other words, the entrepreneurial know-how of marketability, whether "selling oneself" as an object or service-provider, or of positioning an object or service for sale in market competition.

Viewed in this manner, these lines of exploration contribute to questioning the inflection of capitalist market dynamics in social experience and artistic creation. Economic self-sufficiency in these works is exhibited through the knowledge and practice of marketability—or, the positioning of objects and selves to be desired in competition. In them, the uniqueness, qualifying features, and use-value of the house and photographer operate to produce desire through a double movement that personalizes the object and objectifies the person as competitive capital in each. Viewers may witness, in other words, the operative mechanisms of a market that conjugates the images in the construction and critique of desire in market competition. According to this logic in the photographs, the more self-objectified the subject or stripped down to qualifications, the more desirable he is; the more personalized the property in its appeal to experiences and feelings, as well. Nevertheless, as the images exhibit the knowledge and practice of economic survival, viewers are reminded that this is not merely a matter of representation but bears material implications. For, both photographs and their captions exhibit the molding of entrepreneurial subjects in the image of neoliberalism's fully autonomous *homo oeconomicus* in order to survive in market competition (Foucault, 2008, 144). Enacted and critiqued in these photographs are specific practices of self-sufficiency that require an entrepreneurial knowledge on how to position an object or subject to be desirable for their competitive capital (marketing). That is, they draw from ideal practices shaped in the likeness of a fully autonomous economic actor, the presumed subject in neoliberal economic policies that require self-sufficiency and entrepreneurial flexibility to meet the exigencies of market demands. It is a form of self-sufficiency in neoliberal thought, I will add, following Foucault, in which the autonomy of one's work in a precarious market shares its place within the presumed economic autonomy and self-care of all citizens through private investments, which are their own responsibility; it is the baseline presumption that serves as one justification to dismantle the welfare state in labor laws that favor "flexibility" (precarity) and in cutbacks to public education, healthcare, pensions, and social programs, among others. Practices and knowledge of market competition and desire in this case, which Berlant would call adjustments made for survival in the impasse, form an inextricable part of the shaping of enterprising practices in the likeness of those envisioned by neoliberal theory's ideal subject of (social and economic) governance. The exigencies of the market demand to be met, in these photographs, is one in which the plain use of photography to sell real estate and family albums eclipses the value of artistic practice for the latter's slim prospects to scrape together an income.

The financial economy, however, encompasses a terrain of economic activity beyond the material exchange of services and goods alone. One of its properties of projection, or speculation, depends on economic forecasts about the future of investment and possibilities for development on a macro scale. Big business and its decisive power to stall or foster development is portrayed in Paco Gómez's stunning photograph of a young woman, eyes closed peacefully, lying down on train tracks (figure 3.3).

In a corporate decision made based on profits and losses, which "desarrollan zonas y hunden en la miseria a otras" [develop some areas and sink others into misery], the caption explains, the train to Lisbon

Figure 3.3 Paco Gómez, "24 de agosto, Arroyo-Malpartida. Cáceres. Vía muerta".
Photo: © Paco Gómez / NOPHOTO.

will no longer pass through this Extremaduran village, which will certify its extinction to become a ghost town ("24 de agosto, Arroyo-Malpartida. Cáceres. Vía muerta"). The ambiguously calm expression of the photographed woman plays upon the viewer's expectations for risk in which life and death are at stake—the great perceived risk of her position despite her relaxed state, and her tranquil, pale look that suggests no risk, as the train will no longer pass through these rails. High risk, in economic and political decisions on development, has determined that it proves unprofitable to invest further in the town's connectivity to the Iberian Peninsula's two capital cities. In this manner, the viewer's speculation about the girl's serene expression and the sensible risk that her position conveys—as either a portrait of the dead or a death to come—is embedded within a greater history of waning ways of life for the town's residents due to macro scale political and economic decisions. It provides an image of a certified death between two times, within a temporal parenthesis whose outcome is already speculatively known to viewers at present. In doing so, the photograph relays between the subject and the collective experience of the crisis as loss, from the photographed woman to whole ways of life for the town's residents. In this story of modernity and development, and their micro scale consequences, corporate and political decision making is called into question for values driven by profits, investments, and risk, as a collective present on the verge of extinction for this small town.

Folded within the photographs' ways of looking at the present crisis are the complex imbrications among the media, the markets, and the state, which prove essential to understanding their address to viewers. They tell the story of an impasse constructed in *El último verano* as a state of living in-between the expectation of greater downward mobility, precarious work and life, and increased flexibility of labor. Their terms, in other words, are not expressed uniquely in subprime mortgages or the Euribor rate, but in the loss of one's house and the most intimate details of the struggle for survival. They are conveyed to viewers as the circumstance of a shared experience that separates loved ones and conditions one's possibilities to find fulfilling work, that places material limits on one's desires and shapes ideal economic actors with savoir faire to adapt to market conditions. In method, then, the photographs assemble ways of looking at an estranged and estranging present mediated through the subjective responses and reported calculations on the experience of the crisis, which inverts the economic exteriority of market abstractions to reveal their direct relationship to shaping the sensible times through which subjects move. In this light, *El último verano* shuttles between reported financial indicators and subjective indices of the crisis (its register of experience, emotion, affect) as, together, they mediate perception across the photographs in a present somehow taking shape with great change. After all, taken quite literally, no specialized knowledge of economic indicators, the Ibex 35 stock index, or other indices used to report, analyze, and make speculations about economic cycles, are required to read the news and understand, as in Valbuena's photograph, that the abstract calculus of the markets may equate to "another Dark Friday" or personal and collective losses.

Juan Millás captures this relation between the individual and the collective circumstance of the crisis precisely by calling attention to the scission between news of the markets and lived experience. Millás posts a graph of price fluctuations in basic goods such as meat and grain, taken directly from the daily press. The caption reflects on the concept of landscape, which Millás remarks, was historically a juridical and economic concept of the commons before it was an aesthetic object of contemplation. This is why, Millás proposes, his choice of image does not provide any distinguishable icon as an aesthetic image of landscape, but nevertheless as a topographic landscape of sorts, it signifies the estranging, shared "horizonte de lo que tenemos por delante" [horizon of what lies before us] ("13 de agosto, Muros de Nalón, Asturias. Esto sí es un paisaje"). Millás interprets the measurable landscape of graphs and numbers, literally and figuratively, as an index for shared lived experience, or a common horizon for the future. He proposes that the graph's foreignness bears its likeness to the familiar as an abstract indicator of the shared effects of the crisis, one that despite its opacity and power to disturb ought to be confronted as a collective history.

Across the project, the photographs echo and speak to—indeed index—each other collectively. For example, if not Nave's comment on his gallery closing, then viewers find several other critical responses to unemployment, such as in Juan Millás' critique of the symbolic violence inherent in the need to abandon one's profession, reinvent oneself, or have a backup plan in times of crisis, which he critiques sarcastically by proposing to profit from patriotism by selling giant Spanish flags ("26 de julio, Santander. Plan B"). Regarding the arts and culture industry, if not Valbuena's comment on film revenues, then in Juan Santos' interior photograph of an abandoned theater he remembers fondly from his childhood ("25 de agosto, Casillas de Coria, Cáceres. Fue en ese cine, ¿te acuerdas?"). And on displacements, if not in Nave's portrait of his brother's departure, then in Jorquera's shot of sailors wading in the sea as an imagined limit to the growing phenomenon of emigration, paraphrased in the caption's allusion to the urgent cry "man overboard," and so on ("16 de julio, Fuengirola. Nos echaremos al mar"). That repetitions across images evoke other entries in the project, in my view, invites viewers to perceive the photographs' radical openness to stand in for other intimate stories. In other words, the photographs' figurative, discontinuous character would have viewers interpret them with contradiction for their mediation of frustrated disappointment, unsettling anxiety, escapist joy, sad appreciation, empathetic care, ironic exacerbation, and so on. Speaking at many times and in many voices, *El último verano* calls attention to the work that this assemblage of photographs accomplishes as a cultural device that translates quantifiable, market data into the composite terms of subjective experience in crisis; and it does so through modes of perceiving loss that piece together individual histories within a shared circumstance. This mediated movement from the measurable to the immeasurable, from the macro to the micro and vice versa, shares its place within the figurative capacity of each image to evoke other entries in the project—across *El último verano* between the part (image) and the whole (project), and beyond it, between individual and collective experience, among photographers and viewers. To draw from Millás's proposal, it is through their ability to evoke other visual and textual narratives of affective attachments to loss—in sum, to index other intimate stories for viewers—that the many parts of this project assemble a greater social history, as both those pictured in these photographs and those presumably *unpictured* here. Much like Bel's spliced image of "for sale" signs seen in Madrid (figure 3.2), Nophoto's project invites viewers to read across the assembled images—in their repetitions, disjunctions, contradictions—and to perceive the present *crisis* legibly as a composite, shared circumstance.

Viewed through Berlant's notion of the impasse, these photographs provide a compelling demonstration, in my view, that adaptation in an ongoing crisis bears no specific formula but consists in surveying the present, in assessing one's affective attachments to ways of life, and whether consciously or not, in making adjustments for economic survival. In them, *la crisis* is made perceptible in the register of affective attachments to losses and likewise in developed strategies to endure ongoing uncertainty. Taking stock of the present at an impasse, in these photographs, seems to be immersed in a strong sense of temporality in which change and loss destabilize the present, evoking senses of return, nostalgia, future projection, escapist fantasy, anxieties about projected risk, and so on. And in the photographs, this composite character indexes for viewers other ways of looking in times of crisis, from plural perspectives, that assemble a collective, shared circumstance of everyday life in times of austerity. Viewers are invited to perceive an unsettling present reconfigured by macro processes developing *elsewhere*, in government and the markets, but which condition responses located *here* in the temporal experience and perception of subjects, presented in text and image.

Amid the reshaping of life at an impasse, can one speak of agency to enact change despite all else, whether manifested with moments of pessimism, disillusion, escape, vulnerability, or otherwise? Of course so, but agency in the possibilities for action will not be located in the measure of reconfiguring one's relationship to the world and others only in the outcomes of structural political (regime) change alone. To presume that this is the case, it seems, would still operate within the logic of productivity, one that seeks the only valued measure for change in the production of an outcome instead of its very process. Rather, the activity of taking stock of the present at an impasse articulates micro changes that are not essentially apolitical or lacking in solidarity. Nor, on the other hand, do these maneuvers inevitably promise political action and solidarity per se. But the activity of assessing the conditions of life at an impasse—a critical activity performed together, for the photographers, while apart from one another during the summer of 2012—entails a process of sense-making akin to the work of interpretation, of assembling individual experiences in the photo project, and within this assembly-work, in articulating a collective circumstance that relays between the photographers' and others' experiences. As a cultural device that brings together multiple affective registers on loss, the project invites viewers to see how the images, photographers, and perhaps they themselves are implicated in each other's *crisis*. In this sense, to return to my original question, the photographs demonstrate in my view that cramped within the micro experience of the everyday, much (historic) change is happening when it seems that not much is happening at all. Yet, over time, "a process will eventually appear monumentally as form—as episode, event, or epoch"—writes Lauren Berlant, but "[h]ow that happens, though, will be determined processually, by what people do to reshape themselves and it while living in the stretched out 'now' that is at once intimate and estranged" (2008, 5). In an amorphous present sensibly shaped by historic crises, these possibilities for action may be conditioned, but not wholly determined, lest viewers consign agency for action to the impotence of an outcome already prescribed, on the one hand, or to the measure of change that favors the result over the process, on the other. Moving from the *capture* of everyday life in crisis to the possible *production* of such attachments in viewers, the photographs in Nophoto's project remain open in their plural, unshaped connections across each other for viewers to interpret (their figurative, indexical character) in which process is favored over any perceptible outcome. This is, in my view, how the photographs prove capable of working on contemporary viewers, or the work that they can accomplish as a cultural device.

In a final chosen photograph, viewers find a critical response to the rise in violent police intervention in civilian demonstrations. In his reflection on political agency within a politics reserved for the state, Carlos Luján photographs the televised image of the anti-riot police, which serves as the colorful focus of an otherwise shaded living room ("14 de julio, Algorta. En sábado"). The photograph offers a clear denouncement of the police state in its dispatch of force against protesters. But as the television brings public matters into the private home, the image also provides a suggestive Foucauldian turn on the molding of subjects in civil society through disciplinary correction, or the development of modalities of self-policing in private life. In this sense, viewers return to the tranquil comforts of the living room and television pictured here, and to the question of representative democracy today as a mediated spectacle of political and economic interests. The photograph taken from home gives the dual image of televised footage from the street, the locus in which political assembly and action overturn the prescribed role of the "represented" as passive spectators to democracy (Hardt and Negri, 2012, n.p.). In Luján's caption, the crux of this political struggle is mediated in affective terms, in police brutality that aims to produce apathy and impotence (or, stasis) among protesters, that is, to return them to a depoliticized role as passive spectators of a televised democracy.

If the variety of these images provides an incursion into the precarious experience of crisis as a shared, composite time at an impasse, the question of this parenthetical temporality exhibits not only the lived moment as a sensibly estranged and estranging moment of uncertainty, as a time on standby in summer, but also a collective space of address in which viewers and the photographers themselves are immersed in working through change and in enunciating perceptible losses with awareness for the shared horizon. If one gets the sense when viewing *El último verano*, as I have, that the present bears its own composite image of a tipping point, then one might also be prompted to question, is it about time? And if so, as the questions have yet to be formulated in the impasse, then time for what?

CHAPTER 4

House Rules

*"This apparatus," he said..., "is our previous Commandant's invention.
I also worked with him on the very first tests and took part in all the work
right up to its completion. However, the credit for the invention belongs to
him alone. Have you heard of our previous Commandant? No? Well, I'm not
claiming too much when I say that the organization of the entire penal colony
is his work. We, his friends, already knew at the time of his death that the
administration of the colony was so self-contained that even if his successor
had a thousand new plans in mind, he would not be able to alter anything of
the old plan, at least not for several years. And our prediction has held. The
New Commandant has had to recognize that. It's a shame that you didn't
know the previous Commandant!" "However" the Officer said, interrupting
himself, "I'm chattering, and his apparatus stands here in front of us."*
  —Franz Kafka, "In the Penal Colony"[1]

*It is my Government's mission to free Spain from the burden of that inheri-
tance... We do not have at our disposal any more law or less criteria than
what necessity imposes upon us. We are doing what we have no other option
to do, whether we like it or not.... I don't ask if I like it; I implement exceptional measures demanded by exceptional times.*
  —President Rajoy, parliamentary address, July 11, 2012[2]

Reading the (Il)Legible State of Exception

I.

In 2012, the Partido Popular's (PP) control of the executive and legislature, with an absolute majority in parliament, quickly became an
exercise of unilateral political power that justified "exceptional" laws
and practices from the emergency of the crisis. Urgent austerity measures and labor reforms were rushed through parliamentary approval

by decree-laws that had largely forgone debate on these proposals, not least public commentary about them before their adoption. In his first year in office, President Rajoy cancelled the Debate on the State of the Nation, which precluded answering publicly to the opposition and the population at large. So too did the PP's absolute majority repeatedly block the opposition's demands for officials to appear before parliament and thus provide explanations about the party's alleged illegal financing since its inception or, beyond the state, the mismanagement of banking and financial institutions as a whole (Gutiérrez-Rubí, 2012). In contrast to this executive-legislative silence, however, the general public was addressed in other ways.

Spanish residents heard a uniform partisan discourse in the media—a clear pedagogical program from local, regional, and national PP representatives—that discredited the Socialist (PSOE) party's tenure for having left an "herencia envenenada" [poisoned legacy] of allegedly empty coffers, "mentiras" [lies] and "facturas sin pagar" [unpaid bills].[3] Good government was rationalized using the household economy as an example, a comparison echoed by media analysts when explaining complex fiscal issues like sovereign debt. Though it merited criticism, the so-called Socialist inheritance was constructed in partisan and official state discourse, in continuation from the general election campaign, as the most tangible culprit for the crisis. On the other hand, the rhetoric on the disaster of the Socialist legacy and its fiscal irresponsibility laid the bases, in turn, for the PP's claims to resolve the crisis through roll-out neoliberal reforms. Unspoken in this language, however, were the roles of confluent economic and political interests that exacerbated Spain's crisis, despite the denouncement of these powers in investigative reports by the media and successive demonstrations in the streets. The Socialist inheritance had been crafted in partisan speech as both the culprit and the legitimated field of action for the cure, thus weaving the optical effect of a break with the Socialist program on austerity rather than an aggressive continuation of it in other forms. In this rhetorical accomplishment, the constructed duality of an inheritance as both the *reason* and *remedy* for action fostered the illusion of dialog between two speakers, a sort of ventriloquism that monopolized the arguments of the opposition, recast them in its own terms, and contested them from a similar position claiming dissimilarities.

A "metaphor," writes David Caron, "gives a system its coherence by concentrating it entirely within a single image. For example, society is a machine or a house or a body" whereby, "without a central, structural metaphor there is no system at all: the metaphor *performs* the system into existence" and is not simply an expression of it (my emphasis, 2001, 6). Likening state fiscal management to a household budget, this metaphor addressed to Spanish residents performed a dual function as it circulated in the media. On the one hand, it sketched out the terms of government as a form of "good housekeeping," certainly with paternalist implications at times, as much as it also performed the assertion of state authority, and its power exercised in measured silence and speech, in different ways. The metaphoric terms of the state-household serve as the conceptual framework for the moral lessons given on minding one's personal finances like those of the state—beware of depleted bank accounts and unpaid bills—and on public shaming for economic insolvency in the age of austerity. In other words, the metaphor partakes in performing an operative paradigm on the "house rules" by articulating proper (economic) choice, action, and behavior for the citizenry in general, as much as it reifies a power relationship in its dictation. Aside from the moral lecture at work in this rhetoric, the character of paternalist authority also dwells in the actions of government officials, and their selective silences, that side-step democratic procedure without a disposition to dialog thereby treating the state, to work within the metaphor, as a form of (home-) ownership whose authority need not answer to the represented. The popular Spanish idiom *como Pedro por su casa* (as though "one owns the place") comes to mind.

Now, some readers might view this discursive re-appropriation by government officials as cynical politics as usual, which is undoubtedly not unique to Spain. This much is certain. At a time when little credit is given to politicians' words, as Jon Beasley-Murray has noted, cynicism "leaves little room for a politics of either denunciation or revelation," on the one hand, while ideologues aim to combat apathy or estrangement by arousing popular belief in political programs, on the other (2011, 176). But this form of discursive re-appropriation and its metaphors should not be underestimated in my view, for it configures one part of the field from within which the illusion of popular sovereignty is both constructed and negated, at once, while government officials assert their authority in speech and silence—or, the choice to address certain issues publicly, on their own terms, and to ignore others altogether. Political discourse, despite and conversely due to its possibilities for deceit, comprises an operative field of social influence that can legitimize power relations and actions in the name of the People, the imagined sovereign subject of state rule. Speech acts likewise form an integral part of state pedagogy and media analysis, in which the predominant language and metaphors in public circulation bear the capacity of partitioning and redistributing the terms of a given debate, strategically, and of wielding power from the criteria of what deserves address and what merits silence. Yet, although certain speech acts may be founded in deceit, they are also instrumental to oppositional readings that interpret, deconstruct, and trope this language for the illusion of sovereignty asserted through them. As the act of dictation hinges upon literal address ("jot this down" or "take note"), one in which words are to be taken literally as the speaking authority delivers them, oppositional readings can mitigate power wherever authority negates room for interpretation; that is, oppositional readings point out that power is necessarily mediated in address, wherever authority asserts itself as literal, to be taken in dictation (Chambers, 1991, 186).

What is at stake in official discourse amid the crisis is more than just talk alone, but the particular positioning of an "exceptional" field of action through which technologies of government can be legitimated publicly in the name of the People. Perhaps nowhere more evidently is this configuration exposed, paradoxically, than in the state's selective abandonment of the People as the imagined sovereign subject of state rule, which overturns the constituent relation of democratic representation in the interests of the represented, claimed for the benefit of the common good. Such a premise is well known in authoritarian regimes that seek exceptional powers for rule in which mandates are dictated to the population, on their very behalf. Articulated in Rajoy's parliamentary address after his meeting with leaders in the European Union, Spain had "no choice" but to pursue neoliberal reforms "that no one likes" in an absolute violation of the PP's electoral program that brought it to power. Whether one reads these claims as disingenuous, perhaps as cynical or literal in their dictation, Rajoy's speech designates a limited terrain of possibilities from which the party (state) can govern, subjugated at once to more powerful forces, past and present: the fiscal inheritance of its partisan opposition (its straw-man) and the European Union as an economic project, respectively. In both cases, the subordination of the state to the markets and fiscal management blows the cover, so to speak, on the illusion of sovereign power as the representation of popular interests imagined in liberal democracy. That the violation of this constituent relation between representatives and the represented should serve as a legitimating terrain of action for the state, however, configures both the conditions and possibilities of sovereign rule as an articulated state of exception. To paraphrase Rajoy's parliamentary address in the epigraph above, the state governs with exceptional measures at exceptional times, which shall go unquestioned for their necessity, whether the represented care for them or not.

In his classic formulation, Carl Schmitt defined the sovereign as he who decides the rule of law and its exception; thus, sovereign decision-ism is constituted from the powerful choice to grant selective impunity and to determine when the law is applied, to whom, and under what circumstances (2005, 5–15). Therefore, the sovereign decides the rule of law and the exception, and particularly, within its auspices of action, the impunity of sovereign power and its protected interests from the rule. Sharing its place within Schmitt's formulation, sovereign decision-ism is a terrain of possible choice and action reserved for a political class by profession and its (capital) interests whereby the political formation, in practice, has become increasingly synonymous with a state that governs alone by fiscal policy and by bolstering its own protections for and from the rule. As professor of constitutional law Javier Pérez Royo argues, the PP had forged its own terms for a state of exception through unilateral mandate within the first few months of its rule, made possible by the PP's absolute majority, despite the social clamor of protest and minority opposition in parliament ("Estado de excepción parlamentario," 2012; "Estado de excepción," 2012). This is not to say that the 1978 Constitution has been suspended de facto, which is precisely what would make the current technologies of government *legible as an exception* by definition. Rather, as Pérez Royo observes, there exists a breach of the constituent relation for a government that acts in the name of the represented without authorization. It is a circumstance that Pérez Royo observes in other European states subject to financial rescue (specifically, Greece, Italy, Portugal) where the return of technocrats to public office serves largely to sustain the European economic project and common currency by subordinating domestic social policies to the priorities of fiscal management. Departing from Pérez Royo's observation, it should not go ignored that the PSOE had similarly violated this constituent relation between representatives and the represented by rushing through the ratification of the constitutional Art. 135 without a popular referendum, which prohibits the Spanish State from incurring a deficit greater than the margin established by the European Union.

On the other hand, this exception has not manifested itself as an outright suspension of democratic procedure or the Constitution itself, nor does it imply the executive administration of justice that sovereign decisionism requires by Schmitt's formulation, even as indications of exceptional rule, scattered and dispersed throughout and beyond the state apparatuses, strongly recall those of undemocratic regimes.

The protections of confluent political and economic interests are, amid the crisis, the greatest operative terrain of impunities offered by this exceptional circumstance, despite popular and minority partisan opposition to them. They are made evident in the legal and judicial limitations that prohibit, or stall, the trial or conviction of political and economic corruption cases as criminal offenses, or for siphoned public funds to be returned to state coffers. They are perceptible in state fiscal policies that vigorously pursue revenue from the population at large while leaving fiscal fraud by the greatest fortunes largely untouched. They are made visible in the circles of elite wealth and influence that benefit from the crisis economically, as the largest fortunes in Spain amass greater capital, and the protections provided from the so-called revolving door of corporate advisory boards and the politicians who serve on them, and so on. In this regard, selective impunity and exemption are woven from juridical limitations, private interests, and the government policies that protect the latter, but not exclusively from the sovereign decision of pardon, self-impunity, and the selective application of the law. Distinctive state protections on the flows and capture of capital, it seems, may have transformed the terms of the exception, in which sovereign decisionism, or the choice powers of (self-)impunity, have been supplanted largely by the state administration of sovereign debt and its selective powers of (self-)exemption.

Aside from these matters in structural (juridical) limitations, fiscal policy, and corporate spheres of social influence, there also exist specific practices among state powers that make this exception readable as a crisis of popular sovereignty. The perceptible forms of exceptionalism are evident in the stronghold of partisan power that relinquishes possibilities for open dialog, partisan opposition, or transparency of information, essential to democratic procedure, in favor of unilateral decisions that protect an establishment increasingly unable to justify its practices or the evidence of corruption allegations against it. The partisan capture of the public media has become another important indication of this exception, as are the new bureaucratic and legal restrictions on the rights to demonstrate and assemble in public space. The opacity of information through process, it seems, whether originating in the sovereign seat of government, in the controls on the public and private media, or in the population's access to the public itself (public space, public information, public social services, and so on) has augmented specific controls and stops that bear exemptions on the procedures and practices of democracy. Met with violence from the policing apparatus against protesters and evicted homeowners, these modalities of enforcement and restriction bear a form of state authoritarianism. And yet, despite these perceptibly undemocratic practices across branches of the state apparatuses, none of them correspond specifically to the question of selective impunity granted by sovereign decision that defines the exception in Schmitt's historic formulation, which deserves further attention here.

The practices of democracy in the Spanish State—those enacted from the transparency of information, accountability for actions, and public dialog and debate; and those engendered by operative structural mechanisms, such as the separation of powers and the autonomy of the public media—had forged the exceptionalism of unilateral mandate within the existing framework of the 1978 Constitution. That democratic mechanisms in their institutional structure or practice should fail to prevent this exception, suggests, as Cristina Moreiras-Menor has noted, that their conditions of possibility have always already been present—in *practices*—since the consolidation of the democratic state. For Moreiras-Menor, the historicist point of view that upholds the *Transición* to democracy as a model for progress, "no ha sido capaz de tomar en cuenta los fascismos subyacentes (neo-fascismos) que todavía forman parte de nuestra vida cotidiana en el mundo contemporáneo" [hasn't been able to take into account the underlying fascisms (neo-fascisms) that still form part of our everyday life in the contemporary world] (2011, 124), an observation likewise nuanced in scholarship by Eloy E. Merino and H. Rosi Song and their contributors as "traces" of the dictatorial past persisting in the present (2005). Even so, argues Moreiras-Menor, the present-time may only bear witness to this inheritance in partially scattered and dispersed, (il-)legible forms.[4] The exceptionalism of state sovereignty in representative democracy, in other words, appears not as the *exception* per se, but as the rule.

I perceive this issue of the *(il-)legibility* of the inheritance to be at the core of questioning the present's relationship to (and memory of) the experience of the twentieth century, in which authoritarian forms and practices of government—never the same as in the past, but transformed into something new—reside in the very conditions of possibility that have materialized the exceptions of state sovereignty, with or without popular consent, as *partisan property* (at once, the presumption of ownership in property, a politics "proper" to corporatism and clientelism, and the private interests implied in them). In this sense, the metaphor of the state-household materializes as more than just language alone, but as a set of practices that shape the terms of authoritarian governmentality, one in which "father (still) knows best." How have the practices of democracy within a given state, whether Spain or another, not developed regulatory mechanisms, so to speak, that dually detect and prevent the exercise of power from acquiring authoritarian forms? The illegibility of these practices as an *exception*—despite official state discourse that articulates its policies and their circumstance *as* exceptional—requires the present to make sense of their fragmentary character in ways that sovereign decisionism cannot fully account for in the current conjuncture, at least not by the terms of the twentieth-century experience with totalitarian regimes. For technologies of government, access to information, and mechanisms of police repression today tend to recall a time in which official politics was not only a matter reserved exclusively for the state, as a separate sphere of activity removed from, and governing in the name of, the People. But also, at my time of writing, official state politics has retreated into a domain of activity that is increasingly abstruse and sheltered within the powerful protections it establishes for itself, in part, through the strategic exemptions of the political profession and capital interests. Paradoxically, however, this circumstance implies a crisis for the state, for the greater its retreat from democratic forms and procedures, the greater difficulties it faces in legitimating its field of possible action as democratic. Selective impunity, in other words, proves a delicate balance for the powerful, at once consolidating relations of power while undermining their legitimacy, thereby opening up greater room for maneuver in opposition to them, even within the state. As Foucault reminds his readers throughout his work, no relation of power is ever absolute or total: "Where there is power, there is resistance, and yet, or rather consequently, this resistance is never in a position of exteriority to power" (1978, 95). The question I propose, then, is one of *readability*, the pretext to engage power relations with oppositionality. State technologies of government and policing may bear authoritarian forms, but they are not exclusively the result of a direct, top-down adjudication on the rule of law and its spaces of amnesty, as in the sovereign exception in Schmitt's definition. How, then, might one read the scattered (il-)legibility of this exception at present?

Writing amid the political, economic, and state crises of the 1970s, Nicos Poulantzas perceived the compounded crises of monopoly capitalism and state sovereignty as bearing the potential to produce forms and practices of authoritarian statism, particularly in the corporatization of government as a striking indication of "the constitution of a new form of capitalist state with characteristics appropriate to the 'authoritarian state' or 'strong state' that could signify simply that a certain form of 'democratic politics' has come to an end in capitalism" ("The Political Crisis" 320). In this sense, the crises of late capitalism are accentuated, and thus more legible, in the compounded character of an economic crisis that exposes a political crisis, against the crisis of the state in liberal democracy (a representative democracy of "the People"). For Poulantzas, this sort of self-reflexivity of multiple crises may bring to the fore the legitimating fields of action from which the state apparatuses must maneuver, some fractured by internal antagonisms and others concordant in apparent unison. Poulantzas understands the state as a plural, shifting ensemble of social and capital (power) relations in institutional arrangements in negotiation (executive, legislative, judiciary, state employees, the police and security apparatuses, bureaucracy and state agencies, and so forth); they constitute, as Manuel Castells attributes some of his work to Poulantzas's influence,[5] a dynamic network of power relations in constant flux. In this manner, for Poulantzas, the state bears the material forms of power alliances and antagonisms, subject to transformation, inscribed within its institutional structures (*Classes in Contemporary Capitalism*, 1975; *Poulantzas Reader*, 2008; *State, Power, Socialism*, 2000). His writings take into account the complexity of evolving antagonisms within and beyond the branches of the state in which opposition is always possible. Several examples from contemporary Spain come to mind: in the unprecedented mobilizations among state employees against austerity and privatization (the multicolored *mareas*, or Tides of protesters in public education, healthcare, justice, research and development, and so forth); in the dissenting positions within the national police corps on the use of violence against demonstrators and undocumented immigrants (Sindicato Unificado de Policía – SUP); or among employees in the Finance Ministry who rebuke executive mandate by proposing to pursue fiscal fraud from the greatest fortunes, and so on—all indications of opposition pursued by state personnel within it.

If one accepts Pérez Royo's assessment (indeed, also that of 15M protesters) that popular sovereignty has been captured exceptionally by the state's technocratic management of debt, fiscal policy, and flows of capital, then the priorities of the state, following Poulantzas, are perceptibly deterritorialized into micro-scenarios of exceptions and impunities no longer consolidated within a specific sovereign figure. It is not my intention here to address Poulantzas's methodology in structural Marxism or to position his conception of the state and capital in relation to the tradition of Marxist critique he draws from[6]; much in the spirit of his unorthodox approaches to state theory in his late work, one could read Poulantzas, as Bob Jessop[7] has, by taking Poulantzas's suggestion to depart from some of the operative critical concepts in his work (class struggle and agency in Gramscian hegemony[8]) and to privilege his turn to the micro-politics of the state as a social relation (2000, 146–53). In this light, I draw from Poulantzas's work for its ability to comprehend the current crises in which democratic practices are perceived to be at risk, while this risk, paradoxically, is not legible as an exception for state maneuvers that continue to operate permissibly within the structural limitations and procedures considered democratic. That is, the illegibility of exceptionalism in state rule guarantees, in part, its plausible survival.

II.

Specifically, Poulantzas conceives of the state as an institutional assemblage of operations and relations that, in Bob Jessop's development of his writings, practice *strategic selectivity* by rewarding allies to the ends and aims of its exercise of authority, and by placing selective stops on others that destabilize its powers or objectives—both within and beyond the state (private and public interests) (1999, 50–6). Thus, not unlike the corporation, internal antagonisms are observed in the powers that seek objectives pursued competitively by some state branches and that short-circuit others within a hierarchical, networked system of power relations (administrative silence and nondecision here also play an important role) (Poulantzas, 2008, 308–9). In practice, "Different organizations, structures, and systems have their own steering media (for example, law, money, coercion, incentives) which they can use to influence other organizations, structures, and systems" toward strategic ends (Jessop, 1990, 360). Despite their contradictions, state operations may accomplish their aims without a global project and may give the appearance of a scattered micro-politics in different contexts, but across their apparent chaos emerges a pattern of governmentality and policy that structures certain actors and their privileges (even impunities) over others.

Whereas the exceptionalism of sovereign power, according to Schmitt's formulation, relies on the exercise of decision to grant impunity and the sovereign's self-exemption from the rule, Poulantzas's suggestion of *strategic selectivity* in the exercise of state powers may provide a more accurate approach in the current circumstance to how exceptions are crafted selectively as impunities and exemptions, a micropolitics in which the adjudication of the law by a sovereign figure is no longer exclusively at hand. Poulantzas's work goes to great lengths to map the state as a shifting field of social relations in which the terms "power" and the "state" itself, for example, always stand in for the relations that produce them. To revisit Poulantzas's writings amid the crises of the 1970s might provide a possible framework, then, to read—or, to make *legible*—the state powers of exemption, the maneuvers to legitimize sovereign rule, and the contradictory practices of strategic selectivity specific to advanced capitalism, distributed and scattered across the operative fields of action for a state managing the "crisis of the crisis management" or the "crisis of the management of the crisis" (Poulantzas, 2008, 320).

In "The Political Crisis and the Crisis of the State" Poulantzas outlines some patterns emerging across these micro-politics, which are "authoritarian" in their effect, akin to those of a "strong state" (2008, 294–322). They include the selective access and controls of public information and services provided to different publics (legally inscribed social and economic exclusions, opacity and bureaucratization, and the state control and corporate influence of the media); the selective application of the law via channels that do not correspond uniquely to the justice system (budgetary policy and finance, policing and surveillance); and the political and economic alliances within and beyond the state that establish exemptions for privileged actors (the guarantee of corporate and financial support for state policies and aims, negotiated corporate privileges as provisions against the application of labor laws, and so forth), among others. These micro-politics operate within the structural limits—in some cases, indeed test the limits—of what are legally and constitutionally permissible actions in democratic regimes. Authoritarian statism is, then, the democratic appearance of politics "as usual," perhaps more than ever a form of corporatism practiced within the state apparatuses and beyond it, in concert with other institutional arrangements. Thus, authoritarian statism is consolidated through operations that conserve and bolster economic-political power relations, which in the case of Spain have been pursued vigorously through a partisan capture of the state governed by capital interests and fiscal policy.

Within the state itself, the concentration of the executive powers at the expense of parliamentary sovereignty constitutes one of the characteristic features of what Poulantzas observed as the new form of authoritarian statism (2008, 321). In Spain, such a concentration of powers is evident in the executive's public announcement of legislative proposals to become law before their rubber-stamp approval by parliament, or in the Constitutional Court's defense of its head magistrate's militancy in and monetary donations to the ruling party (Fabra, 2013). Therefore, the "organic confusion" of executive, legislative, and judicial actions and competencies exposes the already prevalent confluence of interests among them (Poulantzas, 2008, 321). These overlapping competencies likewise extend to financial and economic interests that inform, if not steer, strategic state policy making and law. Take, for example, the express-law approved by the PP-controlled legislature that effectively revoked the Spanish judiciary's competencies for universal jurisdiction, a measure aimed at coercing judges to shelve their ongoing investigations into international war crimes, originating in pressures from investors abroad.[9] The case reveals a clear overlapping of executive and legislative powers, working in concert to limit the competencies of the justice system in international law from financial interests. In domestic affairs, the fiscal and legal protections provided to corporations could also be construed to fall into this category. In government, Poulantzas notes, state powers see the return of (economic) technocrats in the bureaucratization and administration against the decline of political parties as channels for popular sovereignty ("The Political Crisis" 321), as Pérez Royo observes in European states subject to financial rescue amid the global crisis.

By 2012, the public media in Spain were also subject to partisan controls. At that time, new executives of Spanish public television and radio (RTVE) were appointed, several of them with clear political ties to, or membership in, the ruling party. Immediately, RTVE executives purged choice journalists, editors, and directors of its news programs—*Asuntos propios, Los desayunos de TVE, En días como hoy, Informe semanal, La Noche en 24 horas,* and *Telediario matinal,* to name a few[10]—who had practiced journalism under the protections provided by the 2006 Press Law that guaranteed the neutrality and independence of the public media from partisan interests. Given that RTVE was subject to censorship under the Franco Regime, the national public media would continue to operate in democracy, until recent memory, with considerable bias toward the ruling party in power (G. Montano, 2006; Hooper, 2006, 362–76). That the state should undertake the purging of journalists and directors who tended to criticize austerity measures, suggested that the partisan tutelage of the public media had returned to the discretionary practices of self-censorship and the manipulation of information in journalism, which the Council of Europe denounced in its public report (Rodríguez, 2013). In Madrid and Valencia, regional governments would pursue actions to close the public television networks TeleMadrid and Canal 9, respectively, where journalists claimed that their news content was, at times, delivered to them (Gil, 2013).

These actions have been a motivating factor for mobilizations among employees in these sectors and regions. On the street, too, these measures threatened the autonomy of the press. Such is the case in the arrest of the journalist Ana García from LaSexta national television network who was detained for filming a protest against a forced eviction. Her camera and footage were confiscated by the police and García received five charges of trespassing, disobedience, undermining authority, and causing property damage and physical harm. The incident stirred alarm among professional journalists, enough for the Federation of Associations for Journalists in Spain (FAPE) and the Press Association of Seville (APS) to declare that "se ha vulnerado de una manera inaceptable y peligrosa el libre ejercicio de la profesión periodística y el derecho de la ciudadanía a recibir una información veraz" [the free exercise of the profession of journalism and the rights of citizens to receive truthful information have been violated in an unacceptable, dangerous manner] ("Asociaciones," 2012).

Tightened controls of information designate what Poulantzas observed as the dislocation of concentrated centers of state power in its apparatuses into networked structures indirectly influenced by the executive (here, in the media), in which public access to information and secrecy are administered by controls or stops that selectively provide some flows of information while restricting others (2008, 322). The executive's staged "press conferences" that deny journalists a round of questions—at times, broadcast to reporters on a television fixed behind the podium where the president would otherwise stand in person—not only look surreal, even Orwellian, but they also provide an indication of the kind of micro-politics pervasive in the selectively strategic control of information that reaches the media and the general public in which elected officials aim to minimize human contact with the press and, with it, the possibility of being asked to provide information that breaches these controls.

Within these intersecting spheres of influence, following Poulantzas, the large-scale orchestration and development of organizational networks parallel to the state, in public, semi-public, and private endeavors, may unify and manage state power in line with its directives and those of private interests at large (Poulantzas, 2008, 322). At once connected to the interests of the state, yet removed from its institutional structure, think tanks hold a privileged position today in their production of research on strategic policy making. The "who's who" of corporate members in nonpartisan and partisan think tanks alike inform strategic planning among elite spheres of influence, at once within and beyond the state. As Spain's most influential think tank, for example, the Elcano Royal Institute membership includes high-ranking representation from former ministers and presidents, the public and private media giants, and Spain's largest corporations in energy, telecommunications, transportation, banking, retail, and so on. That the Spanish State should charge Elcano Royal Institute with the task of researching *the positive international perceptions* of "the trademark Spain" ("la marca España") amid the crisis, provides a double indication of both the confluent corporate and political interests inside/outside state operations among these sectors, and the capitalist paradigm of strategic policy making within the state that aims to market "Spain" as a *brand* for foreign investment. Perhaps the greatest danger of think tanks, however, is their paid production of knowledge, which tends to follow the given editorial (ideological) line of the institution. This argument is made by the economist Gonzalo Bernardos, who in his critique on the glaring lack of diverse assessments on Spain's crisis among economists, notes that there exists little autonomy among professionals hired to act as independent advisors, for "we [economists] are the voice of our masters" in which one's own salary and future employment are often perceived to be at stake.[11] Consensuses may be forged, following Bernardos's claim, from institutional arrangements that hire supporting evidence for their own policy agendas.

Other signs of exceptionalism are furthermore legible elsewhere, scattered and dispersed throughout state administration and its apparatuses, which directly infringe on democratic rights and practices in Spain, thereby giving the appearance of an authoritarian statism to which Poulantzas refers. Among them, the penal state and policing state are enhanced in laws that justify the use of police force and the restrictions to assemble in public space. The Ley de Seguridad Ciudadana [Law of Citizens' Security], popularly called *La Ley mordaza* or "The Gag Law," strengthens the competencies of the policing apparatus by restricting citizens' rights to demonstrate and assemble without state authorization; by criminalizing practices of protest and passive resistance through immediate sanctions without a judicial hearing; by extending the rights of the police to potentially arbitrary search, seizure, and arrest for "security purposes"; and by writing into law the justification for video camera surveillance of public space, on the one hand, and the prohibition of any form of photography or video recording of on-duty security forces, on the other (Gobierno de España, Ministerio del Interior, "Anteproyecto," n.d.). Police repression, surveillance, and limitations on public demonstration and assembly strongly recall the years of Francoism and its *grises* (Armed Police corps), as these measures, then and now, are forged from the presumption that the whole of society is "dangerous," "guilt passing from accomplished act to mere intent, [and] repression extending from punishment to policies of prevention" or monitoring that erode democratic rights (Poulantzas, 2008, 322). In tandem, material restrictions to access are enforced around one's private capital, due to Spain's adoption of court fees for all individuals who pursue legal recourse on matters ranging from civil cases and contentions against state administration, to consumer claims, labor issues, and protest fines. Access to the justice system, then, is shaped by one's ability to pay the costs of pursuing legal recourse.

In the case of forced evictions, security forces are dispatched on judicial orders to pursue an eviction, solicited by the bank for a homeowner in default on mortgage payment. That the policing apparatus should be dispatched toward this end provides a clear use of state violence to protect banking institutions and monopoly capital. On the other hand, the legislature and executive have worked in concert to block civilian initiatives on forbearance, spearheaded by Plataforma de Afectados por la Hipoteca (Platform for People Affected by Mortgages – PAH), that aim to modify the law with a substantial impact for those at risk of eviction. Continued police force, met with the legislature's unresponsiveness to proposed initiatives from experts, provides an indication of the administrative controls and stops placed on established channels for direct participation in representative democracy.

Before adjourning for summer vacation in 2012, Rajoy's administration announced the sharpest measures of its austerity program at that time, which equated to the greatest cutbacks to public spending in Spain's democratic history, approved unilaterally by the ruling party. The select ledgers targeted for these austerity measures rolled back social protections for women, undocumented immigrants, the disabled, the disadvantaged, and so on, and annulled the Law for Historical Memory de facto, which the party had opposed in prior legislatures, by depleting it of state funding. There exist, in other words, clear methods of selective enforcement and simulated repeal of the law that bypass conventional legislation alone; budgetary policy can be used to annul a given law by administering no funds to enforce it. Among these measures, labor law reforms that minimized employees' rights before an employer (enabling employers to draw up successive part-time and temporary contracts, to reduce severance pay, to legalize firing practices based on projected corporate losses), inaugurated new permissible contractual terms that favored labor precarity, and with it, corporate profits across labor sectors. On the one hand, whereas the law does not discriminate between sectors or labor segments, largely affecting workers across them in favor of capital interests—and indeed may serve as one point of transversal solidarity for workers mobilizing across these sectors—certain "corporate cultures" continue to provide severance bonuses, securities, and other negotiated benefits for managers and high-ranking executives who remain largely unaffected by the law's application. Thus, generally, the labor law comes to bear evenly upon vast segments of the working population, but it also provides negotiable contractual terms with an employer for an elite class of managers and executives. The former case provides an example of how the state may enforce legislation selectively and strategically through budgetary policy alone, whereas the latter illustrates how corporate contractual practices may provide privileged protections from the law itself.

These measures and their rapid introduction into state policy and law constitute what Poulantzas refers to as the structuring of an emergent relation between the public and private that places individual controls on vast segments of the population (2008, 321). Stated otherwise, they constitute the exercise of strategic selectivity—to uphold some laws and social protections, while divesting others in practice or policy—according to the criteria of political (partisan, capital) interests. Their selectivity resides in the possibilities of advancing certain aims by maneuvering structural state limitations (such as the separation of executive, legislative, and judicial powers) on the one hand, and of restricting access to state provisions for certain segments of the population, on the other. Thus, state powers bear new forms of acting upon individuals through restrictions to access, controls, and the rolling-back of social protections and rights, which may provide a characteristic incoherence or illegibility of reactive state "micro-politics" without a greater project other than that of curtailing welfare services while incrementing "security." In sum, these micro-politics, Poulantzas observes, are "the current forms of 'reform-repression' that mark the policies of Western capitalist states" in different ways (2008, 322).

Bureaucracy can contribute to shaping the selective and, at times, strategic controls and stops on the individual's access. The bureaucracy of specific branches of the state, such as immigration, exemplifies these limitations placed upon access, which operate from the opacity and contradiction of public information between the Police, the Ministry of Justice, and the Civil Registry, and the subjective criteria for immigrants to pass immigration filters (or, reported cases of discrimination). That state employees from the Civil Registry should denounce the executive's maneuver to bypass their competencies in favor of notaries, for private profits, indicates both the economic restrictions placed on equal access and the antagonisms between the state apparatuses as some branches' competencies are minimized and granted to other privileged organs (or, privatized) within and outside the state. So too are undocumented immigrants subject to new restrictions on their access to public healthcare unless paid out of pocket, the procedures for which are obfuscated in the division of competencies between healthcare professionals (who may or may not choose to honor the law), the regional government that administrates healthcare services, and the state mandate itself. Therefore, equal access to healthcare services is not guaranteed; such disparity can partake in embedding discriminatory practices within institutional structures in which a given state employee at any stage within this bureaucratic circuit operates as a "switch" to permit or deny individual access in specific contexts, based on a range of factors (economic ability to pay, ethnicity, language competence, socioeconomic status, and so on). Therein also resides the possibility, however, for networks of state employees to oppose laws and policies by granting access whereby it is otherwise restricted (say, in providing medical treatment to an undocumented immigrant who cannot pay out of pocket).

Gatekeepers who can allow, restrict, or fully deny access selectively may exercise a form of decisionism proper to the sovereign figure in a micro-politics of power relations in specific contexts. The contingent criteria to grant or disallow access discriminatively depend on the circumstance, of course. But in all cases, gatekeepers can be said to perform their function based on either a directive of power or the self-corrective modalities, for example, such as those developed in the professions against the threat of litigation. It is what Andreas Kalyvas has observed in Poulantzas's "authoritarian statism" as comprising, in part, an "authoritarian legalism" in the practices of documentation against the threat of litigation in corporate cultures at present (2002, 123). This form of self-regulation bears a disciplinary character in the Foucauldian sense, but not necessarily within a given disciplinary enclosure, implied in the term "gatekeeper." Rather, the exercise of the gatekeeper to grant or deny admittance, relates specifically to access along circuits, as one would flip a switch. Copyright laws serve as a tangible example that restrict and thus privilege access to information and cultural material, in which institutional or individual gatekeepers (say, a university library or a professor who assigns readings for her course) are expected to perform their roles in providing and restricting distribution according to institutional policy and law. Modalities are forged in the expectation that the individual will comply with her role as gatekeeper against the threat of sanctions or litigation.

On the other hand, the modalities of compliance with state objectives are forged through new instruments. Individuals who exercise the protected right to refuse copayment on pharmacy prescriptions in Madrid must sign a legal statement of noncompliance with tax liability and, at once, a voluntary release for personal information to be included in a database administered by the regional government. Actions such as these work on individuals in micro-political contexts as a form of state interpellation in different scenarios of everyday life. Althusser's classic example of interpellation as a form of policing, or the subject who turns around when hailed, acquires a depersonalized bureaucratic medium for self-correction in the legal release, through which the state, in its vague threat of surveillance and litigation, attempts to mold compliance with its restrictions on access against the standing laws (1971, 170). In this manner, the stops or controls on access to information forged in state policy and law—in parliament, the executive and ministries, and so forth—may bear an uncanny resemblance to the operative mechanisms of compliance with the restrictions to access among individuals who navigate the bureaucracy of state administrations (public healthcare services, social and legal protections, and so on). Specifically, the ways in which access are shaped constitute the institutional materiality of the state within an individual's practices, criteria for decisions, and modalities of compliance, which by the character of the exclusions they can uphold, are inherently a political matter.

When challenged publicly, the ruling party has tended to decry its mandate as justified by the popular will expressed in ballot boxes in the elections. There exists, in other words, no disputable horizon beyond the "will" of a party that recasts its political legitimacy, however undemocratic its practice or design, as the very "will of the People." Not even the social clamor that demands explanations and greater transparency has provoked institutional reflection on this wholesale partisan mandate; rather, the party's representatives, again across local, regional, and national levels, resort to citing its popular support from a "silent majority" (*la mayoría silenciosa*) of constituents—a term that, the journalist Gabriela Cañas notes, might seem to borrow from Nixon's response to protests against the Vietnam War, but in Spain, rather, harkens back to the late years of the Franco Regime (Cañas, 2012). The imagined sovereignty of the People whom the state represents is continuously reimagined, selectively and strategically to a given circumstance, in order to legitimize statutory actions and decisions in its name, at times even abandoning its premise altogether in the dictation of measures "without choice." Thus, discourse forms one part of the legible material of this exceptionalism exposed for its contradictions, even as the democratic procedures of the state are largely conserved and followed in practice, giving the appearance of politics "as usual." Yet, it is within the networked spheres of privileged political and private interests, and the impunities and protections provided to them, where the orchestration of selective flows of information and restrictions to the public, the circumvention of the law by selective enforcement and simulated repeal, and the aleatory micro-maneuvers of the state in its management of *las crisis*, expose new practices and forms of authoritarianism that become legible as a state of exception despite the illusory effect of democracy they provide.

Desiring Scenarios for Change in Zamora's Theater

I.

Drawn to this description in the playbill for Abel Zamora's *Temporada baja*, I am led to wonder about missed encounters occurring at a given time and place shared by contemporaries:

> Un hotel. Dotze persones en un procés forçat de canvi. Set contes de ciutat que s'entrecreuen en uns llargs passadissos plens de portes. Cada porta una historia. (Zamora, 2013, n.p.)
> [One hotel. Twelve characters in a forced process of change. Seven city stories crossing each other in long hallways filled with doors. Each door has a story.]

Conveyed in the verb *entrecreuar* in Valencian language is the crossing of paths, or an encounter of sorts—in this context, among dramatic characters in their exchanges—but not necessarily their entanglement in each other's stories. In a word choice consistent with the dramatic action in *Temporada baja*, each scene of encounter develops the possibility of having the characters' stories entwine into each other, before they turn awry, frustrated and unrealized. The play provides a dystopian portrait of isolation, of solitude spent in the company of others, and of only fleeting moments of connection among the characters, returned to atomization or departure. In this sense, here the missed encounter is not one of two parties that never meet, nor an untimely arrival as one would miss a train. Nor is it of contingency or failure that somehow proves productive, if by chance. Rather, their "missed" quality resides in perceiving how the exchanges are underpinned by desires for substantive change held in abeyance, which bear the kernel of unfulfilled possibilities for the characters.

Zamora's *Temporada baja* stages induced change for characters unable to implicate themselves reciprocally in each others' crises, conditioned in different ways by the predominant relational powers in which they participate. During their stay at this modern, urban hotel, the characters experience a shared isolation from each other, conveyed in the title's allusion to both a "low season" (for tourism) and gloomy times, for a space whose norms serve, in part, to regulate the exchanges among visitors. One of Zamora's signatures as a playwright is his extensive register of references to popular culture in Spanish television, celebrities, commercial brands, and pop songs from the 1960s to the present, which situate the audience's points of reference within a fiction shaped by its allusions to the contemporary. Of the real, it is likewise against the underlying social circumstance of the crisis in *Temporada baja*—unemployment, wage cuts, precarity, improvised measures to secure food and income, and so on—in which the dramatic action transpires in conspicuous differences between the struggling and privileged characters that in one way or another, share in their vulnerable condition. In a point I should like to bring out here, these missed encounters can perhaps nuance some of the limitations to forging connections addressed in chapter 3, when their failure to reshape the scenario at hand, at least for these characters, is in question. To do so, I pay particular attention to the ways in which these encounters are mediated between characters that more often than not, prove incapable of producing the changes they desire.

Zamora crafts specific worlds inside the rooms of his imagined hotel, each one distinct with its own theatrical, even cinematic, genre. Behind different doors, viewers find the comedy of a failed blind date, the conflictive drama of a couple in a damaging relationship, the thriller of a serial murderer who cannibalizes his victim, the family tragedy of an awaited death by suicide, a slapstick brawl between two girlfriend "frenemies," and a choreographed musical theater finale, among others. In this sense, the performance accomplishes a different kind of assemblage-work than the indexical character of Nophoto's project addressed earlier. Zamora develops a dynamic patchwork of scenarios and contrasting moods transpiring in separate rooms where each space (and scene) is made identifiable to the audience for its familiar borrowings from diverse genres in film and drama (romantic comedy, musical theater, thriller, suspense, tragedy, slapstick, and so on), pieced together in crisscrossing stories. Key to these scenes is the space of encounter produced in the characters' interactions. Each scenario transpires largely unbeknownst to the other hotel occupants compartmentalized into the private spaces of their own dramas unfolding in each room. If the distinct genre of the rooms tends toward accentuation, perhaps even exaggeration, for viewers it has the effect of reinforcing the compartmentalized character of each world, pigeon-holed into private, separate spaces of the hotel and, in turn, calls attention to the walls between these spaces and the characters among them. Keeping in mind that during the play's run at Teatre Rialto in Valencia, the two-story set had no walls to partition the adjacent rooms on stage, then the augmented dramatic genre of each scene tends to reinforce the separation between these worlds as an imaginary, constructed boundary (one of distinct genre). The distribution of segmented spaces has viewers note the invisible quality of these walls, that is, in lieu of their physical separation, the powerful forces in each scene that partition the characters into their own individual dramas. These partitions in Zamora's work will be one of my lines of questioning here. What structures of relational powers constitute the "invisible walls" that keep the characters from undergoing desired transformation, on the one hand, and from implicating themselves in each others' stories (only to *criss-cross* each other), on the other? In times of induced change, what forces folded within speech and action in the encounters, shape the characters' desires against their will?

After a speed-dating event to meet other thirty-something singles, Dana (Cristina García) asks her chosen bachelor Ferrán (Xavo Giménez) about his dream profession, in a question that supposes, from the outset, an aspiration to work in something other than his current employment. His response, which deflates Dana's interest momentarily, expresses his contentment with his current job as a city bus driver working long hours, which allows him to spend less time at home, he admits, ever since wage cuts required him to move in with his elderly mother and brother (Zamora, 2013, 48). Changing the subject quickly, Dana aims to maintain a romantic interest in Ferrán, which upstages her disappointment for his complacency as he desires little else from his current situation. As the comedic dialog unfolds, it becomes apparent that Dana is searching in Ferrán for a form of identification with her own desire for something more from life. She encounters it in Ferrán's confessed "unusual" taste for theater instead of soccer matches—unlike most men, he remarks—which has him drink alone while imagining an interlocutor with whom he can comment on the plays he has seen (2013, 50). His solitude and sensitivity are read as an overture, as Dana then discloses an intimate secret to Ferrán. In successive relationships, she feels overpowered and controlled by men's obsession for her sex and the pleasures she is capable of giving (her "superpowers," as she elaborates for the audience), a matter she addresses with her therapist. All in all, Dana's date with Ferrán promises to go well, amid clumsy remarks and nervous distractions, as each character develops identification with the other's solitude.

In contrast to their mutual physical approach in the hotel room, Ferrán's energetic monologue after sex stands in opposition to Dana's hunched, seated position on the bed. Disparagingly for her, Ferrán also ends up fascinated with Dana as an object of pleasure. He begs her not to leave in the second-person plural ("No...os vayáis..." [Don't....go...]), as she abandons him immediately, ashamed and blaming herself ("No es culpa tuya. Es mía, como siempre" [It's not your fault. It's mine, like always]) (2013, 59). Suggested in the objectionable "doubling" to which Ferrán refers, viewers might take note of how this encounter develops in mediation between characters through a form of double. Dana is looking to identify with another who, like herself, wishes for something more from life, which she locates in their mutual loneliness—the point in common capable of mediating her growing attraction to Ferrán. Whereas Ferrán's mediation in their sexual union—his doubling of her, as Dana and her sex, which takes precedence over her person—subjects her to the very pattern of male objectification she desires to escape. Portrayed as entirely unobservant of Dana's reaction, Ferrán in his inability to read her shame and self-blame, in body and speech, renders him oblivious to his machismo and lacking empathy about the damage he has done. While Zamora develops Dana's character as the more dynamic of the two, here and in a later scene, Ferrán's lack of intentions are shown to matter little, for his unawareness participates uncritically in a pattern of male domination that renders him incapable of empathy. The (in-)capacity of the characters to read each other, in body and speech, comprises one of the driving lines for the missed encounters in Zamora's script.

After sex, there is little reciprocity in the dual mediation between Dana and Ferrán, which is why I have chosen to address this scene first, admittedly not the first in the play. Viewers will note that whereas Dana feels ashamed by the repeated machismo of her dating life and the implicit control it exerts over her, it is through Ferrán's "unusual" interest in theater ("no creo que eso sea...sólo para gays" [I don't think that's...only for gays]), against a given social presumption about male heterosexual taste, in which the audience is led to believe, like Dana, that his behavior will be different from that of other men (2013, 50). The established genre of romantic comedy, here, lends itself to the readability of the scene, generating certain audience expectations about the presumed outcome, but which instead reveal presumptions about the normative constructs of gender when the story moves in a different direction. In this sense, much like the audience reads the scene's familiar genre before it takes a turn, Dana reads the social attributes of gender decoded from a social construct of "normal" taste and behavior, in contrast to Ferrán who is entirely incapable of reading her feelings of subjugation, and his responsibility for them, at all. Actions and speech come to light as mediating gestures (in body and language) capable of opposing or reifying the ways in which prevailing power relations work on the characters in their encounters. Reading norms and normalcy in the hotel is part and parcel of Zamora's play. A sort of square-one for the exchanges to follow, the audience might perceive a certain precondition that frustrates this exchange, that is, a disposition to read one's own potentially powerful role in the encounter (Ferrán) and the damage it can prove capable of doing to another.

In contrast to Ferrán's incognizant machismo, other powerful figures engage in seduction and manipulation with similar overpowering results. Such violence when acted upon characters is made explicit in the controlling power of Toni (Sergio Caballero) over the young Chelo (Maria Maroto). Possibly his former student ("Podría caber perfectamente en el traje de mi colegio"[I could still fit perfectly in my school uniform], she remembers), Chelo is introduced to the audience as Toni's longtime lover, which plays upon their age difference, at first, to convey the uneven power dynamic between them as perhaps one of reprimanding schoolmaster and pupil (2013, 23). Typecast in the boredom of a comfortable, loveless middle-class relationship, the dramatic couple in crisis portrays increasingly throughout the scene that Toni's emotional and verbal abuse of Chelo aims to keep her subdued to his authority. Toni ridicules her "childish" desires for a more exciting home life, on the one hand, and her sexual fantasies to be desired, on the other—a scene that turns briefly to physical violence when he tugs at her dress, ripping the buttons ("te lo has regalado tú con mi puto dinero" [you gave it to yourself with my goddamn money] (2013, 23). The verbal abuse Toni spouts is highlighted for the audience as equally as damaging as this physical aggression, which has Chelo assume a kneeling position in the corner—the image of disciplinary humiliation in the classrooms of yesteryear—crying and turned away from her aggressor.

Toni's consistent reaffirmation that he is the material provider of the relationship articulates his paternalist role within this power dynamic that shuttles in the exchange between an abusive lover, schoolmaster, and paternal figure.

However, the violence of Toni's power over Chelo is not exerted uniquely from a top-down position, for Toni, vulnerable at the thought of a breakup, tries to seduce Chelo in his appeal to conserve their relationship, or rather, to conserve his authoritarian role within it. In an attempt to appease her erotic fantasies, he performs the role of a corrupt "bad cop" who demands to search her, before he breaks from his policeman character with further ridicule. Toni returns again to the kind of remarks throughout the scene that reaffirm his power over her decisions—she is incapable of leaving him, he quips. His seduction is played out as a form of doubling, then, in assuming this dual role of drawing Chelo in and of exerting control over her, only made possible by the doubling of his character (Toni and the "bad cop"). Notably, when he breaks from the role-play, his retort is articulated through an observation on the times:

> Las aventuras están en las películas. El paro alcanza cotas elevadísimas. La gente está amargada, no hay tiempo para jugar a las princesas ni a las casitas. (2013, 30–31)
>
> [Adventures are for movies. Unemployment is reaching its highest peak. People are bitter, there's no time to play princesses and dollhouses.]

These are not times for infantile fantasies, he sneers, in an assertion that reinforces his authoritarian role, much like the imaginary "bad cop" he plays to seduce her, who dictates Chelo's desires against her will. It is the backdrop of the crisis that polices, in part, the characters' realization of desires, as Toni does Chelo, evident in other scenes. In this complex psychological portrait of the couple, Toni contradictorily negates and plays out Chelo's fantasies (that is, he mediates them on his terms) in order to entice her to conserve the status quo, and it is Chelo's submission to Toni's reassertion of his paternal authority ("yo te cuido, yo te protejo, Chelo" [I'll take care of you, I'll protect you, Chelo]), which has her delay any decision to end the relationship as the scene closes (2013, 33). Her return is played out even as Toni hushes her, interrupting her final words in the exchange. His role, then, in reaffirming his dominance over Chelo, is one that dictates limitations on her desires, decisions, and the sayable, which extends beyond the case of their relationship in the play. For, Toni is portrayed as an authoritarian double that forcefully shapes the exchange in violent ways; he polices her through seduction and the powerful imposition of dominance by force. Taken up together, the authoritarian norms he enforces by violence— the limitations of desire, decision, speech—are those that regulate the permissible, much like the circumstance he quotes for the other characters in later scenes.

In *Anti-Oedipus*, Deleuze and Guattari make their case that desires are produced, structured, and shaped (ordered and partitioned) in part within prevailing power relations, though never determined or static (1983, 1–42). In their process of production, desires are transformed by and, in turn, can transform the real, begetting the *becomings* that the authors describe in the subjugation and emancipation of desiring subjects (1983, 30). In this light, a forced process of change, due to its forced character, may involve the involuntary shaping or repression of desires by the structures of power (their ordering function), experienced with considerable violence for the subjection they prove capable of producing. Therein also reside, however, the possibilities that decision, action, and speech can, in turn, shape desire (to produce desire, desiring-production), whether these powers have an emancipating or policing effect. It is in this manner in which I refer to desire here, as mediated by and produced within power relations that can shape it, rather than as a lack or metaphoric displacement.[12] Just as Ferrán unknowingly subjects Dana to the powers of male dominance she aims to escape, her shame is made readable to the audience in this production, as is Chelo's own subjection to the dually seductive and aggressive reassertion of Toni's authority that polices her permissible desires, decisions, and words. I should like to propose by taking Zamora's play as my case, then, that power relations are not abstract forces existing somehow outside the scenario; rather, they speak and act through speech and action within the mediated scene of encounter as they ensue relationally within it among the characters. Hence, their two-way or double, mediated character, is discursive in part, capable of shaping and conditioning the possible. It is through this dramatic artifice of body, language, and movement in which Zamora's theater calls the spectator's attention to the scene of encounter as capable of mediating desires shaped, repressed, or conditioned (or, ordered and partitioned) by the predominant power relations that act upon the characters relationally in their individual dramas. In them, policing performs the role of an ordering function, as in Deleuze and Guattari, dividing and disciplining the characters amid invisible partitions, while restoring them to the "norms" of the house rules. How this works, though, requires taking a look at other scenes.

Policing and enforcing limitations extend to the proprieties of behavior in the spaces of the hotel. Outside the hotel rooms, there are transient figures and spaces that have these narratives crisscross each other, in chance encounters in the hallway and hotel bar. Notably, the encounters taking place in the hotel's common spaces are those that bear no specific augmented genre as in the private spaces of each hotel room. Such is the case with the wandering character Irina (Maria Zamora), whose story opens and loosely closes the play, and the scenes in which she appears. A young, unemployed mother in poverty, Irina pushes her baby carriage through the common areas of the hotel while waiting for her husband throughout the dramatic action, where she encounters the occupants and staff. Her character, transient and out-of-place, is constructed from the question of belonging, or rather of *not belonging* in the modern hotel, on first account because she is not a client, but also due to the visible markings of her socioeconomic status, in her simple clothes, that might have the hotel staff identify her as a loiterer ("¿No me dirán nada por estar aquí, no?" [They won't say anything because I'm here, will they?]) (2013, 17). Irina, who does not belong in any of the spaces she traverses, is somewhat like the genre of the scenes in which she appears: indeterminate and visibly marked (in outward appearance to others) as not fitting into any specific, categorical attributes that would shape her story through the conventions of a genre.

Having escaped her disastrous blind date, then, Dana sits at the hotel bar and orders a coffee where she meets Irina. In a similar disposition to connect with a stranger, Dana invites her to a coffee, given that Irina carries only 23 cents lifted from the change found at another table. As with Ferrán in the previous scene, Dana opens up to her interlocutor by expressing her solitude, particularly, as a single woman who is only remembered by her married girlfriends when they care to have a night out. The two of them even establish a chance connection, reminiscing about how they attended the same primary school together long ago, in what suggests that Irina may have also come from a middle-class background, having once seen better times. Nevertheless, Irina quickly monopolizes the conversation, dominating it on her own terms. In monologue, Dana hears about Irina's troubles, their family love despite desperate poverty, the doctor's assessment of their baby's developmental disability, unwelcomed flattery about Dana's fine clothes and perfume, and so on. After Irina interrupts Dana several times, the scene ends abruptly in an explosive rant by Dana, who warns, "Te has tomado el café pues deja de monopolizar y cierra un poco el pico, hija. Déjame también meter baza... No puedes ir avasallando a las personas con tus miserias" [You've had your coffee, so stop monopolizing the conversation and shut your trap a little. Let me butt in, too . . . You can't go pushing other people around with your miserias.] (2013, 96). In an animated leap from her bar stool, Dana spouts derogatory classist insults as she exits the scene, leaving Irina with a bill for two coffees she cannot pay while the bartender intervenes to call security. Irina, in other words, has been identified in public for her out-of-place status.

In her appeal to charity from Dana, Irina is less a character portrait of a class unable to represent itself to others, than of one that in its appeal to be heard cannot engage the conversation on her interlocutor's predominant terms for the exchange. In this regard, Irina's character functions as a subaltern, wandering, indeterminate, and out of place in the hotel, the spaces of which loosely begin to acquire their resemblance to a social architecture of norms that structure privilege and exclusion, belonging and unbelonging. Alluding to their shared class background as schoolgirls, the scene sets up a sharp contrast between the grown-up versions of a struggling and a well-to-do character in the possibility that Dana could also find herself in Irina's situation, which she disavows disparagingly, leading to Irina's expulsion. Dana's desire to share mutually in her solitude with an-other, as she did with Ferrán, has her turn away from alterity (literally, in body, as she departs) in the suggestion that she herself could be this other, which charts her disavowal for the audience in body and speech. In dialog, the relational powers between them come to the fore in the socioeconomic hierarchy at this turning point (her turning away from the other), highlighted in Dana's explosive remarks that reassert her class difference, violently, from Irina's own. And Dana's public embarrassment of Irina leads to the policing of a destitute character that has no place with the others, according to the house rules.

Speaking to power, then, goes horribly wrong for Irina when she indulges in telling her story on her own terms. Yet, ironically, in the power dynamic that Dana establishes for their exchange, Dana is no longer willing to listen in her desire to be heard ("to butt in" the conversation). Dana's two encounters turned foul provide a contrast between cases in which social atomization among the characters is as much a question of engagement on equal terms, or of address and reception against the backdrop of unspoken power relations structuring the conversation (cross-cut by gender, sexuality, class), as it presumes reifying in practice and language the very power structures to which both parties are subject. As such, Dana problematically exerts the humiliation she herself suffers in the previous scene, to the detriment of Irina, by making a scene (figuratively) in public. The scene made (literally, on stage) is one in which the class hierarchy structures Dana's disavowal, leaving Irina ashamed, in debt, and identified publicly for her unbelonging, that is, outcast from the spaces reserved for its clientele and their privacy.

Policing the practices and uses of space constitutes one part of the framework shaping the terms of dialog and action in these encounters. These are the house rules, so to speak, the norms that regulate exchange in this space. Zamora's modern hotel, as a transient space, stages the form of social contract and right to usage noted by Marc Augé in *non-places* proliferating in advanced capitalism, forged between "spaces formed in relation to certain ends (transport, transit, commerce, leisure), and the relations that individuals have with these spaces" (1995, 94). Particularly, notes Augé, the interstices between usage and their relation to the social uphold an unspoken contract of behaviors in which the privilege and right to occupy these transient spaces presumes that the "user of the non-place is always required to prove [her] innocence," somewhat like subway passengers subject to random checks by security, who must demonstrate they have purchased a ticket (1995, 94, 102). The right to belonging and the policing of characters in Zamora's hotel (the question of access), in a similar vein, comes to bear unevenly upon them based on their socioeconomic status, particularly when one considers the privacy and privilege enjoyed by some clients whose stories never leave their respective "rooms" (Toni and Chelo who order room service; Belén's inebriated groom who sleeps in the wedding suite), in contrast to the roaming of Irina and the traveling of the working-class bartender Antxón on hotel staff. The only clients to leave their rooms before the final scene, Belén and Dana, do so to escape their frustrations with their own private "stories"—for Belén, due to an intoxicated groom on her wedding night—whereby they encounter the working-class Antxón in the hallway and Irina in the hotel bar, respectively. In the common areas, their encounters transpire without the legible features of a genre, as a *non-place*, that would have the audience associate them with those of the private rooms. Even so, their encounters are likewise fraught with disconnections and abrupt endings that in Dana's case, "make a scene" by invoking the prevailing power relations on the right to usage (and in turn, policing) in this space, in which the house rules come to bear upon Irina. Rather than a disciplinary enclosure, the hotel without walls resembles an open space of transit regulated, segmented, and ordered by a social contract of conduct and (un-)belonging. Norms can be invoked to enforce the policing of the characters, and their access, at any time.

In the hallway, sitting on the floor outside the nuptial suite where her inebriated groom sleeps, Belén (Paula Llorens) encounters Antxón (Miguel Seguí) leaving his shift, who calls out to her for loitering in a space where she doesn't belong ("Disculpe, aquí no se puede estar, eh?" [Sorry, but you can't stay here, alright?]) (2013, 98). At first, Antxón, as hotel staff, upholds his prescribed role by policing the well-to-do client Belén as he did Irina. Inversely, the client's power is also given in their encounter, for Belén demands room service, and Antxón refuses, noting her rude forms and sense of entitlement ("Son las normas y la educación, vaya" [Those are the rules and, well, have some courtesy]) (2013, 99). But through their conversation, the established hierarchy between speakers transforms, first in Antxón's backtalk and then in Belén's developing interest, in what portrays the erotic appeal of a coarse working-class "other" to an affluent character who considers herself somewhat more refined. In this light, their mutual attraction begins to unfold against a specific condition. For, Antxón reveals to Belén that the security cameras posted throughout the hotel are fake, serving only to suggest that the inhabitants are subject to surveillance in a manner that would have them police their own behavior. Once this myth is exposed, the characters begin to engage in a mutual conversation in which they gradually shed their prescribed roles in action and speech that would have them make demands or regulate the behavior of the other.

Unsure why Antxón looks so exhausted after working a double shift, Belén is made aware for the first time that her fantasies for the perfect wedding day, now spoilt, bore a working-class toll, for Antxón is tired "En hablar de usted. En *mantener la boca cerrada...*, en dejar que me pisoteen, en cargar cajas, en subir botellas, en ascensor para arriba, en ascensor para abajo. En limpiar los vomitados de los invitados de tu boda" [Of talking about you. *Keeping my mouth shut...*, letting them step on me, carrying crates, going up for bottles, up and down, up and down the elevator. Tired of cleaning up the puke from your wedding guests] (my emphasis, 2013, 99–100). Being stepped on and keeping silent about it, while cleaning up the aftermath of the affluent guests' excesses, are a servile toil. In difference to the disposition of other characters, Belén is at least willing to consider her role in this power relation. Following her apology, the attraction between the two develops in their physical proximity on stage and in dialog that banters in mutual interest, in Belén's reference to Antxón as a waiter and his retort, "Soy mucho más que un camarero" [I'm much more than a waiter] (2013, 101). That Belén views Antxón typecast in his profession as "any other waiter" reveals her social position through the very act of reading him according to his generic qualities, that is, his working-class status (his *genre* or social category). In turn, Anxtón's response has Belén reconsider her *manner of reading* him. Their attraction, then, is played out in Antxón's spoken fantasy about performing sexually in surrogate for the impotent groom, interrupted mutually at different times: first, by Antxón's remembrance of his girlfriend and later, by Belén's encouragement for him to call her and express his love, a gesture she herself would wish for. Antxón also becomes the surrogate for Belén, in playing out her desire to be told that she is loved by her unperforming husband. The conversation between the two transforms the given terms of power through a mediation that diverts Antxón's sexual fantasy toward his girlfriend, and Belén's own towards her husband, as the scene ends before she can catch Antxón's name, while she charges back into her suite ("¡Despierta ya! ¡Despierta!" [Wake up already! Wake up!]) (2013, 106). Their departure, in a farewell in which Antxón repositions Belén's loose hair behind her ear, is the culminating point of physical contact in touch that has drawn them together in the dialog, repositioning momentarily the power dynamic between the two through the mutual mediation of the other's desires for yet another.

The reciprocal exchange between Belén and Antxón serves as a counterpoint to all others in the play in which the predisposition of the characters to change the terms of the conversation in mediation can also thereby shape its implicit relation of power between speakers. And building upon previous scenes, it is their open recognition that this policed framework for their exchange is simply a construct—if the security cameras are phony, so too must be the house rules—which lays the bases for their exchange to take place on a more equal grounding. However, as the structures of (class) power are shown to be inscribed within action and speech, as in this exchange, it is only once Belén is made to reconsider her presumptions and her manner of reading Antxón's *genre* (class) that the transformation between the two begins to develop. Such is the nature of navigating predominant relations capable of partitioning and ordering the exchanges between characters in which, perhaps as lesson, speaking to power goes horribly wrong for Irina, however undeserved or unjust the consequence, when she engages her interlocutor from the terms she alone establishes for their exchange. The key to transformation, it seems in each scene, whether frustrated or partially fulfilled, is one that requires certain recognition of the constructedness of the powerful conditions acting upon the scenario at hand and an engagement of the very limitations they impose.

II.

Zamora scripts both the unformed possibility and frustration of trans-formation in which the unspoken social contract (the invisible walls) prevails more often than not. In this manner, the notion of desire in Zamora's play is attached less to any object than to an imagined scenario of realization conditioned by limitations, that is, to a policed scene that the characters are prevented or prevent each other from fulfilling (their repression). Observed in the very circumstance of the crisis that Toni observes to support his recriminating claims against Chelo, policing need not be physically exerted for its control to prove capable of forcibly molding the scenario at hand. In this sense, the characters are left in suspension, desiring scenarios for change.

In what stands as perhaps the play's most productive, developed implication of characters entwined in each other's stories—their turn to alterity—the encounter between Belén and Antxón is also unsettled by its allusion to violence replayed within the circumstance of the crisis. Antxón, employed by a temp agency, steals food from the weekly deliv-ery truck, which he calls the "economía de la supervivencia" [economy of survival] (2013, 100). Given his low-wage precarious employment, a disenfranchised Antxón confesses that he cares not if they fire him for stealing, for joking with fellow workers on the job, or for smoking marijuana on break. Yet, his angers are taken home where he sometimes "roce la línea" [crosses the line] with his girlfriend, in what suggests that the unspoken physical abuse he exerts is played out problematically as the violence he himself experiences on the job (2013, 105). That the other characters should serve as the displaced object of violent subjec-tion, which they themselves experience in other ways (Dana, Antxón, Toni), is one of the dramatic mechanisms repeated in *Temporada baja* as a powerful force capable of atomizing the characters, on the one hand, while replaying their subjugation in repetition toward others, on the other.

The dynamics of this violent subjection—in the shaping of permis-sible desires, decisions, and speech against the characters' expressed will—are made most explicit in the murder and suicide in the play. In the opening act, Irina's husband Jordi (David Matarín), desperate for income, bids a nervous goodbye to his wife and infant son before prostituting himself for the first time to a male client in one of the hotel rooms. Much of the play transpires while, drifting or leafing through a gossip magazine, Irina awaits Jordi's return, unaware that her hus-band has been drugged, victimized, and eaten by the serial killer Peter

(Paco Trenzano) in one of the rooms. Staged in this pulp fiction genre of thriller and suspense, Jordi's encounter with his assassin introduces the audience to the young victim's wishes to be a published writer. Thus, the act of cannibalization acquires an added dimension as the devouring of unrealized desires and dreams, clipped short by his murder. As a nervous Jordi asks about the electric drill next to the bed, Peter's sparse words explain that he "climbed his way" to the top of his business (*trepar*) and now proudly owns a few hardware stores downtown. While the drug begins to paralyze Jordi, Peter searches his victim's backpack to read aloud from his writings gathered in a notebook. In them, Jordi expresses his desire to flee his current situation in desperate poverty as a young married man with an infant son, conveyed to the audience through the pressures imposed upon him to perform an impossible role as male provider for his family ("Tengo capacidades, pero no la de volar. A veces pienso en marchar...pienso en marchar..." [I have abilities, but I can't fly. Sometimes I think about walking away...I think about walking away...]) (2013, 44). As pulp fiction would have it, the image of the calculating assassin, an upwardly mobile type, offers a representational portrayal in his devouring the low-income character who dreams of escape from despair. As inextricably bound notions of class, gender, and sexuality shape this story, notably, it is also Jordi's lack of economic means that requires him to prostitute himself to a male client—stated otherwise, to subjugate himself to the desires of the upwardly mobile type—in order to uphold his role, paradoxically, as the heterosexual head of household and family provider. At least, that is what Jordi's character believes, until he succumbs slowly to the drug that makes him realize that his client has deadly intentions.

In this sense, the two deaths in the play—Jordi's murder and Pablo's suicide—are staged in conversation with each other as cases of desired, yet unrealized, future plans that parallel the other characters' own. In a doubling of types, both are also frustrated writers for different reasons. Jordi is an aspiring writer whose amateur status prevents him from breaking into the profession, and Pablo (played by Zamora himself) is a young, somewhat successful playwright who fails at seeking comprehension from his family through his dramatic work. The contrast in genres, in the suspenseful thriller of Jordi's murder and the somber tragedy of Pablo's awaited death, share in common the question of waiting for the audience, of not knowing what will happen to Jordi as the drug slowly impairs his movement on stage (the suspense of expectations in thriller) and of knowing the end for Pablo revealed in the scene (the fatalism of recognition in tragedy). Waiting, then, much like Irina's awaited return of Jordi, unresolved by the play's end, is shaped by desirable "alternative scenarios" that never come to fruition for the characters.

In the staging of Pablo's suicide, the audience awaits his expected death from an overdose of ingested tranquilizers, a scene that transpires while his twin sister Mari Carmen (Lorena López) attempts to comfort him in their last moments together. This is not his first attempt at suicide, the audience learns, as Pablo's character is portrayed as one whose dramatic work is not accepted by the general public for its references to homosexuality, specifically, in the damaging suspicions it raises that he might be a "marica" [fag] or "transsexual," even from his loving sister (2013, 62). Foregrounding this implicit violence of social stigma, Pablo's death transpires while an important soccer match is on television, the reason why Mari Carmen's husband will not notice her absence, she remarks, which returns the audience to the predominant heteronormative masculinity developed in earlier scenes. Much like Jordi, it is inferred that Pablo is also cannibalized, though in a different way. His death, largely unnoticed, is portrayed as one that is devoured in the celebratory cheers of television spectators watching the game.

Silence and speech are shown to be shaped, in part, by powerful norms acting through them in the scene. In Pablo's final moments, Mari Carmen holds her brother in the bathtub, which reenacts a gesture in parallel to the childhood memories they recall together growing up in a poor family ("nunca tuvimos Reyes" [There were never gifts at Christmas]) (2013, 70). While the audience is made to await Pablo's death, their conversation is spoken through the lyrics of pop tunes and ballads (Dorian, José Luis Perales, Julio Iglesias, Camilo Sesto). The banality of these words, cited verbatim from a stock of pop songs, is furthermore accentuated by the spaces of silence in the dialog between the characters close to Pablo's death, marked by ellipsis, pauses, and trailing sentences. In this manner, the song lyrics serve as a vehicle to convey the only substantive content of their spoken exchange after Pablo's fate is made known to the audience. As such, bringing closure to the scene, Mari Carmen hushes her brother while he sings Camilo Sesto's "Decir te quiero" (To Say I Love You): "Las palabras sinceras las que tienen valor, son las que salen del alma...y en mi alma nacen...solo palabras blancas, preguntas sin respuesta llenas de esperanza" [Sincere words, the ones that take courage, are the ones that come from my heart...and in my soul are born...only blank words, questions without answers, filled with hope] (2013, 75). Truncated aspirations and desires, expressed through the "sincere, blank words" of the pop ballad, are drawn to the audience's attention as the vehicle capable of mediating the emotional bond between brother and sister articulated in Pablo's final moments, against the censure of Pablo's "other" forms of speech. If viewers take the literal translation of these "courageous words," they are also the only "words with value" at all (*las que tienen valor*), as Mari Carmen silences his (lip-synched) final enunciation.

The duality between the stock of given words and silence that go *heard*, on the one hand, versus the playwright's original words that go *unheard*, on the other, bring to light the predominant terms of address and reception in this encounter in which the sayable ("the only courageous/valued words," to paraphrase the lyrics) is policed by prejudice against nonnormative enunciation, as Mari Carmen silences her brother's final sentence. In this light, Zamora constructs the involuntary shaping of desires and the sayable as a burden capable of "devouring" Pablo's character in the end, which is not attributable specifically to any one character's actions (as in Peter's cannibalization of Jordi), but rather to the powers of a policed scenario in which character speech and action participate in censoring the impermissible. As I mentioned earlier, reading (social) norms and normalcy are part and parcel of Zamora's play, brought to light here for the ways in which they work on (to order, partition, police) permissible decision, speech, and desire. Viewers are shown, then, the symmetric, double stage exit of Pablo and Jordi after their respective deaths, as an off-stage voice reads from Jordi's unpublished writings once again.

Cannibalization in the double deaths of Jordi and Pablo, presumes the devouring of two characters and their unfulfilled desires expressed in each scene—that is, their desire for a scenario (of escape, of comprehension) that goes unrealized. In this manner, the consumption of the selfsame implied in the cannibalistic act provides the image of devouring the self and other, captured in the same figure, within the social body to uphold the (house) norm(s). Just as Jordi is cannibalized by the upwardly mobile type who subjects him to his own desires, Pablo is consumed in the celebratory cheers of spectators whose disinterest in non-normative enunciation, and its censoring of the sayable, proves capable of devouring his character in the end. Rooted in the mechanisms of disavowal—of the rejection of alterity and its annihilation of an-other—cannibalism in both scenes consumes the characters and their unrealized desires for a different scenario, left without a trace. Taking the dual deaths of Jordi and Pablo as an example, there exists a certain equivalence—or, doubling—between waiting and expecting in Zamora's play, captured in the Spanish verb *esperar*. For the time of these characters' impasse is also a time of waiting and of fantasizing about other desired realities, "eaten up" in the case of Jordi and Pablo, but also for the others. The parallel between standing by and dreaming within this space could be said to frame the dramatic action in *Temporada baja*, given that the crisscrossing of stories that builds to narrative closure is also clipped short—it is consumed—by an uplifting, comedic musical theater finale, which leaves all other stories suspended in unresolved action.

On waiting and hoping, daydreams on the job provide a form of escapism that channel unrealized desires in the fantasies about what one could have been. In a separate room, two girlfriends and co-workers at a retail clothing store, Paloma (Raquel Hernández) and Enri (Vanessa Cano), share intimate secrets about each other in a scene that escalates into a physical row with slapstick elements. Notably, the scene permissibly earns the audience's acceptance as hilarity and comic release because the characters are constructed as equals, unlike the abuses of powerful characters in other scenes. On the eve of her wedding rehearsal, Paloma admits her same-sex attraction to her co-worker Enri, confessing that she has fantasized about Enri in the sex act with her own fiancé. Conveying her disgust for the term "lesbian" in the performance, with contorted facial expressions and hesitant pronunciation, Paloma contests that the l-word "es una palabra rara. Si fuera lesbiana, que no lo soy, no me gustaría que me llamaran lesbiana" [is a strange word. If I were a lesbian—and I'm not—I wouldn't want to be called a lesbian] (2013, 81). Again, the social contours of gender and sexuality, in a same-sex desire that pleases Paloma but has her disavow the confines she associates with the word lesbian and its social stigma, censor the language of her character with disgust in the suggestion of an unfulfilled desire.

The sharing of intimate secrets bears the possibility of forging a closer relationship, at least as Paloma hopes, which culminates in her planting an unexpected kiss on a hesitant but receptive Enri. On her behalf, Enri participates in sharing secrets by confessing that it was she who stole from the cash register in retribution for her reassignment by store management. So, too, does Enri offer that every time she enters the storage room at work, she envisions herself as a dancer in a Broadway number, a fantasy that both delights and deeply embarrasses her, she admits (2013, 83). However, the humorous banter of insults between friends ("tú sí que eres un mal chiste, tía" [no, *you're* some kind of a bad joke]) establishes the tone and the terms for an unraveling series of petty confessions that increasingly aim to do harm to the other: Enri was Paloma's fifth choice for a bridesmaid; Paloma's co-workers despise her for her irritating positivity; Paloma has insider knowledge that Enri is about to be fired from her job; Enri confirms the rumor that she had a sexual encounter with Paloma's fiancé, and so on, which sparks the brawl between the two (2013, 79). In this light, Zamora conveys feelings of precarity within the same indiscriminate string of associations. In it, vulnerability provides little distinction between causes or their relation to the social, to labor, or to the shadow cast over dubious future plans, in which the circumstance of the crisis is folded reciprocally into the social and vice versa, as in the other scenes in the play. Enri's daydream at work, her unfulfilled fantasy, is staged in the choreographed musical revue that closes the play (figure 4.1).

Enri's employment as a salesperson for Spain's retail giant the Inditex Group sets the stage for her starring role in the musical number "The Inditex Girl." Known for its designer clothing styles sold at discount prices, Enri's place of employment is a campy choice to convey the low-cost glamour of her fantasy, itself an imitation conditioned by material restrictions. The grand finale ends *Temporada baja* on a comedic high-note in which all characters appear on stage singing lines about their respective roles and frustrated dreams in the dramatic action, woven into the story of Enri who, "Dejé un curriculum allí. Un nuevo mundo frente a mí. Sé que la cosa está muy mal—me dije—y nos tendremos que apañar" [I left a résumé over there. A new world in front of me. I know that things are pretty bad, I said to myself, and we're gonna

Figure 4.1 Enri's musical theater fantasy "The Inditex Girl" in Abel Zamora's *Temporada baja*.
Photo: © Vicente A. Jiménez.

have to get by] (2013, 110). Viewers will remember from the previous scene that Enri's self-realization in fantasy is marred by the suspended expectation that she too will lose her job. Against the scenario of the crisis affecting all characters in different ways, in a new world in which one has to "get by" as one can (*apañar*), Enri has sought low-paid precarious employment from the multinational retail store where she is largely overqualified: "Sé valenciano y alemán. Pues no te sirven para doblar" [I know Valencian and German. But they're not much use to fold (clothes)] (2013, 110). Knowledge of several languages is not required for retail, the characters remind her mockingly in their repeated chorus, "Dobla, pliega, sube y baja" [Fold, crease, go up, go down], that parodies the repetitious, mechanical action of the store employee folding and arranging the merchandise on display.

This manual activity on the job, and its choreographed rendition on stage, mechanically replays the worker's action in bodily gestures. It provides the audience with the concluding image of an ensemble of characters that, throughout the dramatic action of *Temporada baja*, repeat the existing power relations mechanically and uncritically through their actions and speech, which returns them to the status quo of a policed scenario, if not to a fatal end. Thereby the final scene brings together the many references to the limitations placed on the characters in their possible realization of a different story, against the circumstance of plural crises, folded indiscriminately within vulnerability for all of them, that powerfully shape their individual realities against their will in different ways. Taken up together, then, across the genres developing in the transient spaces of the hotel, the "low season" to which the title refers is more than a mood, but conveys an inherent violence acted upon unwilling subjects in the shaping of their desires to materialize another scenario and their incognizant participation in making this so in their encounters with the other characters.

In the hotel's resemblance to a social architecture of regulatory norms, traversed by prevailing power relations of class, gender, and sexuality, the actors participate in policing the permissible—of possible decision, speech, and desire—in ways that reinforce or betray predominant power relations in their encounters. In each case, the encounter provides a mediated scenario of body, language, and movement in which the characters perform and read each other uncritically despite their participation in their regulation of others. Yet, if one keeps in mind the encounter between Belén and Antxón, these given terms and their ability to partition the characters are also subject to negotiation and change in their mediation. In this manner, hoping and waiting for substantive change bears the kernel of unfulfilled possibilities for the characters that appear to coast through the transient nonplace of the hotel, bound to the presumed social contract on its right to usage that can be enforced at any time. Viewed in this manner, the invisible walls between the spaces and individual dramas unfolding in private rooms provide an image of the imaginary partition I spoke of from the outset, as one that inverts the interiority of the hotel to become, as a nonplace without walls, an open space of conditioned possibilities acting upon the characters in each scenario. It also supposes, for the audience that recognizes the familiarity of the augmented cinematic and dramatic genres transpiring in each room, an act of *reading* that situates the audience in a parallel activity to that of the characters as they read each other by attributes, categories, and positions that reify their difference and distinction (alterity) from others. The *illegibility* of the hotel space, and its architecture of rules shaping access and social conduct, is conveyed by Dana and Ferrán who mistakenly try to open another room, unable to read the disorienting signs: "Es que los números son tan modernos" [It's that the numbers look so modern] (2013, 43). The unreadability of the hotel space structuring the rules of conduct, after all, extends to the ways in which they see each other conditioned by it: "Eres como la habitación...como las cortinas, como la moqueta..." [You're like this bedroom...like the curtains, like the carpet] (2013, 49). From the audience's point of view, the staged effects of their separation, like the invisible walls that partition the characters, are shown to be inscribed within their actions, speech, and perceptions that shape each other's scenario at hand.

The desires to realize a different scenario are produced and molded for the characters, whose atomization from each other amid these invisible walls is largely a question of how they reenact or disengage the relational powers underpinning their exchanges in conversation with the "other." Within each context, the disposition of addresser and addressee to recognize their roles in the powerful terms between them, the reconsideration of the characters' presumptions (the manner of *reading* each other), and the identifiable tools of mediation between speakers (the conduits to speak and be heard on readable terms for both), are what prove capable of transforming the given terms of the conversation in Zamora's work, if at all, before their encounters go awry. The anatomy of how they do so, however, is dynamic, based on the context of each exchange, offering no set case. A determinant within the power dynamic in address resides in how the characters police each other and themselves, in part, within the hotel as a space of social contact in its right to usage among them, which serves as a framework governing permissible action and speech, according to the house rules. Even in certain scenes, actions and speech replay the violence experienced by characters, displaced toward others in repetition, through forms of disavowal capable of expelling or devouring the other. And on the other hand, the violence of subjection and control, which places limitations on their desires, speech, and decision in different ways, is one that is exerted from within the powers of a top-down subjugation that is shown to require, inversely, their seduction and control to reify subordination to an abusive authority. This subjugation is made more readable for the audience when its violence is exerted by a character, such as Toni. But in the case of a policed scenario, which Toni both performs and cites in the crisis, no specific actor can be attributed with conditioning the scenarios on stage. Instead, the characters themselves in their scenes of encounter mediate the very power relations inflecting their speech and actions in conversations with others, whether unknowingly, desiringly, or otherwise. What is at stake, following Deleuze and Guattari, resides in comprehending, first, the ways in which these characters participate in producing each other's desires in powerful ways, or rather, in policing each other's unfulfilled realization for a different scenario altogether. Once identified for its constructed character, once the terms of power shaping the scenario are made legible, therein also resides the transformative possibility for change within the encounter. But, then again, this presumes that spectators are in a willing disposition, like Belén, to perceive how this might work by considering the *manner of reading* the other in the exchange.

III.

If I have paid specific attention to the ways in which the dramatic genres of different scenes are made legible to the audience, and may prove to mold and perhaps even defamiliarize the spectator's expectations in certain scenes, it is because Zamora establishes, as I see it, an intimate relation between spectatorship as a form of reading and recognition, and the actions of the characters on stage who likewise read, misread, and are sometimes led to question their own manners of reading. In closure, then, I should like to address the question of these invisible walls as those that partition the characters for their effect of reenacting the powerful relations that shape and limit desires, specifically, as they relate to the activity of spectatorship for the audience. For the activity of recognizing the familiarity of augmented genres transpiring in distinct spaces is one that implicates the audience in reading the invisible walls separating each room, much like the characters read and misread each other in their encounters.

In *The Emancipated Spectator*, Jacques Rancière problematizes the diametric opposition between the prescribed roles of the (passive) spectator and the (active) actor, naturalized within the dramatic and visual arts as a self-evident presumption. The experience of theater-going illustrates his argument; conventionally, the viewing audience performs a specific role in the theater space, comprising seated, pensive observers whose social behavior is prescriptive to this passive reception as addressees, separate from the action on stage. In this manner, he writes, "viewing is the opposite of knowing," on the one hand, for the spectator is presumably introduced into the scene of contemplation (the theater, the art gallery, and so on), while observant viewing is presumed to be "the opposite of acting," on the other, in which the role of the active agent is conceived in opposition to the passive contemplation of the viewer (2009, 2). The crux of Rancière's argument is a political one, in which the possibility of emancipation,

> begins when we challenge the opposition between viewing and acting; when we understand that the self-evident facts that structure the relations between saying, seeing, and doing themselves belong to the structure of domination and subjection. It begins when we understand that viewing is also an action that confirms or transforms this distribution of positions. (2009, 13)

Rancière views in the scripted active (actor) versus the passive (spectator) roles a paradigm and practice of politics that one might note translates suggestively into the partitioned roles of governors and the governed in representative democracy—but also, for my purpose here, to the possibilities of ordinary observation, action, and speech.[13] If, for Rancière, a political act is one that redistributes the powerful operative relations that structure saying, doing, and seeing, then I should like to propose that the encounter, in its mediation of permissible speech and action in the given terms for the exchange, is one that bears the possible kernel of a political act capable of engaging critically the prevailing power relations that shape the scenario at hand. In Zamora's theater, spectators are shown that this is an ordinary, everyday occurrence that holds to or strays from participating in the policing of the impermissible, on the one hand, and that speaks and acts through personages unknowingly or desiringly so, on the other. Within this micro-scenario,

redistributing the terms of power speaking and acting through actors—
a small, but a political act—is one that presumes a disposition in address
and reception to speak and listen, to read and be read, but that proves
capable of transforming the terms of the exchange through mediation,
and thus potentially the prescribed roles of actors within the scenario.
In this manner, Zamora's one-act play *Pequeños dramas sobre arena azul*
serves as a concluding remark to illustrate this point, for which the
play's title, incidentally, might be taken as the small (*pequeño*) act of
encounter in which the roles of neither actors nor spectators is prescribed by theatrical conventions.

As in Zamora's other work, the notion of space proves key to the
development of the characters in relation to their stage of action.
Written specifically for the underground venue La Casa de la Portera in
Madrid, *Pequeños dramas* stages an intimate yet sardonic performance
of house pets and their abusive master, staged in a space for some 25
spectators seated around the periphery of a large living room. Featuring
a cast of stage, screen, and television actors (Marta Belenguer, Raúl
Prieto, Nuria Herrero, Mentxu Romero, David Matarín, and Zamora
himself), the three-act play defamiliarizes the audience's expectations to see a stage drama about human characters, pitched vaguely
in its publicity, when the actors enter the room in costume as domestic animals. Their common plight is their inescapable place, an urban
apartment where their master keeps them cooped-up and unjustly
disciplined, reproducing the violence she herself experiences in everyday life. So, too, are their dramas quite human, at least for pets. The
audience is introduced to the mother housecat who cannot mourn her
disappeared litter, due to her painful un-milked udder that reminds
her incessantly of loss; to the mother's stray macho lover who desires
more stability than his compulsive promiscuities allow; to the spayed
male cat seduced into escaping with the alpha male, which leads to an
unknowing leap to his death from the apartment window; to the comi-
cal lice-ridden pigeon, a scatter-brained addict of breadcrumbs, who
consistently reveals tragic news without understanding its emotional
impact on the characters; and to the abused lapdog empathetic to all
others including his abuser, who returns to her time and again. The
only human character in the play is the emotionally unstable housemaster, addicted to social media, Zamora scripts, who keeps her dwell-
ing space in isolated, orderly suffering through beatings and portioned
doses of tranquilizing catnip. One might perceive the parallel correlation between these character types and the limitations imposed upon
their desires to realize a different scenario, in a sort of double to the

crisscrossing stories of Zamora's urban hotel. The colorful casting of human dramas into animal characters estranges the audience enough to call consistent attention to its artificial, even surrealist, imagination (like the plush, full-body costumes of the actors), and thus makes for an element of absurdity that can achieve the heightened range of emotions that the performance aims to convey.

The cramped space of the production has the animal characters search at times for props under the seats of spectators, in what implicates the audience directly in the action of the play, to move and be moved physically in response to the ongoing action around them. Noteworthy, too, is the distribution of seats around the periphery of the room. In contrast to the aisles in conventional theaters that face a separate scene of activity on stage, here spectators see each other seated in a circle, and thereby themselves, as part of the spectacle. The large mirrors hanging on the walls, typical of living room décor, allow spectators seated around the room to view the characters at the center from different angles, above the heads of the other seated audience members. This plural fragmentation of gazes among and toward other audience members and actors constitutes the unique character of spectatorship in the venue and, specifically, in Zamora's play, in which the disciplinary modes of spectatorship in the theater are called into question as the action unfolds. What constitutes "proper" behavior from theater-goers, given the nature of an ongoing performance in which the audience is, as much as the actors, being watched "on stage"? And what of movement, as actors require seated spectators to move and be moved throughout the play? Specific scenes tend to highlight this dynamic more than others, such as those of the housemaster who violently disciplines her cast of pets.

In one particularly violent scene, in which the master beats her dog, the characters are "off-stage" in the hallway, where only the whelps can be heard, in a theatrical convention that proves disturbing by depriving the audience of sight (one might think of Medea murdering her children off-stage). The concealed action implicates spectators by requiring them to imagine its violence against the overheard cries, which proves unsettling. Given the absence of activity "on stage" during this scene, spectators in the audience are left to look at each other while hearing the whelps, in a crisscrossing of observational gazes on the reactions of others. In Zamora's brilliant parallel, then, the disciplinary action of the housemaster's abusive rage on her dog resonates with the activity of seeing and being seen in reaction, which despite and due to its potential discomforts, calls into question the disciplinary modes of spectatorship in conventional theater. After all, one might presume that if the audience were not seated in an inward-looking circle, the discomfort of this scene, barring its explicit overheard violence, would bear less impact on spectators. The parallel raises a series of questions, with potentially political implications in other contexts. How uncomfortable are spectators when forced to step out of the prescribed roles of spectatorship, which move them towards the role of an actor? What of this discomfort involves moving and being moved physically by actors in an ongoing play that draws others' attention to the spectator's own movement? What of it entails seeing and being seen in collective reaction to the overheard violence of a scenario, of which spectators are fully aware, transpiring "off-stage" and out of sight? In what ways do spectators assume and perform the disciplinary (theater) house rules of conduct? For a moment, the audience members in their behavior, and perhaps discomfort, are invited to see other spectators and themselves as a well-trained dog.

In the play, the lapdog's loyalty proves detrimental to his own well-being, as he returns empathetically to his abusive master, time and again. But by this point, at which viewers have already been invited to see themselves as a well-trained animal, Zamora scripts his character's submission as akin to his audience's own, to have them perceive that discipline, and its potential violence, keep him domesticated, and vice versa. As tragedy, *Pequeños dramas* offers no solutions to the characters who, confined in their housemaster's space, cannot escape their own circumstance. Or, if they do, then the sole attempt to run away, for a character seduced into the illusion of escape, has him jump to his death without knowing that the apartment is several stories above the ground, having never been outside the master's space. Instead of solutions, Zamora's performance escapes in a sense by "getting away" with something else altogether. That is, through Zamora's human-like pet characters, the audience spectators are invited to see themselves and others as disciplined, perhaps even domesticated, within this space. And to see oneself and others as trained animals is, after all, getting away with enough to incite one to question, rather than to resolve completely, just how this might be.

Notes

Introduction Urban Multitudes: 15M and the Spontaneous "Spanish Revolution"

1. I use the term *indignadxs* to refer to 15M participants, from the protesters' own words, rather than the masculine plural *indignados* for the gender exclusions implied in the latter. Another gender-neutral choice, also used interchangeably among protesters, is *indignad@s*. In this light, Manuel Castells refers to the *indignadas* in his work in the feminine plural (2012). Here, readers will note that the masculine plural *indignados* appears in reference to published works bearing this name.

2. As Alex Thomson explains, "Traditionally, *poiesis* is distinguished from *praxis* or action, on the grounds that *poiesis* aims at, and is subsequently judged in terms of its success at, the production of a work, but *praxis* is consumed in the action" (2011, 212).

3. According to Sáenz de Santamaría, "Entiendo que en un país con un 45% paro juvenil la gente se indigne. En 1995 los jóvenes vivimos una situación similar. Había un 40% de paro y mucho malestar. Entiendo indignación frente a la inoperancia de las medidas que se han adoptado por parte del Gobierno socialista. La gente merece medidas serias, y las hará un gobierno del PP, ya en 1996 se cambiaron las cosas" [I understand why people are angry in a country with 45 per cent youth unemployment. In 1995, we young people experienced a similar situation. There was 40 per cent unemployment and great unease. I understand outrage before the ineffective measures adopted by the Socialist Government. People deserve serious measures, and the PP government will deliver them, given that things changed in 1996]. See Cué, "Rajoy delega" (2011).

4. For Mariano Rajoy, "Lo fácil es descalificar a la política y los políticos... Es verdad que a veces hay gente que no cumple con sus obligaciones, gobiernos que no están a la altura, es lo que está sucediendo ahora, pero yo he visto a mucha gente trabajando, estirando los presupuestos, atendiendo a sus vecinos, y cumpliendo con su deber que es servir" [It's easy to discredit politics and politicians... It's true that sometimes there are people who don't fulfill their obligations, governments that don't rise to the challenge, and that's

what's happening now, but I've seen many people working, stretching their budget, assisting their neighbors, and fulfilling their duty, which is to serve]. See Cué, "Rajoy contesta" (2011).

5. In reference to 15M, per Deleuze and Guattari, as a nomadic war machine, also see Gutiérrez (2012).

6. To temper Deleuze and Guattari's theoretical model, the authors conceive of the "line of flight" within the rhizome as capable of escaping "outside" the existing structures of power in this *becoming-other*, which is not necessarily substantiated beyond their conceptual model, a point addressed in chapter 2. Here, I refer to *becoming-other* never as a transformation that completely sheds its former properties, or the structures of power conditioning them, but rather, understood through Ross Chambers's re-reading of Deleuze and Guattari, as necessarily shaped within the prevailing relational powers that produce, in part, desire. See the Preface to Chambers (1991, xi–xx).

1 Lessons Felt, Then Learned

1. In an effort to prevent a further downturn in construction, the Socialist government financed public works through the Plan-E stimulus package. For a history and analysis of the housing bubble and construction boom from 1995 to 2007, see Observatorio Metropolitano (2013, 25–75). For information on the devaluation of property in Spain, see Gobierno de España, Ministerio de Fomento (2012).

2. In Redondo's photography Patricia Keller argues for waiting as a political gesture, one of decelerating time against the speed of events in the Spanish crisis (Keller, 2015). For artist Hans Haacke's exhibition on the abandoned suburb "Ensanche de Vallecas" in Madrid, see Borja-Villel et al. (2012).

3. For a history of corruption in democratic Spain and similar practices in Francoism, see Heywood (2005, 39–60).

4. From 2008 to 2011, Spain's unemployed rates sailed from 8.60 percent to 22.85 percent of the active workforce. See the Instituto Nacional de Estadística database, http://www.ine.es.

5. Among other polemical decisions made during the Socialist tenure of Felipe González, which contributed to the disenchantment of the political left, was the vote to grant Spain's entrance into the European Economic Community in 1985; the call for a national referendum approving Spain's permanent membership in NATO in 1986; and favorable relations with the United States under Reagan's administration (Vilar, 1986).

6. See Mayor Oreja (2009), and a replication to this assertion repeated in the media by Pastor Guzmán (2012).

7. The average monthly net income in Spain rounded out to 1,345 euros in 2010. The National Institute for Statistics observes that this figure is much higher than the most common salary in Spain, due to the wealthiest salaries that raise the average; see the Instituto Nacional de Estadística,

"Encuesta de Estructura Salarial" (2010) and Navarro's analysis "Por qué los salarios son tan bajos" (2012).

8. "Trabajar hoy –además de un privilegio– es un acto subversivo, reaccionario y, por lo tanto, perseguido por esas milicias gubernamentales que ahora se llaman sindicatos [...] lacayos del poder, estómagos agradecidos que sólo esperan que no se acabe ese chollo de buen marisco y viajes en barcos" [To work, aside from a privilege, is today a subversive, reactionary act, consequently persecuted by those governmental militias that are now called labor unions...lackeys to power, thankful stomachs that only hope their gravy train of good seafood and boat trips never ends] (Genoveva, 2010, 2).

9. This controversial article, for its outrage, quickly became a trending topic in Twitter, notably, with commentary from prominent journalists such as Juan Ramón Lucas and Jordi Évole, among others. See Millás (2012).

10. In reference to Millás's article, Spain's "soft" bailout from the ECB was granted under certain conditions. As Navarro summarizes, the possibility of future financial assistance from the ECB came with a directive, since made public from Chief Mario Draghi to Spain's President Mariano Rajoy: "In a recent press conference (August 9, 2012), Mr. Draghi was quite clear. The ECB will not buy Spanish public bonds unless the Spanish government takes tough, unpopular measures such as reforming the labor market, reducing pension benefits, and privatizing the welfare state" ("The Euro," 2012).

11. In this sense, "outrage" and "anger" are preferred in English over the more literal translation "indignation," given that the latter implies some form of contempt according to the OED, such as "an action of counting or treating (a person or thing) as unworthy of regard or notice," or an implicit victimization to some form of wrongdoing. The actions of the *indignadxs*, however, cannot be construed as seeking public validation or entrance into the political sphere through victimism, a performative and/or appropriated maneuver ubiquitous in political discourse that is not wholly unique to Spain, as Justin Crumbaugh has noted. See Crumbaugh (2007, 365–84).

12. For a comprehensive overview of current literature on affect and its intersections with sociology, psychology, political theory, and neuroscience, among other disciplinary approaches, see Neuman et al. (2007). For a Deleuzian-Guattaridian reading of political affect in contemporary issues in United States politics, see Protevi (2009), and specifically, on affect and the notion of the war-machine in Latin America, Beasley-Murray (2011).

13. On affect and emotion formed by thought, and thought attached to emotion and affect, see Brennan (2004). For an analysis of the emotions from antiquity to neuroscience, see Gross (2006).

14. For an excellent reading of the culture of fear, threat, and preemptive military action instrumentalized toward political ends, see Massumi (2010, 52–70).

15. See Berlant, particularly *Cruel Optimism* (2011), and Clough and Halley, and their contributors (2007).

16. Although I pay greater attention to *Explicaciones* than Apesteguía's other publications, readers will note that this section also draws from his literary fanzines *(Otras) Reglas para la dirección del espíritu* (2012) and *Manual para seres vivos* (2013).

17. See Foucault (1977) and on the notion of "dressage," Lefebvre's chapter by the same name in *Rhythmanalysis* (2004, 38–45).

2   On Affect, Action, Urban Intervention

1. On the practices of cognitive democracy and technology platforms before 15M, which aim to involve immigrants and residents without the right to vote by citizenship, see Moreo Jiménez (2006, 313–3). On the effectiveness of cognitive democracy to resolve complex problems, see Farrell and Shalizi (2012).

2. "Although the bodies on the street are vocalizing their opposition to the legitimacy of the state, they are also, by virtue of occupying that space, repeating that occupation of space, and persisting in that occupation of space, posing the challenge in corporeal terms, which means that when the body 'speaks' politically, it is not only in vocal or written language" (Butler, 2011, n.p.).

3. María Luz Congosto offers quantitative data analysis of the most frequently used hashtags on Twitter during the encampment to find that the volume of public "noise" about the movement created through this social medium (with nearly one million Tweets in six days) was produced from over 160,000 unique users, showing that these users were highly active when disseminating information repeatedly over the first few days of the Sol encampment ("Del 15M a la #acampadasol," 2011; "Evolución," 2011).

4. This refusal is what Hardt and Negri have called an *exodus*, defined in terms of "a process of *subtraction* from the relationship with capital by means of actualizing the potential autonomy of labor-power" (2009, 152). Hardt and Negri tend to argue for subtraction as a "line of flight" capable of escaping the predominant structures of power, at least as it is proposed by Deleuze and Guattari. I should like to temper this observation while holding to one of its claims in practice. I argued earlier that critical responses to the crisis—to one's own economic hardship or that of others, to the powerful instruments aimed at legitimizing the art of government for the governed—bear an affective intensity to move one to act from the immediacy of thought, which are here brought into practice.

5. A weblog of the first few days of the Sol encampment may be found at its original web address, at *Acampada Indefinida en Sol* (2011).

6. For information on the expansion of 15M into neighborhood and town assemblies, see Pérez-Lanzac (2011). For an account on the history of 15M, updated occasionally by its participants, see "15M" (*15MPedia*, n.d.).

7. For an analysis on the impact of this bill if passed into law, see Cortizo (2012). For information on the restriction of media access to demonstrations before parliament in 2012, see *El Público's* account of events reported live ("#29S en directo," 2012).

8. Teaching and learning from one another are contingent upon chance encounters and disconnects in mobilizing activities, observed by Alberto Corsín and Gabriel Estalella. The authors argue that these social practices produce space through action and temporal-spatial relations—or, urban rhythms, as Lefebvre understood them. Corsín and Estalella analyze the assembly's activities as a rhythmic arrangement, one that produces forms of care (the ambulatory), as the "assembly is an urban object of care—and an object of urban care" ("What Is a Neighbor?", 2013, 3). The construction of space and time as a spatial arrangement, which the authors view through Lefebvre's rhythmanalysis, is one that shapes and is shaped by the social practices of providing care for others.

9. For a discussion on consensus in activism and the "structuring" of an emotional hierarchy within queer activist groups (one that tends to repress "personal" emotions in favor of collective affects), see Wilkinson (2009, 36–43).

10. However, these hierarchies of emotion associated with collective decision should also be taken with precaution, notes Eleanor Wilkinson, given their ability to structure a social consensus of feeling around group decision driven by cooperation, determining which emotions are appropriate and which ones are not (2009, 39). Though I have no evidence of Wilkinson's observation in the case of 15M, this is not to discard this possibility.

11. For a list of commissions and working groups in Madrid, see Asamblea Popular de Madrid (n.d.).

12. According to the Election Board: "En los días de reflexión y votación nuestra legislación electoral prohíbe realizar acto alguno de propaganda o de campaña electoral. Asimismo, el día de la votación prohíbe formar grupos susceptibles de entorpecer, de cualquier manera que sea, el acceso a los locales electorales, así como la presencia en sus proximidades de quiénes puedan dificultar o coaccionar el libre ejercicio del derecho del voto. Todas estas medidas legales están destinadas a garantizar el ejercicio con plena libertad del derecho fundamental de sufragio reconocido en el artículo 23 de la Constitución" [On reflection and voting days, our election legislation prohibits the celebration of any act of propaganda or election campaigning. Moreover, on voting day it prohibits forming groups susceptible to obstructing, in whatever manner, the access to voting sites, as well as the presence in the proximities of those who could impede or coerce the free exercise of the right to vote. All of these legal measures aim to guarantee this exercise with total freedom of the fundamental right to vote, recognized in Art. 23 of the Constitution]; the Board writes in conclusion, "es un comportamiento no acorde a las previsiones de la

LOREG y que excede del derecho de manifestación garantizado constitu-
cionalmente" [it (to assemble) is a conduct that is incompatible with the
provisions of the LOREG (election law) and that exceeds the constitutionally guaranteed right to demonstrate]. See Gobierno de España, Junta
Electroal Central (2011).

13. Deleuze argues: "However, the eternal return itself, in turning, gives rise
to a certain illusion in which it delights and admires itself, and which it
employs in order to double its affirmation of that which differs: it produces
an image of identity as though this were the *end* of the different. It produces an image of resemblance as the external *effect* of 'the disparate.' It
produces an image of the negative as the *consequence* of what it affirms, the
consequence of its own affirmation" (1994, 301).

14. Luis Moreno-Caballud notes that practices of the commons have come
to the foreground amid the crisis in Spain: "Junto a la desesperanza, la
pasividad y la victimización (que sin duda han estado y están presentes),
hemos visto cómo se han desarrollado y consolidado en estos últimos años
importantes redes de solidaridad, auto-organización, colaboración, denuncia y protesta, que se han movilizado activamente ante la crisis, y cuyo
estudio revela la emergencia de todo un caudal de 'imaginación sostenible'
particularmente importante para comprender en qué se está convirtiendo
la cultura española contemporánea" [Together with desperation, passivity,
and victimization (which undoubtedly have been and are still present),
in recent years we have seen how important networks of solidarity, self-
organization, collaboration, denouncement and protest have developed
and consolidated, which have actively mobilized faced with the crisis—a
study of which reveals the emergence of an entire current of "sustainable
imagination" particularly important to understanding what contemporary
Spanish culture is turning into] (2012, 536–7).

15. Žižek writes, "even if we do not take things seriously, even if we keep an
ironical distance, *we are still doing them*" (1989, 33). On the castration of
power, see his work *First As Tragedy, Then As Farce* (2009, 6–7).

16. An independent news source reports the proceedings of the assembly on
May 29, 2011: "Aludieron a importantes problemas de convivencia interna
y con los vecinos y comerciantes de la zona y de infraestructura (eléctricos y
de alimentación principalmente). Su propuesta fue 'reestructurarse', lo que
podría implicar, según explicaron, reducir el campamento y reorganizar
los puestos y los grupos de trabajo" [They alluded to important internal
problems on living together and also with the neighbors and business owners in the area, as well as with infrastructure (electricity and food, primarily). They proposed "restructuring," which could mean, as they explained,
reducing the encampment and reorganizing the information points and
working groups] ("Última hora," 2011).

17. For an excellent reading on the concept of "love" and the turn to the
"other" in resistance movements, particularly in 1968 Mexico City, see

Williams (2011, 117–52). On love and collective labor, also see Hardt and Negri (2009, 189).

18. My thanks to Megan Saltzman for sharing with me the "mind map" of 15M's transformations and confluences with existing platforms and activist groups; see "Mapa mental" (2014).

19. On the results of the regional and local elections in May 2011, see Gobierno de España, Ministerio de Interior ("Elecciones Locales," 2011). On the results of the general elections in November 2011, see Gobierno de España, Ministerio de Interior ("Elecciones Generales," 2011). All election statistics cited here come from these sources.

20. The terms "sphere of consensus" and beyond it, the "sphere of legitimate controversy," are attributed to Daniel C. Hallin's analysis on the role of the news media in the United States to have influenced public opinion about the Vietnam War. Hallin argues against this claim, noting that the news media continued to operate according to its reporting function in the late years of the war, to the extent that the shifting sphere of controversy (disagreements among government officials about the war) was reflected in this news coverage (1984, 2–24).

21. In a similar vein, writing before 15M, H. Rosi Song and Eloy E. Merino note that the general constituency's "proclivity to accept political measures without contestation has produced what [Juan Luis] Cebrián calls a 'fundamentalismo democrático' [democratic fundamentalism], which has converted democracy (and consensus) into the ideology practiced until recently by the governing conservative party Partido Popular" (2005, 14). The formulation of an oppositional discourse on CT in the wake of 15M would tend to challenge what Noël Valis noted as the "loss of oppositionality" which the author observes after the death of Franco in 1975 and the *Transición* era (2002, 295).

22. On Gran Vía as a symbol of early twentieth-century modernity, see Larson (2011). On the avenue's signature architectural *colosalismo,* I refer to Baker (2009).

23. For an extensive selection of the Situationist International's texts translated into English, see McDonough (2002). A comprehensive critique of the philosophical aims and origins of Situationism can be found in Plant (1992). For a review of Situationism's role in the events of 1968, see Hecken and Grzenia (2008, 23–30).

24. "The trajectory of Situationist discourse—stemming from an avant-garde artistic movement in the postwar period, developing into a radical critique of politics in the 1960s, and absorbed today into the routine of the disenchanted discourse that acts as the 'critical' stand-in for the existing order—is undoubtedly symptomatic of the contemporary ebb and flow of aesthetics and politics, and of the transformations of avant-garde thinking into nostalgia" (Rancière, 2004, 9).

3   The Biopolitics of Neoliberal Governance

1. In recent history, these reforms have proved "damaging [to] the welfare of the common people in those countries, causing enormous suffering," writes Vicenç Navarro. "[T]hese policies had consequences for the welfare and quality of life of ordinary people, creating death, disease, and social unrest" ("The IMF's Mea Culpa?", 2013, n.p.).

2. It would seem that, wherever the visible signs of poverty disturb neoliberal myth, such as Spain's reported 70 percent increase in extreme poverty since the crisis (Fundación Foessa, 2013), proof can be downplayed, discredited, or simply denied, to quote Finance Minister Cristóbal Montoro, as figures that "do not correspond to reality" ("Montoro critica," 2014).

3. Beyond the state, notes David Harvey, the advocates of neoliberalism "occupy positions of considerable influence in education (the universities and many 'think tanks'), in the media, in corporate boardrooms and financial institutions, in key state institutions (treasury departments, the central banks), and also in those international institutions such as the International Monetary Fund (IMF), the World Bank, and the World Trade Organization (WTO) that regulate global finance and trade" (2005, 3).

4. Cristina Moreiras-Menor argues that desires "to be modern" in *Transición*-era Spain, which entailed producing and "selling" a new democratic image to an international market were economically and psychologically motivated: "emerge la imperiosa necesidad de integrarse activamente en el ámbito internacional, funadmentalmente en Europa, para así transformarse en un sistema político, social y culturalmente moderno que la haga partícipe de los avances económicos, tecnológicos e informáticos que caracterizan el mundo internacional" [there emerges the imperative need to integrate actively into the international arena, fundamentally in Europe, in order to transform into a politically, socially, and culturally modern system that can make (Spain) a participant in economic, technological, and informational advances characterizing the international world] (2002, 60). After nearly four decades of isolation under Francoism, Spain was eager to participate in international political and economic modernization, which Joan Ramon Resina argues, contributed to the political *Transición*'s illusion, its "sleight of hand": "[r]ather than an event, the Transition was the special effect [. . .] of a collective installation in a present that wished itself absolute: the present of the market" (2000, 93).

5. In his introduction to Albarracín et al., José María Zufiaur spells out four features of neoliberalism in 1990s Spain, summarized here for brevity: (1) political discourse aimed to situate the struggle against inflation at the center of public debates, positioning it as an antagonism to growth and job creation; (2) to overturn the incremented taxation scale thereby favoring the greatest fortunes; (3) to condemn all things public and broaden areas for private profits, socially and culturally, by casting public services and aid in a negative light while, conversely, identifying privatization and

market reach in a positive one; and (4) to force a change in the balance of social powers, weakening labor unions and social organizations in favor of market functions and influential financial interests (1994, 8).

6. The first wave of privatizations under Socialist rule involved two main methods, either the direct sale of the company to impartial corporations or the gradual, and often total, divestment of state shareholding in the company's stocks on a case-by-case basis. Regarding labor, during González's tenure the unions UGT and CCOO opposed the introduction of temporary employment and a plan to create 800,000 jobs for Spain's youth given its impact to foster flexibility and minimize job security, thus making workers vulnerable to subpar salaries and labor securities. The year 1988 marked a definitive rupture in the PSOE's relation with the union UGT (Encarnación, 2008, 119). Also, for a brief history of privatizations in Spain's democratic history, see the Sociedad Estatal de Participaciones Industriales (SEPI), an organization dependent upon Spain's Ministry of Finance ("Privatizaciones de 1984 a 1996"; "Privatizaciones de 1996 a actualidad," n.d.).

7. The authors continue, "Las subvenciones y el sistema de adjudicación de las ayudas está matando a las empresas y está destruyendo los incentivos a la creación de un cine que tenga mercado" [Subsidies and the system of allocating aid are killing companies and destroying incentives to create a cinema that has a market] (Albert and Biazzi, 2009, 8).

8. Chueca, Malasaña, La Latina, Lavapiés, and the Sol and Plaza Mayor historic district are but a few exemplary neighborhoods transformed by privatization efforts from Madrid City Hall and its urbanization plans. For an excellent reading of La Latina neighborhood's self-managed initiatives against the effects of gentrification and privatization in recent years, see Feinberg (2014).

9. See Amador Fernández-Savater's two-part interview with Begoña Santa-Cecilia, Luis Moreno-Caballud, Susana Draper and Vicente Rubio, participants in the Occupy movement. In it, Draper draws a contrast to the United States where "no hay el mismo ambiente de crisis que en España, la crisis no organiza la conversación cotidiana" [there isn't the same air of crisis as in Spain; the crisis doesn't organize everyday conversations] ("Occupy más allá de Occupy II," 2012). My agreement with Draper's observation is admittedly informed by my experience as a resident of Madrid.

10. The nine participating artists are Jonás Bel, Paco Gómez, Jorquera, Carlos Luján, Juan Millás, Eduardo Nave, Eva Sala, Juan Santos, and Juan Valbuena. I cite the photographs using the format for weblog entries, available online for interested readers (Nophoto, "El último verano," 2012).

11. In the photographers' words: "Tras los recortes anunciados por el Gobierno el pasado 11 de julio, NOPHOTO ha decidido documentar la evolución del verano más inhóspito y desalentador de nuestra historia reciente. Por si después de éste ya no hubiera otro. Por si desaparece de nuestras vidas el verano. Este blog narra por tanto un estado de inquietud. Sus contenidos son frágiles y discontinuos, asociados a la naturaleza precaria de los

tiempos que vivimos. Pretende describir y rememorar las emociones de esa experiencia en vías de extinción que llamamos verano" [After the cutbacks announced by the Government last July 11, NOPHOTO has decided to document the evolution of the most discouraging, inhospitable summer in our recent history. In case there would be no others after this one. In case summer disappears from our lives. Therefore, this blog narrates an unsettling state. Its contents are fragile and discontinuous, associated with the precarious nature of the times we live in. It aims to describe and recall the emotions of that experience on its way to extinction, which we call summer] (Nophoto, 2012).

4 House Rules

1. English translation by Ian Johnston (Kafka, 2008).
2. "Es misión de mi Gobierno liberar a España del peso de esa herencia [...] No disponemos de más ley ni de más criterio que el que la necesidad nos impone. Hacemos lo que no nos queda más remedio que hacer, tanto si nos gusta como si no nos gusta. [...] No pregunto si me gusta, aplico las medidas excepcionales que reclama un momento excepcional" ("Frases de Rajoy," 2012).
3. The same language—"herencia envenenada" and "facturas sin pagar"—was used prior to the campaign for the 2011 General Elections ("Cospedal," 2011; "Mentiras," 2011).
4. On Franco and sovereign exceptionalism, "Law is on Franco's side; he is the law precisely because he is the suspension of the same law that is applied to those around him but not to himself or to those who are like him. That is, he is the state of exception due to the fact that while he applies the law, he is excluded from its framework, from its territory of applicability," as a sovereign power that defines and is always already excluded from the law he mandates (Moreiras-Menor, 2008, 6).
5. Also see Castells's dedication to *Communication Power* (2009, 15).
6. For a review of Poulantzas's work in relation to a tradition of Marxist criticism, see Kalyvas (2002, 105–42).
7. Jessop has developed some of the hermetic conceptual terms in Poulantzas's work, bringing them into the question of practices and structures that Poulantzas referred to as the institutional materialism of the state, in which these structures, divisions, and practices create a separation of labor and production. On Poulantzas, he notes: "There is a continuing movement of state power upward, downward, and sideways as attempts are made by state managers on different scales to enhance their respective autonomies and strategic capacities. One aspect of this is the loss of the de jure sovereignty of national states in certain aspects of rule- and/or decision-making powers are transferred upward to supranational bodies and the resulting rules and decisions bind national states," such as in the European Union (2002, 206).

8. For Poulantzas, political and economic actors do not simply "control" the state to protect monopoly capital, but rather these ensembles work separately toward objectives that bear the image of coherence in their aims, despite their haphazard execution. On his notion of hegemony in the state and the alienation of labor: "Unity-centralization is written into the capitalist State's hierarchic-bureaucratized framework as the effect of the reproduction of social division of labor within the State (including the division of manual and intellectual labor) and of its specific separation from the relations of production. It also arises from the State's structure as the condensation of a relationship of forces, and from the predominance over other classes or fractions of the power bloc that is commanded within the State by the hegemonic class or fraction" (2000, 136). The diffuse operations of power are not exclusively a question of ideology, but of the inscriptions of power within the actions of the state, for example, in the division of labors in bureaucratization that favor certain reproductions of difference, exclusion, and influence.

9. In a most recent example of how Spain's international law has been steered by the priorities of financial interests and sovereign debt, in 2014, the People's Republic of China urged Rajoy's administration to cease judicial investigations into the genocide of the people of Tibet, following the Spanish Magistrate Ismael Moreno's warrant for Interpol to arrest five government officials, among them, the former President Jiang Zemin. Given that the separation of powers between the executive and judicial branches of government does not allow Rajoy's administration to intervene in the investigation, the PP-controlled legislature passed urgently into law a wholesale limitation of the competencies of the Spanish justice system to try crimes abroad, which effectively forced the Spanish judiciary to file its investigation into the Tibet case, while placing into doubt the future of some 15 other cases. According to *El País*, a reported 20 percent of Spain's sovereign debt is held by investors in China, which political opposition and human rights groups alike have claimed is the motivating factor behind the PP's express law ("China," 2014; Fernández, 2014; "Crímenes," 2014).

10. These journalists and executives are, respectively, José Luis Agudo, Xabier Fortes, Toni Garrido, Alicia G. Montano, Fran Llorente, Juan Ramón Lucas, and Ana Pastor, to name a few.

11. See Professor of Economics Gonzalo Bernardos (University of Barcelona) for his critique on the lack of autonomous decision for economists hired by private sectors and the state to act as independent advisors: "somos la voz de nuestro dueño, ya sea político, ya sea algún consejero de alguna empresa. Decimos lo que quieren oír, porque si no, sabemos perfectamente que peligra nuestra retribución económica o peligra nuestro puesto de trabajo" [we're the voice of our master, whether a politician or some advisor to a company. We say what they want to hear because if we don't we know perfectly well that we risk our salary or our job] (Bernardos, 2014).

12. If there is a case to be made today about how desires are produced, rather than formed around a lack, then a cultural investigation into the methodologies of marketing strategies taught to business students would provide significant material. In order to prolong the profits of a given product, some marketing strategies chart a linear sequence of events (say, a ten-step process) for a product to reach a consumer, and then target one of these steps in order to generate added value for the consumer in her access to and consumption/use of the product. This kind of method, in other words, does not hinge upon identifying and then exploiting an "existing lack" in the market, but rather aims to "manufacture consumer desire" in the language of Sturken and Cartwright (189–236), particularly by installing added value in the expectations or comforts of consumers for the future (one's next purchase).

13. Rancière's argument, elaborated from his earlier work in *Aesthetics and Its Discontents* (2009), finds its roots in the paradoxical notion that this concept of the (passive) spectator is inherited from a classical triangulation between *mimesis*, or the regime of artistic representation (its grammar, so to speak), *poiesis* or artistic creation, and their bridge of continuity in *aisthesis*, or the reception of the work, in the domain of affects and sensations (aesthetics) conveyed from the work to spectators.

Bibliography

"#29S en directo: La Policía carga una noche más contra los manifestantes." *Público*, September 30, 2012. Accessed February 5, 2013. http://www.publico.es/443166/el-29s-en-directo-la-policia-carga-una-noche-mas-contra-los-manifestantes.

"15M." *15MPedia*. n.d. Web. Accessed September 17, 2012. http://wiki.15m.cc/.

Acampada Indefinida en Sol. May 16, 2011. Accessed August 10, 2014. http://concentracionsolmadrid.blogspot.com.es/2011_05_01_archive.html.

Acampada Sol. "Acampada Sol continuará en la Puerta del Sol." May 22, 2011. Accessed January 10, 2012. http://madrid.tomalaplaza.net/2011/05/22/acampada-sol-continuara-en-la-puerta-del-sol/.

———. "El Grupo de Trabajo de Economía Sol convoca una Asamblea con Carácter de Urgencia para tratar la reforma constitucional anunciada por el presidente del Gobierno." August 23, 2011. Accessed January 9, 2012. http://madrid.tomalaplaza.net/2011/08/23/.

———. "Propuestas aprobadas en la Asamblea de hoy día 20 de mayo de 2011 en ACAMPADA SOL." May 20, 2011. Accessed July 28, 2014. http://madrid.tomalaplaza.net/2011/05/20/propuestas-20-mayo/.

———. *Propuestas del Movimiento 15M.* Press Release. Madrid: Acampada Sol, May 20, 2011. *RTVE.es.* Accessed September 17, 2012. http://www.rtve.es/contenidos/documentos/propuestas_movimiento_15M.pdf.

Acevedo, Carlos et al. *CT o la Cultura de la Transición. Crítica a 35 años de cultura española.* Barcelona: Random House, 2012.

Agencia EFE. "Botella propone cubrir con voluntarios parte de los servicios públicos." *ElMundo.es,* January 26, 2012. Accessed September 17, 2012. http://www.elmundo.es/elmundo/2012/01/26/madrid/1327601221.html.

———. "Bruselas recuerda a Cataluña que la independencia implicaría salir de la UE." *ABC,* April 29, 2013. Accessed July 27, 2014. http://www.abc.es/20120911/espana/rc-bruselas-recuerda-cataluna-independencia-201209111914.html.

Ahmed, Sara. *The Cultural Politics of Emotion.* New York and London: Routledge, 2004.

Albarracín, Jesús et al. *La larga noche neoliberal. Políticas económicas de los 80.* 2nd Ed. Barcelona: Icaria, 1994.

Albert, Rocío and Rogelio Biazzi. "Mentiras y gordas (un thriller español): Los socialistas no frenan el desplome de espectadores pese a dar 87,7 millones de euros de subvenciones al cine." *Papeles FAES* 102 (5 June 2009): 1–8. Fundación para el Análisis y los Estudios Sociales. Accessed November 22, 2012. http:// www.fundacionfaes.org/record_file/filename/2417/papel_102.pdf.

Alcaide, Soledad. "Movimiento 15M: los ciudadanos exigen reconstruir la democracia." *El País*, May 17, 2011. Accessed September 17, 2012. http://politica.elpais. com/politica/2011/05/16/actualidad/1305556621_810419.html.

Althusser, Louis. "Ideology and Ideological State Apparatuses." In *Lenin and Philosophy and Other Essays*, translated by Ben Brewster, 127–86. New York and London: Monthly Review Press, 1971.

Amin, Ash and Nigel Thrift. "Doreen Massey: The Light Dances on the Water." In *Spatial Politics: Essays for Doreen Massey*, edited by David Featherstone and Joe Painter, 204–12. Somerset, NJ: Wiley, 2013.

Apesteguía, Gregorio. *(Explicaciones) Acerca de lo que está pasando. Ética para desheredados valientes*. Madrid: Dos Sardinas Ediciones, 2013.

———. *Manual para seres vivos*. Madrid: Dos Sardinas Ediciones, 2013.

———. *(Otras) Reglas para la dirección del espíritu*. Madrid: Dos Sardinas Ediciones, 2012.

Asamblea Popular de Madrid. n.d. Accessed January 10, 2013. http://madrid. tomalaplaza.net/contacto/.

"Asociaciones de la prensa censuran la detención de una periodista de La Sexta." *El País*, Seville Edition, November 26, 2012. Accessed December 30, 2013. http:// ccaa.elpais.com/ccaa/2012/11/26/andalucia/1353933143_114451.html.

Augé, Marc. *Non-Places. Introduction to an Anthropology of Supermodernity*. Translated by John Howe. London and New York: Verso, 1995.

Aznar, José María. "Ideas para salir de la crisis." *Una invitación al debate FAES* 1 (30 March 2009): 1–16. Fundación para el Análisis y los Estudios Sociales. Accessed July 31, 2014. http://www.fundacionfaes.org/file_upload/publication/ pdf/20130521152551una-invitacion-al-debate.pdf.

Baker, Edward. *Madrid Cosmopolita. La Gran Vía, 1910–1936*. Barcelona: Marcial Pons Historia & Villaverde Editores, 2009.

Banet-Weiser, Sarah. "Branding the Crisis." In *Aftermath: The Cultures of the Economic Crisis*, edited by Manuel Castells et al., 107–31. Oxford and New York: OUP, 2012.

Barroso, F. Javier. "La Juna Electoral de Madrid prohíbe la concentración en la Puerta del Sol." *El País*, May 17, 2011. Accessed September 17, 2012. http:// politica.elpais.com/politica/2011/05/16/actualidad/1305579962_497160.html.

Barthes, Roland. *Camera Lucida. Reflections on Photography*. Translated by Richard Howard. New York: Hill and Wang, 1981.

———. *Mythologies*. Translated by Annette Lavers. New York: Hill and Wang, 1972.

Basu, Sanjay and David Stuckler. *The Body Economic: Why Austerity Kills: Recessions, Budget Battles, and the Politics of Life and Death*. New York: Basic Books, 2013.

Beasley-Murray, Jon. *Posthegemony: Political Theory and Latin America*. Minneapolis: University of Minnesota Press, 2011.

Benjamin, Walter. *The Arcades Project*. Translated by Howard Eiland and Kevin McLaughlin. Cambridge, MA: Belknap Press of Harvard University Press, 1999.

——. *Illuminations*. Translated by Harry Zohn. New York: Schocken, 1968.

Berardi, Franco "Bifo." *The Uprising: On Poetry and Finance*. *Semiotext(e) Intervention Series* 14. Los Angeles: Semiotext(e), 2012.

Berlant, Lauren. *Cruel Optimism*. Durham and London: Duke University Press, 2011.

——. "Thinking about Feeling Historical." *Emotion, Space, and Society* 1 (2008): 4–9.

Bernardos, Gonzalo. "Entrevista: Gonzalo Bernardos, profesor de Economía en la Universidad de Barcelona." *Para Todos La 2*. RTVE, Madrid. Television. June 2, 2014. Accessed June 6, 2014. http://www.rtve.es/alacarta/videos/para-todos-la-2/para-todos-2-entrevista-gonzalo-bernardos-profesor-economia-universidad-barcelona/2594138/.

Blanco, Patricia R. "Santamaría: 'Por la crisis los españoles han recuperado valores perdidos.'" *El País*, June 6, 2012. Accessed September 17, 2012. http://politica.elpais.com/politica/2012/06/06/actualidad/1339012473_225979.html.

Blyth, Mark. *Austerity. The History of a Dangerous Idea*. Oxford and New York: OUP, 2013.

Borja-Villel, Manuel J. et al. *Hans Haacke: Castillos en el aire*. Madrid: Museo Nacional Centro de Arte Reina Sofía, 2012.

Brennan, Teresa. *The Transmission of Affect*. Ithaca and London: Cornell University Press, 2004.

Brown, Gavin and Jenny Pickerill. "Space for Emotion in the Spaces of Activism." *Emotion, Space, and Society* 2 (2009): 24–35.

Brown, Wendy. *Edgework: Critical Essays on Knowledge and Politics*. Princeton: Princeton University Press, 2005.

Buenafuente, Andreu. *Buenafuente*, Episode 305. La Sexta, television. Broadcast September 18, 2007.

Butler, Judith. "Bodies in Alliance and the Politics of the Street." Lecture. Venice (September 7, 2011) European Institute for Progressive Cultural Policies. Accessed January 9, 2014. http://www.eipcp.net/transversal/1011/butler/en.

Cañas, Gabriela. "Cómo interpretar a la 'mayoría silenciosa.'" *El País*, October 1, 2012. Accessed December 30, 2013. http://sociedad.elpais.com/sociedad/2012/10/01/actualidad/1349118911_488847.html.

Carmona Pascual, Pablo et al. *Spanish Neocon. La revuelta neoconservadora en la derecha española*. Madrid: Traficantes de sueños and Observatorio Metropolitano, 2012.

Caron, David. *AIDS in French Culture. Social Ills, Literary Cures*. Madison and London: University of Wisconsin Press, 2001.

Casa Real, "Mensaje de Navidad de Su Majestad el Rey Juan Carlos I." Archive. 24 Dec. 2009–12. Accessed September 18, 2013. www.casareal.es.

Castells, Manuel. "#12M#15M." Editorial. *La Vanguardia*, May 5, 2012. Accessed September 17, 2012. http://www.lavanguardia.com/opinion/articulos/20120505/54289233400/manuel-castells-12m15m.html.

———. *Communication Power*. Oxford and New York: OUP, 2009.

———. *Networks of Outrage and Hope: Social Movements in the Internet Age*. Cambridge, UK: Polity, 2012.

Chambers, Ross. *Room for Maneuver: Reading (the) Oppositional (in) Narrative*. Chicago and London: University of Chicago Press, 1991.

"China pide a la justicia española que 'corrija su error' en el caso del Tíbet." *El Mundo,* February 12, 2014. Accessed July 31, 2014. http://www.elmundo.es/espana/2014/02/12/52fb51e522601d75228b4572.html.

Clough, Patricia Ticineto and Jean Halley, eds. *The Affective Turn: Theorizing the Social*. Durham and London: Duke University Press, 2007.

Congosto, María Luz. "Del 15M a la #acampadasol: Topologías para un experimento político urbano." Address. Medialab Prado, Madrid, July 8, 2011. Accessed January 17, 2012. http://medialab-prado.es/article/investigacion_social_de_internet_y_las_tecnologias_digitales.

———. "Evolución de la propagación del 15M en la plaza de Twitter." May 22, 2011. Accessed January 14, 2013. http://www.barriblog.com/.

Comisión Europea. *Diario Oficial de la Unión Europea*. "Recomendación del Consejo de 12 de julio de 2011 relativa al Programa Nacional de Reforma de 2011 de España y por la que se emite un dictamen del Consejo sobre el Programa de Estabilidad actualizado de España (2011–2014)." 2011/C 212/01 Brussels: European Commission, July 19, 2011. Accessed January 13, 2015. http://eur-lex.europa.eu.

———. *Documento de Trabajo de los Servicios de la Comisión. Evaluación del programa nacional de reforma de 2011 y del programa de estabilidad de España que acompaña al documento Recomendación de "Recomendación del Consejo" relativa al programa nacional de reforma de 2011 de España y por la que se emite un dictamen del Consejo sobre el programa de estabilidad actualizado de España (2011–2014)*. Brussels: European Commission, June 7, 2011. Accessed January 13, 2015. http://eur-lex.europa.eu.

Comisión de Información Acampada Sol. "Compilación final de propuestas." April 24, 2012. Accessed September 17, 2012. http://madrid.tomalaplaza.net/.

Comisión Legal Sol. Madrid, n.d. Accessed September 17, 2012. http://legal15m.wordpress.com/.

Compitello, Malcolm A. "Sketching the Future Furiously. *La Movida*, Graphic Design, and the Urban Process in Madrid." In *Toward a Cultural Archive of la Movida: Back to the Future*, edited by H. Rosi Song and William Nichols, 203–31. Plymouth, UK: Rowman & Littlefield, 2013.

Corsín Jiménez, Alberto and Adolfo Estalella. "Asambleas al aire: La arquitectura ambulatoria de una política en suspensión." *Etnografías de la indignación*. Spec. issue of *Revista de Antropología Experimental* 13.4 (2013): 73–88. Universidad de Jaén. Accessed March 12, 2014. http://www.ujaen.es/huesped/rae/articulos2013/MEI_04%2013.pdf.

———. "What Is a Neighbor? Notes on #Occupying the urban relation," *Prototyping*, September 2012. Accessed January 13, 2013. http://www.prototyping.es/wp-content/uploads/2012/09/Corsin_Estalella_What-Is-Neighbour.pdf.

Cortizo, Gonzalo. "La prohibición de difundir imágenes de policies, vista por los jueces." *ElDiario.es*, October 18, 2012. Accessed January 4, 2014. http://www.eldiario.es/politica/policia-imagenes-manifestaciones_0_59494526.html.

"Cospedal: 'La mayoría de los españoles respira aliviada por el Adelanto electoral.'" *RTVE*, July 30, 2011. Accessed December 30, 2013. http://www.rtve.es/noticias/20110730/cospedal-mayoria-espanoles-respira-aliviada-adelanto-electoral/451059.shtml.

"Crímenes que pueden quedar impunes con la reforma del PP para limitar la justicia universal." *Público*, February 12, 2014. Accessed July 31, 2014. http://www.publico.es/politica/501300/los-crimenes-que-pueden-quedar-impunes-con-la-reforma-del-pp-para-limitar-la-justicia-universal.

Crumbaugh, Justin. "Are We All (Still) Miguel Ángel Blanco? Victimhood, the Media Afterlife, and the Challenge for Historical Memory." *Hispanic Review* 75.4 (Fall 2007): 365–84.

———. "*Poiesis*, producción, trabajo." *ALCES XXI Journal of Contemporary Spanish Literature and Film* 0 (2012): 41–53. Accessed June 25, 2014. http://revista.alcesxxi.org/.

Cué, Carlos E. "Los indignados agitan la campaña y los partidos les piden el voto." *El País*, May 19, 2011. Accessed September 17, 2012. http://politica.elpais.com/politica/2011/05/19/actualidad/1305788356_860217.html.

———. "Rajoy contesta: 'Lo fácil es descalificar a los políticos.'" *El País*, May 17, 2011. Accessed September 17, 2012. http://politica.elpais.com/politica/2011/05/17/22m/1305637087_714623.html.

———. "Rajoy delega en Sáenz de Santamaría para hablar de los indignados." *El País*, May 18, 2011. Accessed September 17, 2012. http://politica.elpais.com/politica/2011/05/18/actualidad/1305725529_450107.html.

Cué, Carlos E. and Anabel Díez. "Zapatero sobre el 15M: 'Hay que escuchar, hay que ser sensibles.'" *El País*, May 19, 2011. Accessed September 17, 2012. http://politica.elpais.com/politica/2011/05/19/actualidad/1305809587_615025.html.

Debord, Guy. *The Society of the Spectacle*. Translated by Donald Nicholson-Smith. New York: Zone, 1995.

"Definition of PIIGS." *Financial Times* Lexicon, n.d. Accessed September 18, 2014. http://lexicon.ft.com/.

Deleuze, Gilles. *Difference and Repetition*. Translated by Paul Patton. New York: Columbia University Press, 1994.

Deleuze, Gilles and Félix Guattari. *Anti-Oedipus. Capitalism and Schizophrenia*. Vol. 1. Translated by Robert Hurley et al. Minneapolis: University of Minnesota Press, 1983.

———. *A Thousand Plateaus: Capitalism and Schizophrenia*. Translated by Brian Massumi. Minneapolis and London: University of Minnesota Press, 1987.

Delgado, Manuel. "La ciudad levantada. La barricada y otras transformaciones radicales del espacio urbano." In *Hacia un urbanismo alternativo*, edited by

Josep Muntañola and Marcelo Zárate, 137–53. *Arquitectonics: Mind, Land, and Society*, 19–20. El Prat de Llobregat, Barcelona: Edicions Universitat Politècnica de Catalunya, 2010.

Derrida, Jacques. *Specters of Marx: The State of the Debt, the Work of Mourning, and the New International*. Translated by Peggy Kamuf. New York and London: Routledge, 1994.

"Descripción." *WikiLibro 15M.cc.* n.d. Accessed September 17, 2012. http://wiki.15m.cc/wiki/WikiLibro_15M.cc.

Díaz Villanueva, Fernando. "15M: del entusiasmo al perroflautismo." *La Gaceta, Intereconomía*, June 16, 2011. Accessed September 17, 2012. http://www.intereconomia.com/noticias-sociedad/15M-del-entusiasmo-al-perroflautismo-20110616.

"Dibujantes que abandonaron *El Jueves* por censura lanzan *Orgullo y Satisfacción.*" *ElDiario.es*, June 16, 2014. Accessed July 19, 2014. http://www.eldiario.es/rastreador/dibujantes-abandonaron-Jueves-Orgullo-Satisfaccion_6_271632854.html.

Draper, Susana. *Afterlives of Confinement. Spatial Transitions in Postdictatorship Latin America*. Pittsburgh: University of Pittsburgh Press, 2012.

Duncombe, Stephen. *Notes from Underground. Zines and the Politics of Alternative Culture*. Portland: Microcosm, 2008.

Elola, Joseba. "El 15M sacude el sistema." *El País*, May 22, 2011. Accessed September 17, 2012. http://politica.elpais.com/politica/2011/05/21/actualidad/1305999838_462379.html.

———. "La silenciosa expansión del 15M." *El País*, May 5, 2012. Accessed September 17, 2012. http://politica.elpais.com/politica/2012/05/05/actualidad/1336234920_810740.html.

Encarnación, Omar G. *Spanish Politics: Democracy after Dictatorship*. Cambridge, UK: Polity Press, 2008.

Erlanger, Steven. "Euro Zone Is Imperiled by North-South Divide." *New York Times*, December 2, 2010. Accessed September 17, 2012. http://www.nytimes.com/2010/12/03/world/europe/03divide.html?pagewanted=all.

Eyerman, Ron. "How Social Movements Move: Emotions and Social Movements." In *Emotions and Social Movements*, edited by Helena Flam and Debra King, 41–56. London and New York: Routledge, 2005.

Fabra, María. "El Constitucional se reafirma en la compatibilidad de la militancia de Cobos." *El País*, October 2, 2013. Accessed December 30, 2013 http://politica.elpais.com/politica/2013/10/02/actualidad/1380717905_793817.html.

———. "Jueces y fiscales progresistas califican la reforma de 'populista.'" *El País*, September 14, 2012. Accessed September 17, 2012. http://politica.elpais.com/politica/2012/09/14/actualidad/1347635139_397000.html.

Fajardo, José Manuel. "Del 11-M al 15-M." Editorial. *El País*, July 8, 2011. Accessed March 9, 2013. http://elpais.com/diario/2011/07/08/opinion/1310076012_850215.html.

Farrell, Henry and Cosma Rohilla Shalizi. "Cognitive Democracy." *Crooked Timber*. May 23, 2012. Accessed July 14, 2014. crookedtimber.org.

Feinberg, Matthew I. "Don Juan Tenorio in the Campo de Cebada: Restaging Urban Space after 15-M." *Journal of Spanish Cultural Studies* (2014): 1–17. Accessed January 8, 2015. http://www.tandfonline.com.

Fernández, María. "La Audiencia Nacional archiva la investigación sobre genocidio en el Tíbet." *El País*, June 23, 2014. Accessed July 31, 2014. http://politica.elpais.com/politica/2014/06/23/actualidad/1403537543_926352.html.

Fernández-Savater, Amador. "El nacimiento de un nuevo poder social." *Hispanic Review* 80.4 (Fall 2012): 677–81.

Fernández-Savater, Amador et al. "Occupy más allá de Occupy (I)." *ElDiario.es*, September 21, 2012. Accessed August 7, 2013. http://www.eldiario.es/interferencias/Occupy_Wall_Street-aniversario_6_49755042.html.

———. "Occupy más allá de Occupy (II)." *ElDiario.es*, September 24, 2012. Accessed August 7, 2013. http://www.eldiario.es/interferencias/Occupy-crisis-aniversario-EEUU_6_51154885.html.

Ferrandis, Joaquín. "El jefe de policía se refiere a los estudiantes como 'el enemigo.'" *El País*, Valencia Edition, February 21, 2012. Accessed September 17, 2012. http://ccaa.elpais.com/ccaa/2012/02/20/valencia/1329764951_838007.html.

Foucault, Michel. *Birth of Biopolitics: Lectures at the Collège de France, 1978–1979*. Translated by Graham Burchell. Basingstoke: Palgrave Macmillan, 2008.

———. *Discipline and Punish. The Birth of the Prison*. Translated by Alan Sheridan. New York: Vintage, 1977.

———. *The History of Sexuality. An Introduction*. Vol. 1. Translated by Robert Hurley. New York: Vintage, 1978.

"Frases de Rajoy: 'No podemos elegir (…) No tenemos esa libertad.'" *RTVE.es*, July 11, 2012. Accessed January 16, 2015. http://www.rtve.es/noticias/20120711/frases-rajoy-podemos-elegir-tenemos-libertad/545301.shtml.

Fundación Foessa and Cáritas. *Análisis y perspectivas, 2013. Desigualdad y derechos sociales*. Madrid: Fundación Foessa and Cáritas, 2013.

G-20 Washington Summit (2008). *Declaration of the Summit on Financial Markets and the World Economy*. G-20 Research Group, University of Toronto. Accessed January 13, 2015. http://www.g20.utoronto.ca/2008/2008declaration1115.html.

G. Montano, Alicia. "Los indignados: causas y estela de un fenómeno." CaixaForum, Madrid, August 29, 2011. Address.

———. *La manipulación en televisión*. Madrid: Espejo de Tinta, 2006.

Galcerán Huguet, Montserrat. "Presencia de los femenismos en la Puerta del Sol madrileña." *Youkali: Revista crítica de las artes y el pensamiento*. 12 (January 2012): 31–36.

García, Ángeles. "Arte para denunciar 'el tocomocho de las élites de la Transición.'" *El País*, January 15, 2013. Accessed October 21, 2013. http://cultura.elpais.com/cultura/2013/01/15/actualidad/1358249536_768482.html

García de Blas, Elsa. "Las 14.700 propuestas de cambio del 15M." *El País*, May 11, 2012. Accessed September 17, 2012. http://politica.elpais.com/politica/2012/05/10/actualidad/1336649244_037483.html.

García Gallo, Bruno. "La acampada supera el examen de los inspectores municipales de Salud." *El País*, May 28, 2011. Accessed September 17, 2012. http://elpais.com/diario/2011/05/28/madrid/1306581859_850215.html.

García-Rosales, Cristina and Manuel Penella Heller. *Palabras para indignados. Hacia una nueva revolución humanista.* Madrid: Mandala Ediciones, 2011.

Garea, Fernando. "El 'escaño 351.'" *El País*, August 14, 2011. Accessed September 17, 2012. http://politica.elpais.com/politica/2011/08/14/actualidad/1313343760_653017.html.

Genoveva. Editorial. *La Gaceta*, September 29, 2010: 2.

GESTHA Sindicato de Técnicos del Ministerio de Hacienda. *Sí hay alternativas. Gestha propone medidas para ingresar 63.800 millones anuales.* Madrid: GESTHA, 2012. Accessed September 18, 2014. http://www.gestha.es/archivos/informacion/comunicados/2012/alternativas-de-gestha-a-la-subida-del-iva-y-recortes-del-rdl-20-2012-sin-anexos.pdf.

Gil, Joaquín. "Las caras de la indignación." *El País*, May 17, 2011. Accessed September 17, 2012. http://politica.elpais.com/politica/2011/05/17/actualidad/1305656044_210451.html.

———. "He trabajado en una televisión manipulada." *El País*, November 6, 2013. Accessed July 14, 2014. http://ccaa.elpais.com/ccaa/2013/11/06/valencia/1383741792_791945.html.

Gobierno de España. Boletín Oficial del Estado. *Ley 35/2010, de 17 de septiembre, de medidas urgentes para la reforma del mercado de trabajo. Núm. 227. Sec. I. Pág. 79278.* September 18, 2010. Accessed September 17, 2012. http://www.boe.es/.

———. *Real Decreto-Ley 3/2012, de 10 de febrero, de medidas urgentes para la reforma del mercado laboral. Núm 2076. Sec. I. Pág. 12483.* February 11, 2012. Accessed September 17, 2012. http://www.boe.es/.

Gobierno de España. Congreso de los Diputados. *Diario de Sesiones del Congreso de los Diputados, Pleno y Diputación Permanente (2012) X Legislatura Núm. 25. Sesión plenaria núm. 24.* April 11, 2012. Accessed September 17, 2012. http://www.congreso.es/.

Gobierno de España. Junta Electoral Central. *Solicitud de que la Junta Electoral Central establezca un criterio uniforme, respecto a las diversas concentraciones, reuniones y manifestaciones promovidas por particulares, en particular en la jornada de reflexión, atendiendo a la existencia de acuerdos contrapuestos por parte de las Juntas Electorales Provinciales. Expediente 293/200.* May 19, 2011. Accessed September 17, 2012. www.juntaelectoralcentral.es.

Gobierno de España. Ministerio de Fomento. *El ajuste del sector inmobiliario español*, edited by Fernando da Cunha Serantes, January 2012. Accessed September 20, 2012. http://www.fomento.gob.es/.

Gobierno de España. Ministerio del Interior. "Anteproyecto de ley orgánica para la protección de la seguridad ciudadana." n.d. *Jueces para la democracia.* Accessed March 30, 2014. http://www.juecesdemocracia.es/legislacion/anteproyecto-de-ley-de-seguridad-ciudadana.pdf.

————. "Elecciones Generales 2011." November 21, 2011. Accessed June 14, 2014. http://elecciones.mir.es/resultadosgenerales2011/99CG/DCG99999TO_L1.htm.

————. "Elecciones Locales 2011." n.d. Accessed September 17, 2012. http://elecciones.mir.es/locales2011/.

Gobierno de España. Ministerio de Justicia. *Anteproyecto de ley orgánica por la que se modifica la ley orgánica 10/1995, de 23 de noviembre, del Código Penal.* July 16, 2012. *Jueces para la Democracia.* Accessed September 17, 2012. http://www.juecesdemocracia.es.

Gross, Daniel M. *The Secret History of Emotion: From Aristotle's Rhetoric to Modern Brain Science.* Chicago: University of Chicago Press, 2006.

Guirao Cabrera, José. *El libro mutante. La auto-edición vista desde España.* Madrid: La Casa Encendida & CajaMadrid Fundación Especial, 2013. Accessed July 8, 2014. librosmutantes.com.

Gutiérrez, Bernardo. "El aparato de guerra nómada del 15M." *ElDiario.es,* June 6, 2012. Accessed September 17, 2012. http://www.eldiario.es/zonacritica/aparato-guerra-nomada_6_12658744.html.

Gutiérrez-Rubí, Antoni. "Sin preguntas, sin ruedas, sin Debate." *Blog Macropolítica. El País,* June 21, 2012. Accessed December 30, 2013. http://blogs.elpais.com/micropolitica/2012/06/sin-preguntas-sin-ruedas-sin-debate.html.

Hache, Eva. "La crisis ha cambiado nuestra depresión post vacacional." *Club de la Comedia,* LaSexta, Television. Broadcast September 2, 2011. Accessed September 12, 2012. http://www.lasexta.com/sextatv/elclubdelacomedia/la_crisis_ha_cambiado_nuestra_depresion_post_vacacional/262803/5401.

Hallin, Daniel C. "The Media, the War in Vietnam, and Political Support: A Critique of the Thesis of an Oppositional Media." *The Journal of Politics* 46.1 (1984): 2–24.

Hardt, Michael and Antonio Negri. *Commonwealth.* Cambridge: Belknap Press of Harvard University Press, 2009.

————. *Declaration.* New York: Argo Navis, 2012.

————. *Empire.* Cambridge, MA: Harvard University Press, 2000.

————. *Multitude: War and Democracy in the Age of Empire.* New York: Penguin, 2005.

Harvey, David. *A Brief History of Neoliberalism.* Oxford and New York: OUP, 2005.

————. "The 'New' Imperialism: Accumulation by Dispossession." *The New Imperial Challenge. Socialist Register* 40. Eds. Leo Panitch and Colin Leys. London: Merlin Press, 2004. 63–87.

————. *Rebel Cities: From the Right to the City to the Urban Revolution.* London and New York: Verso, 2012.

Hecken, Thomas and Agata Grzenia. "Situationism." In *1968 in Europe: A History of Protest and Activism, 1956–1977,* edited by Martin Klimke and Joachim Scharloth, 23–30. Basingstoke: Palgrave Macmillan, 2008.

Hessel, Stéphane. *¡Indignaos! Un alegato contra la indiferencia y a favor de la insurrección pacífica.* Translated by Telmo Moreno Lanaspa. Barcelona: Destino, 2011.

Heywood, Paul M. "Corruption, Democracy, and Governance in Contemporary Spain." In *The Politics of Contemporary Spain*, edited by Sebastian Balfour, 39–60. London and New York: Routledge, 2005.

Hooper, John. *The New Spaniards*. London: Penguin, 2006.

Horkheimer, Max and Theodor W. Adorno. *Dialectic of the Enlightenment. Philosophical Fragments*. Edited by Gunzelin Schmid Noerr. Translated by Edmund Jephcott. Stanford, California: Stanford University Press, 2002.

Huete Machado, Lola and Virginia Collera. "Emigrantes otra vez." *El País*, Sunday Edition, December 11, 2011. Accessed September 17, 2012. http://elpais.com/diario/2011/12/11/eps/1323588415_850215.html.

"Indignados." *Informe Semanal*. RTVE, Madrid. Broadcast May 21, 2011. Television. Accessed September 17, 2012. http://www.rtve.es/alacarta/videos/informe-semanal/informe-semanal-indignados/1108047/.

Instituto Nacional de Estadística. "Encuesta de Estructura Salarial 2010." *INEbase*, n.d. Accessed September 17, 2012. http://www.ine.es.

International Monetary Fund. *Poverty and Social Impact Analysis by the IMF. Review of Methodology and Selected Evidence*. Edited by Robert Gillingham. Washington, DC: International Monetary Fund, 2008. Accessed October 14, 2013. http://www.imf.org/external/pubs/ft/books/2008/posocimp/posocimp.pdf.

———. *World Economic Outlook, October 2012. Coping with High Debt and Sluggish Growth*. Washington, DC: International Monetary Fund, 2012. Accessed October 14, 2013. http://www.imf.org/external/pubs/ft/weo/2012/02/pdf/text.pdf.

Jameson, Fredric. *Postmodernism, or the Cultural Logic of Late Capitalism*. Durham: Duke University Press, 1991.

Jessop, Bob. "Globalization and the National State." In *Paradigm Lost: State Theory Reconsidered*, edited by Stanley Aronowitz and Peter Pratsis, 185–220. Minneapolis: University of Minneapolis Press, 2002.

———. *State Theory: Putting the Capitalist State in Its Place*. University Park, PA: Pennsylvania State University Press, 1990.

———. "The Strategic Selectivity of the State: Reflections on a Theme of Poulantzas." *Journal of the Hellenic Diaspora* 25.1–2 (1999): 1–37.

Kafka, Franz. "In the Penal Colony." Translated by Ian Johnston. October 2003. Accessed January 4, 2015. http://www.kafka.org.

Kalyvas, Andreas. "The Stateless Theory: Poulantzas's Challenge to Postmodernism." In *Paradigm Lost: State Theory Reconsidered*, edited by Stanley Aronowitz and Peter Pratsis, 105–42. Minneapolis: University of Minneapolis Press, 2002.

Keller, Patricia. "Espera, Andalucía: la crisis, el tiempo de la espera y la fotografía de Markel Redondo." In *La retórica del sur: Representaciones y discursos sobre Andalucía en el periodo democrático*, edited by Antonio Gómez-López Quiñones and José Manuel del Pino Cabello, 289–324. Seville: Ediciones Alfar, 2015.

Kövecses, Zoltán. *Metaphor and Emotion: Language, Culture, and Body in Human Feeling*. Cambridge : CUP, 2000.

La Parra-Pérez, Pablo. "Revueltas lógicas: el ciclo de movilización del 15M y la práctica de la democracia radical." *Journal of Spanish Cultural Studies* (2014): 1–19. Accessed January 8, 2015. http://www.tandfonline.com.

Labanyi, Jo. "Doing Things: Emotion, Affect, and Materiality." *Journal of Spanish Cultural Studies* 11.3–4 (2010): 223–33.

Labrador Méndez, Germán. "Las vidas subprime: la circulación de historias de vida como tecnología de imaginación política en la crisis española (2007–2012)." *Hispanic Review* 80.4 (Fall 2012): 557–81.

Lamo de Espinosa, Emilio. "El 11-S y el nuevo escenario estratégico." *Cuadernos de pensamiento político. Fundación para el Análisis y los Estudios Sociales* 13 (Jan–Mar 2007): 9–36.

Lara, Ángel Luis. "Virgil Starkwell en la Puerta del Sol: públicos en revuelta, políticas hacia el ser por venir." *Hispanic Review* 80.4 (Fall 2012): 651–65.

Larson, Susan. *Constructing and Resisting Modernity: Madrid 1900–1936.* Estudios de la Cultura de España, 20. Madrid: Iberoamericana and Vervuert, 2011.

Lazzarato, Maurizio. "Neoliberalism in Action: Inequality, Insecurity, and the Reconstitution of the Social." *Theory, Culture & Society* 26 (2009): 109–33.

Lefebvre, Henri. *Rhythmanalysis. Space, Time, and Everyday Life.* Translated by Stuart Elden and Gerald Moore. London and New York: Continuum, 2004.

Lemke, Thomas. "'The Birth of Bio-Politics': Michel Foucault's Lecture at the Collège de France on Neo-Liberal Governmentality." *Economy and Society* 30.2 (2001): 190–207.

Librería Bakakai, ed. *Vacaciones en Polonia.* 6 vols. to date. Granada: Editorial Bakakai, 2006-.

Likki, Tina. "15M Revisited: A Diverse Moment United for Change." *Zoom Político* 11 (2012). Fundación Alternativas. Accessed September 17, 2012. http://www.falternativas.org/laboratorio/libros-e-informes/zoom-politico/15m-revisited-a-diverse-movement-united-for-change.

Lustig, Nora, ed. *Coping with Austerity: Poverty and Inequality in Latin America.* Washington, DC: Brookings Institution, 1995.

Madrid 15M, "Grupos de Trabajo." n.d. Accessed September 17, 2012. http://madrid.15m.cc/ 2012/06/grupos-de-trabajo-de-15mcc-v.html.

"Mapa mental de Mutaciones, Proyecciones, Alternativas y Confluencias 15M." AutoConsulta Ciudadana, March 2, 2014. Accessed August 10, 2014. http://autoconsulta.org/mutaciones.php.

Marcus, Greil. "The Long Walk of the Situationist International." In *Guy Debord and the Situationist International. Texts and Documents*, edited by Tom McDonough, 1–26. Cambridge and London: MIT Press, 2002.

Martín Cabrera, Luis. "The Potentiality of the Commons: A Materialist Critique of Cognitive Capitalism from the Cyberbracer@s to the Ley Sinde." *Hispanic Review* 80.4 (Fall 2012): 583–605.

Martín Rodrigo, Inés et al. "La crisis del libro, según los editores." *ABC*, May 5, 2012. Accessed July 10, 2014. http://www.abc.es/20120511/cultura-libros/abci-cinco-editores-hablan-cambiar-201205102052.html.

Martínez Soria, Carlos Julián, ed. *UNELibros. Publicación de la Unión de Editoriales Universitarias Españolas.* 26 (Spring 2013). Accessed July 10, 2014. http://www. une.es/media/Ou1/Image/webmayo2013/UNE%20Libros%2026.pdf.

"Más de seis millones de españoles han participado en el Movimiento 15M." *RTVE.es*, August 6, 2011. Accessed September 17, 2012. http://www.rtve.es/ noticias/20110806/mas-seis-millones-espanoles-han-participado-movimiento-15m/452598.shtml.

Massumi, Brian. "The Future Birth of the Affective Fact: The Political Ontology of Threat." In *The Affect Theory Reader*, edited by Melissa Gregg and Gregory J. Seigworth, 52–70. Durham: Duke University Press, 2010.

———. *Parables for the Virtual: Movement, Affect, Sensation.* Durham: Duke University Press, 2002.

Mayor Oreja, Jaime. "La deuda moral de la crisis económica." Editorial. *ABC*, January 7, 2009. Accessed September 18, 2012. http://www.abc.es/hemeroteca/historico-07-01-2009/abc/Nacional/la-deuda-moral-de-la-crisis-economica_912300689861.html.

———. "Reforma, regeneración y rectificación." *Papeles FAES* 141 (23 July 2010): 1–16. Fundación para el Análisis y los Estudios Sociales. Accessed November 25, 2012. http://www.fundacionfaes.org/es/publicaciones/ papeles_faes?year=2010&order=&size=50.

McDonough, Tom, ed. *Guy Debord and the Situationist International: Texts and Documents.* Cambridge and London: MIT Press, 2002.

"Memoria vecinal." Asociaciones de Vecinos de Madrid. Madrid, n.d. Accessed January 12, 2013. http://www.memoriavecinal.org/.

"Mentiras y facturas sin pagar." *La Razón*, July 18, 2011. Accessed December 30, 2013. http://www.larazon.es/detalle_hemeroteca/noticias/ LA_RAZON_387087/3700-mentiras-y-facturas-sin-pagar-herencia-socialista.

Merino, Eloy E. and H. Rosi Song. "Tracing the Past: An Introduction." In *Traces of Contamination: Unearthing the Francoist Legacy in Contemporary Spain*, edited by Eloy E. Merino and H. Rosi Song, 11–26. Lewisburg: Bucknell University Press, 2005.

"Merkel alaba la reforma constitucional española para limitar el déficit." *ABC*, August 31, 2011. Accessed September 17, 2012. http://www.abc.es/20110831/ economia/abci-merkel-alaba-deficit-201108310918.html.

"Metodología asamblearia." Asamblea Popular de Madrid. Madrid, n.d. Accessed September 17, 2012. http://madrid.tomalosbarrios.net/metodologia-asamblearia/.

Millás, Juan José. "Un cañón en el culo." *El País*, August 14, 2012. Accessed September 22, 2012. http://cultura.elpais.com/cultura/2012/08/13/actualidad/1344875187_015708.html.

Mohíno, Fran, perf. *We_Love_You.* In *No hay banda. Un experimento en el tiempo*, curated by Abel H. Pozuelo. El Matadero, Madrid, April 5, 2013. Performance.

"Montoro critica los informes de Cáritas sobre la pobreza infantil en España." *Cadena Ser*, February 28, 2014. Accessed July 31, 2014. http://cadenaser.com/ ser/2014/03/28/espana/1395967833_850215.html.

Moreiras-Menor, Cristina. *Cultura herida. Literatura y cine en la España democrática.* Madrid: Ediciones Libertarias, 2002.

———. *La estela del tiempo. Imagen e historicidad en el cine español contemporáneo.* La Casa de la Riqueza Estudios de la Cultura de España, 21. Madrid: Iberoamericana & Vervuert, 2011.

———. "History against the Grain: The State of Exception and Temporality in the Spanish Transition." *Tiresias* 2 (April 2008): 3–13. Accessed December 30, 2013. https://www.lsa.umich.edu/rll/tiresias/previous%20issues/pdf2/TIRESIAS%20Issue%202.pdf.

Moreno-Caballud, Luis. "La imaginación sostenible: Culturas y crisis económica en la España actual." *Hispanic Review* 80.4 (Fall 2012): 535–55.

Moreno Jiménez, José María. "E-Cognocracia: Nueva sociedad, nueva democracia." *Estudios de Economía Aplicada* 24.1 (April 2006): 313–33. Red de Revistas Científicas de América Latina y el Caribe, España y Portugal, Universidad Autónoma del Estado de México. Accessed June 14, 2014. http://www.redalyc.org/pdf/301/30113179013.pdf.

Muñiz, Andrés. "El número de desahucios bate todos los récords: 46.559 en tres meses de 2012." *Público,* July 21, 2012. Accessed July 25, 2014. http://www.publico.es/espana/439864/el-numero-de-desahucios-bate-todos-los-records-46-559-en-tres-meses-de-2012.

Muñoz-Alonso, Alejandro. "Democracia y pobreza." *Papeles de la Fundación FAES* 10 (January 1995): 5–28. Fundación para el Análisis y los Estudios Sociales. Accessed January 7, 2012. http://www.fundacionfaes.org/file_upload/publication/pdf/20130426153518democracia-y-pobreza.pdf.

"N-1." N-1, n.d. Accessed September 17, 2012. https://n-1.cc/.

Narváez, Diego and Lourdes Lucio. "Zapatero culpa del paro al urbanismo salvaje del PP y pide ayuda a Rajoy." *El País,* February 22, 2010. Accessed September 26, 2014. http://elpais.com/diario/2010/02/22/espana/1266793202_850215.html.

Navarro, Vicenç et al. *Hay alternativas: Propuestas para crear empleo y bienestar social en España.* Madrid: Sequitur & ATTAC, 2011.

Navarro, Vicenç and Leiyu Shi. "The Political Context of Social Inequalities and Health." *Social Science and Medicine* 52 (2001): 481–91.

Navarro, Vicenç. "The Euro Is Not in Trouble. People Are!" *Social Europe Journal,* August 17, 2012. Accessed July 27, 2014. http://www.social-europe.eu/2012/08/the-euro-is-not-in-trouble-people-are/.

———. "The IMF"s Mea Culpa?" *Revolting Europe. On Europe, the Left, Labour, and Social Movements,* January 17, 2013. Accessed July 30, 2014. http://revolting-europe.com/2013/01/21/the-imfs-mea-culpa/.

———. "Por qué los salarios son tan bajos en España." *Dominio público,* Editorial. *Público,* August 30, 2012. Accessed September 17, 2012. http://www.vnavarro.org/?p=7775.

Neuman, W. Russell et al. *The Affect Effect: Dynamics of Emotion in Political Thinking and Behavior.* Chicago and London: University of Chicago Press, 2007.

Nieuwenhuys, Constant. "A Different City for a Different Life." In *Guy Debord and the Situationist International. Texts and Documents*, edited by Tom McDonough, 95–101. Cambridge and London: MIT Press, 2002.

Nophoto. *El último verano*. Madrid, 2012. Accessed August 7, 2013. http://elultimoverano.nophoto.org.

———. *El último verano. NOPHOTO ha decidido documentar la evolución del verano de 2012*. Exhibition catalog. Madrid: CentroCentro & Nophoto, 2012.

Observatorio Metropolitano de Madrid, eds. *Paisajes devastados. Después del ciclo inmobiliario: impactos regionales y urbanos de la crisis*. Madrid: Traficantes de sueños, 2013.

Ortega Almón, María Ángeles, and María Ángeles Sánchez Domínguez. "La política de privatizaciones en España." *Momento económico* 122 (July–August 2002): 32–40. Universidad Nacional Autónoma de México. Accessed January 14, 2013. http://www.ejournal.unam.mx/contenido.html?r=17&v=S/V&n=122.

Partido Popular. "Súmate al cambio, Vota Partido Popular." Campaign Advertisement. October 25, 2011. Accessed August 10, 2013. https://www.youtube.com/watch?v=DWcDF3DY50Q.

Pastor Guzmán, Francisco. "Por encima de las posibilidades ¿de quién?" Editorial. *El País,* January 17, 2012. Accessed September 20, 2012. http://elpais.com/diario/2012/01/17/opinion/1326754806_850215.html.

Patton, Paul. "Deleuze and Democracy." *Contemporary Political Theory* 4 (2005): 400–413.

———. "Multiculturalism and Political Ontology." In *The Ashgate Research Companion to Multiculturalism*, edited by Duncan Ivison, 57–71. Surrey: Ashgate, 2010.

Peck, Jamie and Adam Tickell. "Neoliberalizing Space." *Antipode* 34.3 (July 2002): 380–404.

Pérez-Lanzac, Carmen. "El 'big-bang' del 15M." *El País*, July 18, 2011. Accessed September 17, 2012. http://elpais.com/diario/2011/07/18/madrid/1310988256_850215.html.

Pérez Royo, Javier. "Estado de Excepción." *El País,* February 4, 2012. Accessed December 30, 2013. http://elpais.com/diario/2012/02/04/espana/1328310006_850215.html.

———. "Estado de excepción parlamentario." *El País,* July 6, 2012. Accessed December 30, 2013. http://politica.elpais.com/politica/2012/07/06/actualidad/1341595862_758523.html.

Perriam, Chris. "Spanish Microcultural Studies: Fleeting Moments and Cultural Structures." *Journal of Spanish Cultural Studies* 11:3–4 (September–December 2010): 291–304.

Pequeños dramas sobre arena azul. By Abel Zamora. La Casa de la Portera, Madrid, February 6, 2014. Performance.

Plant, Sadie. *The Most Radical Gesture: The Situationist International in a Postmodern Age*. London and New York: Routledge, 1992.

Poulantzas, Nicos. *Classes in Contemporary Capitalism*. Translated by David Fernbach. London: NLB, 1975.

————. "The Political Crisis and the Crisis of the State." In *The Poulantzas Reader. Marxism, Law, and the State*, edited by James Martin, 294–322. London and New York: Verso, 2008.

————. *State, Power, Socialism*. London and New York: Verso, 2000.

Protevi, John. *Political Affect: Connecting the Social to the Somatic*. Minneapolis: University of Minnesota Press, 2009.

Rancière, Jacques. *Aesthetics and its Discontents*. Translated by Steven Corcoran. Cambridge: Polity, 2009.

————. *Dissensus. On Politics and Aesthetics*. Translated and edited by Steven Corcoran. London and New York: Continuum, 2010.

————. *The Emancipated Spectator*. Translated by Gregory Elliott. London and New York: Verso, 2009.

————. *The Politics of Aesthetics*. Translated by Gabriel Rockhill. London and New York: Continuum, 2004.

Read, Jason. "A Genealogy of Homo-Economicus: Neoliberalism and the Production of Subjectivity." *Foucault Studies* 6 (Feb. 2009): 25–36.

Resina, Joan Ramon. "Short of Memory: The Reclamation of the Past since the Spanish Transition to Democracy." In *Disremembering the Dictatorship: The Politics of Memory in the Spanish Transition to Democracy*, edited by Joan Ramon Resina, 83–126. Amsterdam: Rodopi, 2000.

Rodríguez, Ana. "El Consejo de Europa denuncia las injerencias del PP en TVE." *El Plural*, January 29, 2013. Accessed July 31, 2014. http://www.elplural.com/2013/01/29/el-consejo-de-europa-denuncia-las-injerencias-del-pp-en-tve/.

Romanos, Eduardo. "Collective Learning Processes within Social Movements: Some Insights into the Spanish 15-M/Indignados Movement." In *Understanding European Movements: New Social Movements, Global Justice Struggles, Anti-Austerity Protest*, edited by Cristina Flesher Fominaya and Laurence Cox, 203–219. London: Routledge, 2013.

————. "Humor in the Streets: The Spanish Indignados." *Humor and Politics in Europe*, Special issue of *Perspectives on Europe*: Council for European Studies at Columbia U 43.2 (Autumn 2013): 15–20.

Romero, José Manuel et al. "Entrevista Economía: Zapatero a examen: 'Es un tema opinable si hay crisis o no hay crisis.'" *El País*, Sunday edition, June 29, 2008. Accessed September 17, 2012. http://elpais.com/diario/2008/06/29/domingo/1214711556_850215.html.

Rose, Nikolas. *Powers of Freedom: Reframing Political Thought*. Port Chester, NY: CUP, 1999.

"Rubalcaba: 'Nos consideramos compatibles con la Monarquía.'" *El País,* June 11, 2014. Accessed July 9, 2014. http://politica.elpais.com/politica/2014/06/11/actualidad/1402477698_946135.html.

Saleh, Samira and Carmen Pérez Lanzac. "Un campamento con calles y baños portátiles." *El País,* May 19, 2011. Accessed September 17, 2012. http://elpais.com/elpais/2011/05/19/actualidad/1305793032_850215.html.

Sampedro, Víctor and Josep Lobera. "The Spanish 15-M Movement: A Consensual Dissent?" *Journal of Spanish Cultural Studies* (2014): 1–20. Accessed January 8, 2015. http://www.tandfonline.com.

Sampedro, Víctor and José Manuel Sánchez. "Del 15M a la #acampadasol: Topologías para un experimento político urbano." Address. Medialab Prado, Madrid, July 8, 2011. Accessed January 17, 2012. http://medialab-prado.es/article/investigacion_social_de_internet_y_las_tecnologias_digitales.

———. "La Red era la plaza." Ciber-democracia, 2011. Accessed July 14, 2014. http://www.ciberdemocracia.es/.

Sánchez Cedillo, Raúl. "El 15M como insurrección del cuerpo-máquina." *Rebelion. org*, Februrary 28, 2012. Accessed September 17, 2012. http://www.rebelion.org/noticia.php?id=145402.

———. "Las elecciones del 20N como no acontecimiento." In *Democracia Distribuida: Miradas de la Universidad Nómada al 15M*, edited by Universidad Nómada, 71–9. Madrid: Universidad Nómada, 2012. Accessed October 5, 2012. http://www.trasversales.net/ddun15m.pdf.

Santaeulalia, Inés et al. "Perfiles de los peregrinos indignados." *El País*, July 23, 2011. Accessed September 17, 2012. http://politica.elpais.com/politica/2011/07/23/actualidad/1311457492_090512.html.

S.C. Agencias, "La Comunidad de Madrid crea los "voluntarios forzosos": la administración podrá hacer trabajar gratis a los parados." *El Plural*, May 29, 2013. Accessed July 25, 2014. http://www.elplural.com/2013/05/29/la-comunidad-de-madrid-crea-los-voluntarios-forzosos-la-administracion-podra-hacer-trabajar-gratis-a-los-parados/.

Schmitt, Carl. *The Concept of the Political*. Chicago and London: University of Chicago Press, 1996.

———. *Political Theology: Four Chapters on the Concept of Sovereignty*. Translated by George Schwab. Chicago: University of Chicago Press, 2005.

Seco, Raquel et al. "La izquierda hace guiños al 15M." *El País*, May 18, 2011. Accessed September 17, 2012. http://politica.elpais.com/politica/2011/05/17/actualidad/1305657705_222458.html.

Serrano, Eduardo. "El poder de las palabras: glosario de términos del 15M." Madrilonia.org, 2011. Accessed April 4, 2013. http://www.madrilonia.org/2011/06/el-poder-de-las-palabras-glosario-de-terminos-del-15m/.

Serrano, María Isabel. "Nadie quiere hospedarse en Sol." *ABC*, June 1, 2011. Accessed September 17, 2012. http://www.abc.es/20110601/madrid/abcp-nadie-quiere-hospedarse-20110601.html.

Sierra, Santiago and Jorge Galindo. *Los encargados*. Madrid, August 2012. Accessed August 12, 2014. http://www.santiago-sierra.com/201207_1024.php.

Snyder, Jonathan. "About Time: Sensing the Crisis in Nophoto"s *El último verano*." *Journal of Spanish Cultural Studies* (2014): 1–17. Accessed September 25, 2014. http://www.tandfonline.com.

Sociedad Estatal de Participaciones Industriales (SEPI). "Privatizaciones de 1984 a 1996." Ministerio de Hacienda y Administraciones Públicas. Ministerio de Hacienda y Administraciones Públicas, n.d. Accessed January 28, 2013. www.sepi.es.

———. "Privatizaciones de 1996 a actualidad." Ministerio de Hacienda y Administraciones Públicas, n.d. Accessed January 28, 2013. www.sepi.es.

Sontag, Susan. "Happenings: An Art of Radical Juxtaposition." In *Against Interpretation and Other Essays*, 263–74. New York: Picador, 1961.

"Spain: After the Fiesta." *The Economist*, November 6, 2008. Accessed September 17, 2012. http://www.economist.com/node/12562353.

Spires, Robert C. *Post-Totalitarian Spanish Fiction*. Columbia, Missouri: University of Missouri Press, 1996.

Strauss, David Levi. *Between the Eyes. Essays on Photography and Politics*. New York and London: Aperture, 2003.

Tanner, Jakob. "Motions and Emotions." In *1968 in Europe: A History of Protest and Activism, 1956–1977*, edited by Martin Klimke and Joachim Scharloth, 71–80. Basingstoke: Palgrave Macmillan, 2008.

Temporada baja. By Abel Zamora. Directed by Sergio Caballero. Teatre Rialto, Valencia, April 13, 2013. Performance.

Thomson, Alex. "On the Shores of History." In *Reading Rancière: Critical Dissensus*, edited by Paul Bowman and Richard Stamp, 200–16. London and New York: Continuum, 2011.

Thrift, Nigel. *Non-Representational Theory: Space, Politics, Affect*. New York and London: Routledge, 2007.

"TomaLaPlaza." *TomaLaPlaza.net*, n.d. Accessed September 17, 2012. http://tomalaplaza.net/.

Townson, Nigel. "El 15M: ¿un nuevo Mayo de 1968?" Editorial. *El País*, June 6, 2011. Accessed September 17, 2012. http://elpais.com/diario/2011/06/06/opinion/1307311211_850215.html.

"Última hora, 30 de mayo: Sigue la Acampada Sol en directo." *LaInformación.com*, May 30, 2011. Accessed August 10, 2014. http://noticias.lainformacion.com/asuntos-sociales/ultima-hora-30-de-mayo-sigue-la-acampada-sol-en-directo_K6fK4IoEBVqKTC4RDdVYe/.

Unión General de Trabajadores (UGT). "Méndez y Toxo expresaron a Rajoy el rechazo sindical a los recortes." *UGT*, July 27, 2012. Accessed September 17, 2012 http://www.ugt.es/actualidad/2012/julio/b27072012.html.

Valis, Noël. *The Culture of Cursilería. Bad Taste, Kitsch, and Class in Modern Spain*. Durham: Duke University Press, 2002.

Vilar, Sergio. *La década sorprendente, 1976–1986*. Barcelona: Planeta, 1986.

Vilaseca, Stephen Luis. "The 15-M Movement: Formed by and Formative of Counter-Mapping and Spatial Activism." *Journal of Spanish Cultural Studies* (2014): 1–21. Accessed January 8, 2015. http://www.tandfonline.com.

"WikiLibro." 15MPedia. *WikiLibro 15M.cc*, n.d. Accessed September 17, 2012. http://wiki.15m.cc/wiki/WikiLibro_15M.cc.

Wilkinson, Eleanor. "The Emotions Least Relevant to Politics? Questioning Autonomous Activism." *Emotion, Space, and Society* 2 (2009): 36–43.

Williams, Gareth. *The Mexican Exception: Sovereignty, Police, and Democracy.* New York: Palgrave Macmillan, 2011.

Zamora, Abel. *Temporada baja. Textos en escena* 17. Valencia: CulturArts Generalitat Valenciana, 2013.

Žižek, Slavoj. *First As Tragedy, Then As Farce.* London and New York: Verso, 2009.

———. *The Sublime Object of Ideology.* London and New York: Verso, 1989.

Index

Printed by Printforce, the Netherlands